Tread
Softly for
You Tread on
My Jokes

Malcolm Muggeridge

Tread Softly for You Tread on My Jokes

COLLINS/Fontana Books

First published, 1966
First issued in Fontana Books, 1968

© *Malcolm Muggeridge, 1966*
Printed in Great Britain
Collins Clear-Type Press
London and Glasgow

Contents

Contents

Introduction

It is a fearful thing to contemplate the output of forty years of assiduous journalism. Let us suppose an average daily stint of round about one thousand words. The total runs into millions. One has written the Bible and the *Encyclopædia Britannica* many times over. Add to this the spoken words on radio and television, and one moves into astronomical figures; a vast verbal outpouring, dealing, for the most part, with topics of no present relevance—notices of books and plays whose authors have long been forgotten, editorials on once burning controversies which now matter to no one, obituaries already out-of-date when their subjects died. Appeals, exhortations, solemn warnings, tributes; massive features and tiny gossip parts, turnovers and middles; every variety of shape, size and substance—from pulp to pulp, oh! printed word, where is thy sting?

Why, then, engage in a *Récherche des mots perdus*? Surely the glory of journalism is its transience. Only the greatest bores like Walter Lippmann imagine that their offerings reach beyond the last edition. Let ridiculous dons—a Rowse, a Leavis—persuade themselves that their convoluted sentences will continue to assail posterity as they have defenceless undergraduates in their lifetime. The journalist may take a saner and more wholesome view. He knows that what he writes exists only to be melted down and dispersed, like the metal on which it is momentarily stamped. Each night the same climax reached, with the same languid aftermath. The rotary presses beginning to turn, like a heart ardently beating; scuttling to and from the stone, poring over damp, limp galleys, shouting, pushing, heaving, and lo! the edition is out. Vans race away with it, trains roll along with it through the silent night, aeroplanes lift it into the sky. In the grey morning light, hands push it through letter-boxes, deposit it beside milk bottles. Then, propped up on breakfast tables, read rocking to and fro in railway carriages, gymnastically held up to view in buses and underground trains; by midday at the latest, finished and thrown aside, thenceforth useful only for lighting fires, wrapping fish and stopping broken windows.

Yet with old age the desire grows to salvage from this mounting dump of lost words some which seem to deserve the slightly longer preservation provided by hard covers. I, at any rate, have succumbed. The pieces here collected have been chosen by me for no other reason than that, re-read, they happened to please me better than others. In some cases, I have revised them, or run two pieces together. Where their subjects have subsequently died, tenses have been altered and other appropriate adjustments made. They are not arranged chronologically, but in a purely haphazard manner. All that can be claimed for them is that they express, I hope cogently and with due emphasis, conclusions I have reached, attitudes I have taken and judgments I have made in course of a life largely devoted to the practice of journalism.

They have appeared in a great variety of publications, daily and periodical. As a journalist, I have preferred the hazards of street-walking to the security, such as it is, of being permanently attached to one of the licensed houses. With all its frustrations and limitations, I cannot imagine engaging in any other profession. Some of the excitement has survived from the first time, so many years ago now, that I opened a newspaper and read in it words I had written. From earliest childhood it always seemed to me that the only thing worth doing in life was to write. Before I knew my letters I had a printing-set, and delighted in their shapes even though I could not identify them; just as I remember turning over the pages of my father's books before I could hope to spell out their contents. It was part of the romanticism, not to say priggishness, of my generation to consider all artistic and scholarly achievements as infinitely preferable to any others; to the point that even now it seems to me quite extraordinary when someone with intellectual pretensions expresses admiration for a general or a millionaire or a politician as such.

It all began for me in Cross Street, Manchester, with the (as it then was) *Manchester Guardian*, under C. P. Scott; a venerable but still sprightly figure in his eighties, with pink cheeks, a ribald beard and bright eyes. At his behest, we leader-writers produced our nightly offerings, conscious—I dare say too conscious—of being the voice of reason and righteousness in an unreasonable and unrighteous world. Many an uplifting sentence did I tap out and lay on Scott's desk, expressing the hope that moderate men of all shades of opinion would draw together, and that wiser counsels might yet prevail. The people of this country, I thundered, will never for a moment tolerate—just precisely what I now forget. In any case, they went on their way, heedless of the admonitions we so eloquently and earnestly addressed to them from our editorial corridor in Cross Street, Manchester.

The next scene of my lucubrations was Moscow, where I acted as *Guardian* correspondent. Here, hopes that wiser counsels might yet prevail were difficult, if not impossible, to sustain, and moderate men of all shades of opinion had a way of disappearing into Lubianka Prison, never to be seen again. Stalin, I came to realise, was no C. P. Scott. In the shadow of the Kremlin, my typewriter acquired a querulous, shrill note consequent upon this disconcerting discovery.

At its next port-of-call—the office of the *Statesman* in Calcutta—some of Bengal's steaming humidity got into its bones. These were the great White Paper days, when from Whitehall and Delhi there flowed a quenchless stream of words about India's constitutional future such as has never, I should suppose, been known on earth before or since. Not one of the words, I may add, bore the smallest relation to what was happening in India, or to that sub-continent's subsequent destiny. In the *Statesman* office we assiduously added our little bucketfuls to the mighty flood.

From Calcutta I transferred myself to Fleet Street, actually to Shoe Lane, there to toil, on the late Lord Beaverbrook's behalf, on the *Evening Standard* Londoner's Diary. No one's education is complete without a spell as a gossip-writer. How otherwise is it possible to know the minutiæ of human vanity; that passion which, in the Century of the Common Man, to a greater or lesser extent afflicts everyone, to be known as an uncommon man. Nor are those who were privileged to witness it likely ever to forget the spectacle of otherwise sane and even amiable fellow-humans striving to translate into terms of ostensible sense the malignancies, the prejudices, the sheer raving absurdities of their exigent master. I hear it still over the telephone, that raucous Canadian voice— 'You've gotta say . . . You've gotta say . . .' We duly said it.

Round the corner from Shoe Lane, in Fleet Street itself, stands the office of the *Daily Telegraph,* a building intended to be dignified but only succeeding in being commonplace. Here it was that the first Lord Camrose devised, with great skill and acumen, the perfect reading-matter to occupy a stockbroker's attention between Tunbridge Wells Central and Cannon Street. It was a highly successful and profitable venture, in whose maquis I managed to lurk with a fair degree of ease and satisfaction, first in the Fleet Street office, and then in Washington, D.C., as the newspaper's correspondent there. In Moscow there was no news, in Washington nothing but news. In each case one was cut off, living among the shadows of pseudo-events which could only be described in pseudo-words. It was the difference between being alone in the Sahara and being alone in Fifth Avenue. In Soviet prison camp slang, a prisoner who confesses is a novelist; in journalistic jargon, a happening is a story. It comes to the same thing. My typewriter tapped sturdily away in my office in the Washington National Press Building, competing with the ticker-tape in the corner which likewise tapped sturdily away, ejecting on to the floor great yellow piles of news upon which, from time to time, I had to make desperate assaults.

Farther along Fleet Street from the *Daily Telegraph*, on the left looking towards Charing Cross, is Bouverie Street. There I next repaired, to the office of *Punch,* whose editor I became. It was a sombre place, haunted by old jokes and lost laughter. Life, as I discovered, holds no more wretched occupation than trying to make the English laugh. I and my staff, all anguished men, would sit together trying to discover what, if anything, was funny, and sadly reaching the conclusion that nothing was. It was with a sense of infinite relief that I went downstairs, past the figure of Mr. Punch, and out through the door for the last time. A sense of almost mystical exhilaration seized me at the thought that I should never again cross that threshold, never again enter the twilit world within, or find myself under the professional necessity of trying to be funny.

10

Thenceforth I was fortunate enough to be able to avoid any comparable commitment. Doubtless for this reason, the succeeding years have been, for me, singularly happy ones. It is out of these years, I confess, that a good many of the pieces included in this volume have come. Perhaps one has to be old and disengaged to be truly interested in, and curious about, one's fellows. Human life, I have come to feel, in all its public or collective manifestations is only theatre, and mostly cheap melodrama at that. There is nothing serious under the sun except love; of fellow-mortals and of God. Everything is ridiculous save ecstasy. So, at any rate, I should like to think and feel and write during the brief span which still remains to me in this world.

Tread softly for you tread on my jokes

I first became acquainted with humour in the professional sense on 1st January, 1953, when I moved across from the office of the *Daily Telegraph* in Fleet Street to Bouverie Street to become the eighth editor of *Punch*. It was, for me, a curious and rather sombre moment. There, looking across at me, I fancied with no great pleasure, was the austere countenance of Sir Owen Seaman Bt.: out of the window I could see rolls of newsprint being hoisted into the *News of the World* for use that coming week-end. I had seldom looked at, and never much cared for, *Punch,* as a publication, let alone contributed to it. Nor had I the faintest notion of how to set about editing it. A mood of doubt and despair settled upon me, intensified by the enormous and unfamiliar quiet in which I found myself. The pursuit of news is accompanied by perpetual and reassuring noise; humour, like love, must, it appeared, be sought silently, invisibly.

What is humour? I idly asked myself, and, like Pilate, did not wait for an answer. There is, I believe, a large literature on the subject, but I have never read any of it, and doubt if I ever shall. All I have learnt is that what makes one man laugh makes another enraged; that the English, particularly, take their humour very seriously, and grow exceedingly angry at attempts to amuse them which they consider to have failed. It is not for nothing that, in the English language alone, to accuse someone of trying to be funny is highly abusive. Humour, I have come to realise, is practically the only thing about which the English are utterly serious. You can bomb them, nationalise them, de-nationalise them, ration and de-ration them, even subject them to teach-ins, without disturbing their equanimity; but touch their humour, and they rise up like lions. Like any other journalist I have long been accustomed to the unbridled insanity of the greater part of the letters addressed to daily newspapers, but they are as lucid as Voltaire, Gibbonian in their urbanity, compared with the ones addressed to the editor of *Punch*. These rage and

13

storm; they insult and they abuse; they demand that the
writer's subscription be cancelled, and avow that never
under any circumstances, no, not even at the dentist's, will
the accursed publication again be opened. I can state without
fear of contradiction that the funniest documents which came
my way as editor of *Punch* were communications from irate
readers.

Curiously enough, what is complained of is, more often
than not, the introduction of a new joke rather than the repetition of an old one. Readers of *Punch* have much the same
attitude to their jokes that port drinkers have to port. They
like them laid down in a cellar to mature. Then, on special
occasions, they can bring them up, encrusted with cobwebs,
and savour again their rich, familiar bouquet. The editor of
The New Yorker, one assumes, has to cater for the American
passion for novelty, the editor of *Punch* for his readers' deep
and passionate conservatism. Humor must seem varied,
humour ever the same. The big hand in an English music hall
was always for the joke everyone knew. It was the same with
Punch. Here, as even its enemies are forced to admit, *Punch*
fulfils its rôle satisfactorily, ladling out old chestnuts with
a generous hand. And anyway, the sad fact is that there are
very few jokes—not more than six or seven at most, and all
by now decidedly well-worn. Every now and then something
happens in the world—as, for instance, a man changing his
sex and becoming a woman—which opens up the faint hope
that a new joke may be born; but this hope is soon disappointed, and it is seen that the seemingly new situation falls
into the pattern of an old joke.

Nearly everyone I met after I became editor of *Punch* would
remark that as a child he had discovered the bound volumes
of *Punch* in his father's library, and been enchanted by them.
This picture of the tiny tot with a cumbersome tome open
on a table, and the evening light coming in through a stained
glass window, lost to Nanny and forgetful of meal times
as Leach, Tenniel, Du Maurier and Partridge were absorbed,
was as standardised as *Punch*'s own jokes. Let me then make
it abundantly clear that in my own lower middle class home
there were no bound volumes of *Punch*, nor, for that matter,
a nanny.

This omission I corrected (the bound volumes, I mean, not

the nanny) by buying a set (the price was disconcertingly cheap), and thenceforth quite often turned over their pages. Alas, they provided me with no guidance as to how *Punch* should be conducted in the middle of the twentieth century. If the early numbers were harsher and more 'political,' and the later ones more whimsical and 'conformist,' no standard for the fabrication of humour was to be derived from them. I myself, as it happened, preferred the earlier, harsher note. Humour, for my taste, has to have an astringent flavour—like Shakespeare's Fools, who usually (for instance, the most splendid of all in *King Lear*) hurt in order to amuse, or vice versa. As for the later whimsy—it seemed to me to express, in the years after the 1914-18 war, the desire of the English middle and upper classes to be convinced that their world remained intact when, in fact, for good or ill, it had ceased to exist. After the 1939-45 war the havoc which had been wrought was so evident that to assume it had not happened became impossible. The only recourse then was self-pity, manifesting itself in wry jokes about washing up, bank overdrafts and other forlorn intimations of a final retreat from the glory of comical housemaids, strayed revellers and children with tousled heads saying their prayers.

Clearly, I decided, the business of a humorous or satirical magazine must be to ridicule the age in which we live, and particularly those set in authority over us. It is the gargoyle grinning beneath the steeple; it is Thersites mocking at pomposity, pretentiousness, self-importance and all the other occupational diseases of the mighty in their seats. Here a difficulty at once arose. Our age (as I dare say every age has seemed at the time) is so overflowing with absurdity that it defies mockery. Who can parody *Hansard* or *Who's Who,* or for that matter, the *Congressional Record*? Where is the humorous genius capable of inventing anything inherently funnier than, say, the British Broadcasting Corporation, or, in its macabre way, the hydrogen bomb? What chance has comic invention with Sir Alec Douglas-Home, George Brown, Mr. Goldwater and the Bishop of Woolwich, not to mention General de Gaulle, about the place? When everything in *The Times* (except the fourth leader) is so hilariously funny, where is the place for *Punch*? Who will be bold enough to undertake to produce absurdities outdoing those which television screens, government press releases, City banquets, the House of Commons, Lord Snow and Professor Hoyle constantly purvey? Try and invent a more comical figure than Lord Reith, a newspaper proprietor more intrinsically absurd than Lord Thomson of Fleet, or a sometime Prime Minister who in the way of clowning outdoes Mr. Harold Macmillan. It just cannot be done. The melancholia to which clowns, radio comedians, gag-writers, editors of *Punch,* and all who are in any way concerned in the humour industry, are notoriously susceptible, is due, I am confident, to being constantly confronted with this tragic dilemma of how to ridicule a world whose reality so often outdoes their wildest and most daring inventions.

I could provide many examples. Take, for instance, newspapers. How often in *Punch* we tried to embellish their vast daily outpouring only to find our own efforts so much more sober, cogent and literate than the originals that we blushed for them. The same difficulty arose in the case of political exhortations, votes of thanks, Royal tours, the English-Speaking Union, not to mention the House of Lords and the *Reader's Digest.* No one who has not tried can form any conception of how truly appallingly difficult it is to find anything in the world serious enough to be ridiculed. An occasion would arise—let us say a Freud or Shakespeare centenary, which, it was decided, ought to be good for a joke or two. And lo, the Freudians and the Shakespearians got going with their authentic celebration of the occasion, making our poor efforts seem, by comparison, restrained to the point of banality. Before the visit of Mr. Khrushchev and Marshal Bulganin to England we drew up what we fondly hoped would be a humorous itinerary for them. Imagine our consternation when, at the last moment, we had to delete a good proportion of it because it coincided with their actual itinerary.

And if ever we did succeed in achieving a valid and adequately barbed comment on the contemporary scene it was pretty well certain that we should thereby lay ourselves open to the charge of having been guilty of execrable taste. Truth itself, I came to feel, is in decidedly bad taste—which, from the point of view of an editor of *Punch,* is a most unfortunate state of affairs, since humour only exists in so far as it is truthful. The moment it departs from truth it is automatically transubstantiated into some ersatz product like whimsy. Mr. Punch, with his crooked back and enormous nose and minute stature, is no respecter of persons. He has a naturally cantankerous disposition, with a natural propensity towards disrespect rather than consideration, towards criticism rather than acquiescence. His uncomfortable disposition makes it difficult, if not impossible, for him to be on good terms with authority. He has never appeared in an honours' list, never been to a good school, never changed for dinner, never shot grouse or otherwise disported himself among his betters. He is, in fact, decidedly non-U.

What is somewhat alarming, if one happens to be responsible for the activities of this deplorable individual, is to observe that the degree of public tolerance accorded him shows a marked tendency to shrink. For instance, in old volumes of *Punch* it is quite common to find the Royal Family being made the subject of highly satirical comment. I doubt very much whether anyone to-day would care to publish an equivalent of so recent a venture in this field as Sir Max Beerbohm's admirable caricature of King Edward VII. And even such transitory and vulnerable figures as prime ministers, I found, are liable to be regarded as in certain respects sacrosanct. Making them look foolish (no very difficult task) can evoke violent protests.

No doubt it is all part of a larger trend towards a collectivist, conformist society, in which humour (except in its meanest aspects) is repugnant, and ultimately has no place. Any orthodoxy protects itself, if it can, by making unorthodoxy a crime—whether against the State, or against the canons of good taste. To laugh is to criticise; to recognise that no human institution is other than imperfect, and no human authority other than derisory. (I discount the laughter of acquiescence—that agonising, mirthless ripple of the face, manifesting obsequiousness rather than amusement, with which the witticisms, such as they are, of important personages are greeted.) Humour, that is to say, is a kind of resistance movement, which is sometimes indulgently tolerated, sometimes barely tolerated, and sometimes not tolerated at all. Shakespeare makes King John refer to 'that idiot, laughter . . . A passion hateful to my purpose.' The

17

degree of tolerance depends on the certainty with which current beliefs are held, and the stability with which current institutions are credited. A decrepit society shuns humour as a decrepit individual shuns draughts.

In a healthy, civilised society, it seems to me, everyone and everything should be open to ridicule. Indeed, I would go further and contend that the degree of health and civilisation in any given society bears a direct relation to the degree to which this principle operates. Taboos, where humour is concerned, are an admission of doubt, and derive from a sense of weakness and insecurity. The truly religious take no offence when attention is drawn to the absurdity necessarily inherent in the dogmas to which they subscribe and the ceremonies in which they participate. Protests invariably come from the conventionally religious; from the formalists for whom the dogmas and the ceremonies constitute the whole content of their faith. It is the same with politicians. Those who most object to being ridiculed have least confidence in the policies they advocate. It is the same with moralists. If they complain that some cherished principle is blasphemed by the humorous treatment of its application, then it is certain that in their hearts they doubt the principle's ultimate validity.

In England the situation recently underwent a welcome change as a result of the great popular success of the B.B.C. Television programme *That Was The Week That Was* (rather feebly copied in America), as well as of the theatrical review *Beyond the Fringe*. For a time, too, the Establishment Club, in a similar vein, enjoyed a considerable vogue, as well as the magazine *Private Eye* which gives every appearance of continuing to thrive. Satire, indeed, became all the rage, to the point that the *Observer* ran a Satire Page, no doubt calculating that, by labelling the page, any danger of confusing its contents with the rest of the paper (otherwise a decided possibility) was reduced, if not eliminated. This widely prevalent satirical attitude of mind was reflected in the ever-growing popularity of novelists like Evelyn Waugh, Anthony Powell and Kingsley Amis. A similar flavour pervaded much of the conversation of the young, agreeably contrasting with the desperate earnestness of a Professor Hoggart or a Raymond Williams—a hangover from the post-

18

war years; still more with the Auden-Spender-Isherwood sense of purpose of the Thirties, not to mention the Reithean solemnity which once blanketed the land, and the Eliotean dirge, a rendering of which was obligatory whenever two or more were gathered together to the greater glory of Eng. Lit. Eliot himself, it is only fair to concede, was in his time a considerable satirist, in a lowering sort of way.

No doubt the change was partly due to contemporary circumstances, which are hazardous, brutish, and may well be short. It was possible to believe at the time that, for instance, the outcome of the Spanish Civil War mattered enormously, though, thanks to Mr. Hugh Thomas's monumental labours any such assumption now would be quite derisory. Again, Soviet idolatry provided a cult to which the forces of enlightenment could plausibly adhere. Mr. Khrushchev, in his inimitable way, has put paid to all that, God bless him. Who nowadays sees the land bright eastwards, or, for that matter, westwards? Man is born in chains and is everywhere free; the Bad Guy has stolen the Sheriff's badge, and it is the Good Guy who neglects to shave.

The booming satire industry which grew up under the shadow of the mushroom cloud had a strongly American flavour, intensified by visiting maestros like Mort Sahl and Lenny Bruce, blown by the wind of change across the Atlantic. Even *The New Yorker,* centuries ago, scattered the good seed, not all of which fell on stony ground. I might even claim to have made puny efforts myself in the same direction, operating from my secret headquarters in Bouverie Street opposite the *News of the World*. With satire as popular as chemmy such maquis tactics were unnecessary. Hard hearts and coronets thronged the Establishment Club; *Private Eye* sold like hot cakes outside the Ritz; and the youthful performers in *Beyond the Fringe* surveyed in their appreciative audiences the living targets of their wit. The lash fell on willing shoulders, and evoked cries, not of pain or outrage, but of delight.

The pleasure that is taken in contemporary satire by its victims necessarily raises certain doubts about it. Can it really be an effective antiseptic when there is absolutely no hurt? There was a cripple who used to hang about outside Buckingham Palace some forty years ago selling, or trying to sell, a publication called *No More War*. I remember him well, in a rather battered wheel-chair which he manipulated with great skill and energy. 'Penny *No More War*,' he would shout, 'Penny *No More War*,' and then would add, to reinforce his appeal, 'Truth hurts!' He, too, obviously felt that prospective buyers would be attracted by the idea of being hurt by truth. Though, as far as could be seen, he by no means enjoyed the vogue of *Beyond the Fringe* and the Establishment Club, it was significant that he should have selected so distinguished a size for his pitch. Lenny and Mort, after all, are for the rich. The poor like *Coronation Street* and *Peyton Place*.

One was struck, at the Establishment Club, by the general air of affluence. One looked round instinctively for Princess Margaret, or at any rate the Duke of Bedford. One was enfolded in Colour Supplements. Laughter was bold as brass. Indeed it was the Brass who laughed. Decaying societies, like decaying teeth, invite the tongue to probe, and touch the exposed nerve. If I had a club I should call it The Hollow Tooth. In the days of the Third Reich, it was said, a Nazi procession included a small, sad contingent of Jews bearing a banner inscribed: 'Down with us.' Patrons of *Beyond the Fringe* and the Establishment Club, one felt, had adopted the same slogan.

Private Eye, too, I should suppose, has a largely Top People clientele. Osbert Lancaster was its John the Baptist; its contributors, if they are not careful, will find themselves before long carving their initials on the *Punch* table alongside A.A.M., O.S., A.P.H., and, alas, M.M. For the moment, however, their satiric zest is young and in the spring. They have managed to be delightfully and offensively rude to one and all, and have earned, even if they have not always been awarded, the coveted accusation of bad taste. Older hands may feel that they are too widespread in their attacks; that they fire a bazooka rather than discharging poisoned arrows. Let us hope that time will correct the fault (if fault it is), bringing discrimination, and the perfect hate which casteth out facetiousness.

Another criticism is that these young practitioners of satire lack a sense of purpose. Older practitioners like Low were Public Eyes, looking with enraged contempt or sorrowful pity at mankind's follies in the vain hope of correcting them. Swift, in the epitaph he wrote for himself, referred to the furious indignation which lacerated his heart. It was because of this furious indignation that he saw mankind as odious little vermin. To the young satirists, on the other hand, authority is a schoolmaster, who, when his back is turned, can be pelted with paper darts and mocked with mimicry and funny faces. Such insubordination can easily be laughed off; boys will be boys. With Swift it was different. He understood too well what he was attacking. When his trumpet sounded the walls of Jericho really did tremble. The trouble with the young satirists is that the walls have already fallen; their trumpets sound across the resultant debris.

Nor did anyone ever accuse Swift's satirical writing of being 'sick,' though he described with hating care nature's necessities, a whore's undressing, and the Brobdingnagian ladies' monstrous toilet. This was because stinks and sores and vilely magnified flesh were, to him, only the obverse side of an elusive perfection. Contemporary 'sick' humour conveys no such obverse side. Therein, perhaps, lies its sickness.

The young satirists, significantly enough, have turned to photography rather than caricature. The funniest material at The Establishment shows was provided by the newsreels, as, in *Private Eye,* by suitably amended press photographs. The camera, not pencil or brush, is satire's instrument to-day. Mimicry and press cuttings suffice. Nature is held up to a mirror; all the stage is a world.

Rooting about in the rubble of an already blitzed citadel, the young satirist advances upon positions long ago evacuated. I am reminded of a missionary who, as an ardent young evangelist, felt it to be his duty to attend a heathen festival, and, in broad Scottish Presbyterian accents, denounce the god who was being worshipped. The worshippers took this amiss, and cursed and stoned the good man, to his great satisfaction and edification. At subsequent festivals opposition grew ever more languid, until it ceased altogether. When the missionary at last retired, his Society received a request from the festival authorities for a replacement. His act had become part of the show.

Such a rôle is particular rather than universal. Yet it is the universality of humour which makes it so sweet an alleviation of life's bitterness. *Cette vie qui est si pénible et si belle*—surely an important element is translated from the category of what is painful to the other, of what is beautiful, by the faculty of laughter. Among the sublime achievements of human endeavour must be counted Cervantes's *Don Quixote,* Shakespeare's Falstaff, Voltaire's *Candide,* Gogol's *Dead Souls,* as well as masterpieces of our time like *Huckleberry Finn, The Diary of a Nobody* and P. G. Wodehouse's Jeeves and Bertie Wooster. As long as we can laugh—at our aspirations as at our disillusionments, at our fears and our pretensions and our vanities and our appetites; above all, at ourselves—there is still hope for us, and for the things we hold dear. Let us, then, laugh.

Many winters ago in Moscow

When I was a newspaper correspondent in Moscow in the early 1930s I used to spend a lot of the day just walking the streets. This was partly because there was nothing else to do, but even if there had been I think I might still have thus employed my time. The unending stream of people, grey-faced, anonymously clothed, treading soundlessly on the snow, had a curious attraction. They seemed to be going nowhere in particular, to have no particular object in view. There was nothing in the shop windows to look at, and they did not, like street crowds in other cities, take stock of one another. Anonymous, inscrutable, drifting along without any evident expectation of better times or fear of worse ones, I found them comforting and companionable. They evoked none of the excitement or despair which make most large cities so uneasy and sleepless an environment. As evening came on, the effect was even more pronounced. It was like living in the mountains of the moon, with no restless desires or insistent ego to trouble the quiet, unmolesting passage of time.

How marvellous the Russian revolution seemed when it happened! A little bearded man wearing a cap, Lenin, had taken over the vast empire of the Tsars on behalf of the

22

workers and peasants; his Jewish lieutenant, Trotsky, had created a Red Army of legendary valour, without officers, gold braid, bands or any of the other contemptible insignia of militarism. How we rejoiced and cheered and exulted at the time! Thenceforth, to us, mounted police were Cossacks and even Ramsay MacDonald, Philip Snowden and J. H. Thomas (otherwise an unedifying trio, as they seemed even well before the 1931 debacle) commissars-to-be. At the 1917 Club in Gerrard Street the intelligentsia—another imported word—offered thanks in an atmosphere of *vin ordinaire*, pipe smoke and progressive promiscuity. In the distant, fabulous land of steppes and vodka the proletariat had seized power and the millennium had begun.

Even so, had I been less uplifted I might have noticed certain danger signals. The intelligentsia themselves were by no means as unanimous on the subject of the Russian revolution as seemed to be the case. Bertrand Russell, to his great credit, very early on detected the trend towards terrorism and oppression in the actual operation of proletarian dictatorship. And Fabians like the Webbs were bitterly hostile to the struggling U.S.S.R. Ironically, but I fear all too characteristically, they only began to admire the Soviet system when it had ceased to be admirable; when Stalin and the G.P.U. had fully taken over, keeping the firing-squads busy and the labour camps full.

Living and working as a journalist in Moscow at the time of the collectivisation of agriculture, disillusionment soon closed in on me. It was not just the almost inconceivable brutality and dishonesty of the régime (as George Orwell was to demonstrate so brilliantly, such is the whole trend of twentieth-century authority); nor even the painful spectacle of all my heroes, from André Gide to Bernard Shaw, displaying towards it an imbecile credulity which an African witch-doctor would have found enviable. The words of the *Magnificat* had been fulfilled, certainly; the mighty had duly been put down from their seats and the humble and meek exalted, and now I had to face the unpalatable fact that the humble and meek, thus exalted, had become mighty in their turn and fit to be put down. That particular *aperta a sinistra* was closed to me for ever, and, as nightmare spectacle succeeded nightmare spectacle—purges, Nazi-Soviet Pact, the East German and Hungarian risings—seen to be so by all but a few zealots so tough, stupid or bewitched that they struggled on, however rough the going may have been, to keep abreast of the Party Line.

Looking back now across more than three decades, I see those months I spent in the U.S.S.R. in a different light. The disillusionment, such as it was, merges into a general sense that power must invariably bring out the worst in those who exercise it, and that the dream of a more humane and just and joyous collective existence, whether entertained by a St. Francis or a Karl Marx or Philadelphia Founding Fathers, must always belong—as the psalmist puts it— to a land that is very far off. What abides with me is the feeling, mystical in its intensity, that in Moscow the drama of our time was being enacted, and that there one was participating in it in some quite unique, umbilical manner. There the world we were to live in, for good or ill, was being shaped. That noiseless, aimless procession through the blank streets and between the blank houses was mankind processing through the twentieth century.

The life of a foreign correspondent in Moscow was even then largely detached from the land, the government and the people whose affairs we were supposed to be reporting. In the mornings we thumbed over the day's newspapers, spelling them out ourselves or with the help of a secretary. They were inconceivably long-winded and flat—enormous, turgid articles about the Five-Year Plan or the collectivisation of agriculture. I used in those days to nourish the hope that the Soviet régime would collapse under the weight of its sheer tedium. No human beings, I would reflect, not even Slavs, could indefinitely sustain this boredom of portentous words, these unillumined sentences meandering down column after column, this endless repetition of the same slogans and propositions. How wrong I was! There is, as I now know, no limit to what contemporary human beings will endure, in what is written, spoken, or visually presented to them, however repetitious, long-winded, and inherently false it may be. The more they venerate literacy, the greater becomes their capacity for suffering gladly any amount of boredom in terms of words and images; the more they persuade themselves that facts

24

and figures can explain their circumstances, the greater is their credulity and tolerance of charlatanry.

Out of the newspapers we managed to extract items which could be made to seem like news. The newspapers were our only source of information. This vast, diverse country in which we were living, as far as we were concerned, might not have existed. In the beginning was the Word, and in the end, too—as propounded by *Pravda* and *Izvestia*.

Having confectioned a message of sorts, it had to be taken to the Press Department and the Foreign Office for censorship. This was a room furnished with gilt and red chairs and divans; a shabby, faded place which had survived unchanged from pre-Revolution days. There were, in particular, three officials with whom we dealt, all now dead; one, Oumansky, in an aeroplane accident, and the other two, Podolsky and Neyman, shot. Oumansky was an unattractive individual, with crinkly hair and a lot of gold teeth. He once, we had reason to believe, climbed into bed with an ageing Commissar's wife in the hope of bettering his chances of promotion; which, indeed, he succeeded in doing, for he was Soviet Ambassador in Washington at the time of his death. Podolsky was a sad, rather charming man with a pointed head who, at official receptions, was skilled at transferring sandwiches and pastries from the buffet into his pockets to take back to his family, whom he adored. As for Neyman—a thin fringe of black beard gave him a rabbinical appearance. He once showed me some snapshots of his children in sailor suits at a seaside resort by the Black Sea.

These three would read over our messages like schoolmasters reading over an essay submitted to them for correction. 'You can do better than this,' one expected to find written in red ink on the message when it was handed back. Occasionally, they would frown, and delete a sentence or two. Newcomers were liable to argue the point, sometimes with heat, but later they too became reconciled to the system. After all, the messages were rubbish anyway—lies culled from lies. It scarcely mattered in what form they went out. Our greatest hope—perhaps I should say mine, for some of the correspondents, especially the Americans, were an earnest lot— was to raise a laugh, or even a faint smile, as a message was perused. This happened extremely rarely. The most notable occasion was when Cholerton, correspondent of the *Daily Telegraph*, in the course of a heated discussion as to whether Habeas Corpus prevailed in the Soviet Union, remarked that, whatever might be the case about Habeas Corpus, without any question Habeas Cadaver prevailed there. Podolsky positively shouted with laughter as he lacerated Cholerton's cable. Not surprisingly, he was the first to be liquidated.

Cholerton was far and away the most interesting and attractive of the foreign correspondents. He had drifted into the U.S.S.R. in the twenties just in time for Lenin's funeral —a leftish, scholarly, bearded figure, a fellow of King's in the Keynes era; extremely amusing, indolent, and companionable. When I think of Moscow, I think more of him than of anyone else. In an odd way, he belonged to the place. All day long he would lie on a sofa and talk mockingly of the régime, its bosses, its monstrous cruelties and stupidities. I delighted in his conversation. Once I said to Podolsky: 'How do you put up with him when you know he loathes the whole show more than any of us?' 'We find him irresistible,' Podolsky replied. 'He reminds us of the old days. He's just like a Russian intellectual.' It was a fascinating remark, with fascinating implications. I should have known that, like his laughter over Habeas Cadaver, it constituted poor Podolsky's death warrant. Cholerton now lives on the French Riviera; another place of shadows, but lengthening backwards instead of forwards.

Some of the correspondents, like Louis Fischer at that time, felt bound to defend the régime. They somehow managed to sustain their Soviet addiction, and to write little homilies in the *Nation* and other such publications on the theme: 'I have seen the future and it works.' They had seen the future all right, but it didn't work, except as the past had worked; brutally, mendaciously, and callously. Occasionally Fischer would go so far as to rebuke the rest of us for our flippancy and scepticism, with the air of a choirmaster calling sniggering, whispering choir-boys to order and due solemnity.

Other correspondents just wanted to stay in Moscow, where they managed to have a fairly prosperous and comfortable time on boot-legged roubles. The official rate was about six to the pound, but it was fairly easy to get four hundred. One would collect them, usually from some minor foreign consular official, and take them away in large newspaper parcels, like fried fish. With our foreign currency we could buy in the Torgsin shops where roubles were not accepted. The windows were arrayed in such a way as to attract the hungry, with sausages and hams and great mounds of butter on display. There was usually a little crowd of starving Muscovites staring in, the idea being that if one of them had some little gold trinket still undisposed of, or could induce some relative abroad to send in foreign currency, this shop window temptation would break down any considerations of prudence about disclosing the fact to the authorities. Quite a lot of precious metal and valuta was procured by this diabolical arrangement, which, like so many things in the U.S.S.R., was an application of capitalist practice at its most barefaced and brutal.

The most touching figures were the eager American journalists who tried to apply, in the bizarre conditions of the U.S.S.R., the ordinary techniques of energetic journalism. They went after non-existent scoops, they prowled about in rubber shoes looking for news, they sought interviews with Stalin—alas, sometimes got them, drenching the front pages of their newspapers with Soviet propaganda in the form of prefabricated questions and answers. This device, astonishingly enough, continues to work. The bait of an exclusive interview still serves to land mighty whales from the Western seas.

Actually, foreign journalists have been a great asset to the Soviet régime. They have to work for their visas. A correspondent knows that if his messages are unfriendly he will soon have to go. On the whole, he wants to stay, for professional, economic, and sometimes personal reasons. The price of staying is to be, by and large, sympathetically disposed to the régime in what he writes about it in his newspaper. He can, it is true, when he finally comes out, write an outspoken series which largely contradicts what he wrote while he was in, but a lot of the effect is lost by virtue of this contradiction.

On the way to the opening of the Dneprostroy Dam, when we journalists had been talking bitterly about famine and terrorism; all the fraudulence to which we were ceaselessly subjected, an official who was travelling with us said: 'I don't know what you're worrying about; you've got plenty to drink.' It was true. We had, and to eat, too. The special train was overheated, and we were plied with food and drink. Most of the stations had been cleared for our passage, but occasionally, at a small one, there would be a little huddled group of starving mujiks. At one such station, a German correspondent threw out a chicken leg he'd been gnawing. The mujiks hurled themselves upon it. It was one of those little, quick scenes which live with one like stigmata.

The truth is that the Soviet authorities despised us, and not without reason. We could so easily be flattered; so easily, in an oblique way, be bribed. We were so manageable. The most we could hope to do was to smuggle out an uncensored piece through the diplomatic bag, and then, if and when it appeared, we would be called in by Oumansky, and read a lecture with threatening undertones. After two or three such piejaws, as we well knew, a correspondent was liable to have his visa withdrawn. The great successes of Soviet propaganda have been due, far more than to its own inherent force and skill, to the ease with which non-Soviet channels have been found for its dissemination.

Comic relief was provided in Moscow by Intourists, who in those days flocked into the country in great numbers. This is a spectacle I would not have missed for anything. It was far more interesting and diverting than the Soviet régime, which, once you got the hang of it, was relatively simple and monotonous. But the Intourists! They were hilarious—clergymen reverently walking through anti-God museums, Quakers smiling radiantly as they were told that in the U.S.S.R. capital punishment had been abolished, Liberals overjoyed to learn that what amounted to proportional representation had been introduced, town planners looking up awed at gimcrack buildings which were beginning to fall down before they were completed, feminists who could not contain their joy when they beheld women sweeping the streets on equal terms with men. I recall, among many such treasured memories, Sir Julian Huxley's statement, in a book he wrote about a visit to the U.S.S.R., that Stalin was in the habit of going to the railway siding and helping to unload potatoes. Someone should make an anthology of what these Intourists said and wrote about the Soviet régime. A brilliant issue of the magazine *Survey* (April, 1962), on the theme 'The Western Image of the Soviet Union 1917-1962,' provides excellent material for such a work. It would be a compilation of folly probably unequalled in history—produced for the most part by those who, even to this day, are accustomed to enlighten and instruct us on B.B.C. panels and other like occasions.

My own state of mind during this time in the U.S.S.R. was troubled and confused. I had gone there from the *Manchester Guardian* with a deep distrust of liberalism. The leading articles I had pounded out for two and a half years about all sorts of subjects, from corporal punishment to the Indian Round Table Conference, nearly always ended up with: 'It is greatly to be hoped . . .' We were always greatly hoping—hoping that some mean and timidly ambitious politician would prove after all a far-seeing statesman; that fanaticism would give place to moderation, violence cease when reason was spoken, and all mankind accept the sagacious guidance proffered from Cross Street, Manchester, without, of course, interfering with the cotton trade. Ramsay MacDonald, then Prime Minister, put it in his inimitable way: 'I want the lion (I don't know which is the lion) to lie down with the lamb (I don't know which is the lamb).' 'It is greatly to be hoped'—over and over again, on a typewriter, in my head as I walked beside the dingy little canal near where I lived, on the train going to London, out in the—at that time—forlorn and desolate Lancashire towns, their streets crowded with idle men waiting for the cinemas to open. What, oh what, was greatly to be hoped? I inwardly groaned.

Oumansky was never tired of praising the *Manchester Guardian*. He gave me dinner in the huge, ornate former residence of a rich Jewish merchant. The furnishings and decorations represented everything he most admired and yearned to enjoy. There were innumerable little mirrors on the walls, and they seemed to be blinking at me as I got drunk. From very far away, I could hear Oumansky's voice telling me how, alone of the Capitalist Press, the *Manchester Guardian* was virtuous and admirable. One of the most satisfactory aspects of human life is the apt manner in which the stage is set, though, alas, the lines which have to be said are often sadly incoherent and banal. I could not have imagined a better décor for Oumansky to flash his gold teeth in adulation of the *Manchester Guardian* and the fine tradition of British Liberalism.

There was another reason for Oumansky to hold me in some regard. I was connected by marriage with Mrs. Sidney Webb, and had, indeed, spent the last week-end before leaving for Moscow at Passfield to receive her and her Consort's blessing. These two extraordinary individuals were then in the high tide of their Soviet enthusiasm. She paced up and down with her large quick strides, while he sat, minute, in his chair. Together they intoned their Fabian admiration for the Soviet régime and all its works, one taking up the refrain when the other paused. His particular admiration was for the Consumers' Co-operatives, hers for the Party élite and their abstemious ways. What they really admired was the régime's sheer power; the fact that there were no votes to be taken, no motions to be referred back, no tedious, bone-headed trade unionists to be coaxed and cajoled. This emerged when Mrs. Webb said: 'It's true that in the Soviet Union people disappear.' She accentuated this last word, '*disappear*,' and I realised, even in my somewhat euphoric condition, how happy she would have been if similar arrangements prevailed in the L.C.C., and recalcitrant councillors and aldermen could be made likewise to disappear.

Their house was comfortably appointed; there were two elderly Scottish maids (one of them asked: 'Do you think the Five-Year Plan answers?') to see that meals were on time, and hot-water bottles duly available. We went for walks over the adjoining scrubland with a dog named Sandy; and still, while neighbouring stockbrokers played golf or took their ease with a glass and a Sunday newspaper, her voice rang out, with his a muffled, sibilant echo, proclaiming the excellence of a dictatorship of the proletariat, and how, because Lenin had translated their *History of Trade Unionism* while in Siberia, they had become Soviet ikons. Rum ikons, I thought, even then—or perhaps, after all, not so rum.

When Oumansky had finished with the *Manchester Guardian,* he moved on to the Webbs. He hoped that he, too, would have an opportunity to visit Passfield, and pay his homage to the estimable couple who lived there. I hoped so, too. The little mirrors were beginning to blink rather frighteningly. It was time to go. I said good night to Oumansky, leaving him, doubtless, like Podolsky, to gather up some of the feast's leavings for his family's consumption. Outside, the snow had been falling. Against its whiteness, buildings were black shadows. The town seemed almost deserted—just an occasional figure hurrying by. Silent and deserted, and yet I still had the feeling that somehow, just now, this was the centre of the spider's web of history. Snow crunched underfoot, and the silence was oppressive in its intensity. I began to shout, but whether in defiance or acquiescence or just out of fatuity, I cannot now remember.

We were all the time trying to formulate thoughts and views about the régime. There was nothing but the régime—nothing else to talk or think or read about; no girls, except the little, grisly band of over-powdered, over-scented ones who were hand-picked to be our companions; no unexpected encounters or chance conversations. We lived in a small, closed world of our own, like forlorn Sahibs in one of the smaller Indian stations in the old days. At public functions we would occasionally see Stalin, Molotov, and the others file on to a platform. From afar we watched them, distant, pygmy figures, who might have been on a television screen.

There was also the British Embassy, where we occasionally visited. The Ambassador, Sir Edward Ovey, had a plan for abolishing unemployment, but somehow I never got the hang of it. This meant that it was an inexhaustible subject of conversation. He had around him the usual staff of first, second, and third secretaries—men in dark suits, with that particular sort of closed, self-satisfied face which the diplomatic service produces. They crop up everywhere, and, as disasters have thickened, it has been interesting to observe how their self-satisfaction has survived intact. Our downhill course as a nation has been followed by these discreet and elegant funeral mutes, who arrive at the graveyard in perfect order, without the slightest sign of breathlessness or disconcertment.

In those days in Moscow there were still some survivors of the pre-Revolution liberal intelligentsia—strange, faded, shabby figures who emerged occasionally like ghosts to recall a Fabian summer school they had once attended, to borrow

31

a copy of the *New Statesman,* to reminisce about a visit to Tolstoy, or to ask for news of Mrs. Besant; ladies in high-necked blouses, men with bad breath and threadbare suits who could quote Walt Whitman and had read William Morris; pacifists, anti-vivisectionsts, feminists, the last poor eddy of a tide which had once strongly flowed. Their company was painful but inescapable; their efforts to uphold and justify the régime which had engulfed them were as unconvincing as protestations on behalf of an old expired love. They have all long since—to use Mrs. Webb's favourite word—disappeared.

I used occasionally also to see Prince Mirsky, whom I had vaguely known in England. He was a sombre, mournful man who obviously regretted his eccentric decision to return to his native land despite an aristocratic background in pre-Revolution Russia, a spell of fighting with the Whites in the civil war, and considerable involvement in extreme reactionary émigré politics in Paris and London. In the course of writing a biography of Lenin he became convinced of the validity of Leninism, and it was on the strength of this that he was given permission to come to Moscow, where, of course, he automatically became a Soviet citizen. His chief utility was to be produced at Intourist gatherings as a proof that one could be a prince and still *persona grata* in the U.S.S.R. Oumansky would point him out, gleefully dwelling upon his title and his record. This did not please Mirsky, but there was nothing he could do about it except get drunk on Intourist vodka, which was usually in good supply. Drinking only made him the more morose, and he would sit with his head sunk on his breast, deeply silent, and quite unresponsive to the Intourists twittering round him.

Mirsky would come from time to time and take a bath in my flat. As he dried, we chatted. His body, I remember, was oddly youthful and graceful, and there on top of it was that bearded, battered old head, with its sunken, forlorn eyes. Occasionally he would take me to a House of Foreign Writers which he frequented. It was a kind of Soviet P.E.N. Club, full of infinitely obscure (at least to me) men- and women-of-letters, for most of whom residence in the House of Foreign Writers constituted their sole literary credentials.

The atmosphere was decidedly old-fashioned. They discussed questions like the nature of Beauty and its relation to Truth, but not without a touch of anxiety, as though even this anodyne topic might, unless they were careful, move into dangerous channels. Their clothing and habits were likewise 'bohemian' in the old Café Royal style. The only name I knew was Aragon's. On one occasion he stood at the back of the room and recited with that particular unction that the French give to verse, a poem he had lately written on the Communist Party.

I imagine that most of the then occupants of the House of Foreign Writers have likewise long ago disappeared, though not, of course, Aragon. Others, doubtless, have taken their places. It is like the audience at the Windmill Theatre; as one row clears another moves up to be nearer the stage. As a Howard Fast turns in his belated apologia some young aspiring student is opening the works of Lenin for the first time, thereby embarking upon a course likely to culminate in his apologia some twenty years hence.

At the House of Foreign Writers Mirsky was as morose as at the Intourist reception. He fixed a female there, for whom he appeared to nourish a passion, with his sombre eyes, and turned for solace once more to the vodka bottle. For the others he appeared to have only contempt. I was glad to be his protégé rather than theirs. He earned his living by writing literary articles for the Soviet Press, mostly about European and American writers like François Mauriac, T. S. Eliot, Osbert Sitwell, and Sinclair Lewis. They were the sort of heavily denigratory articles which he would have been writing in Paris or in London. The last to appear was, in a similar strain, on the occasion of a Pushkin anniversary. Unfortunately, all unknown to him, the line had changed, and Pushkin had become once more a great national poet instead of an odious court lackey. Thenceforth Mirsky was seen no more, and presumably died in a concentration camp or at the hands of a firing-squad. He, too, disappeared.

Journalists, in my time, were still allowed to travel, and I went off by myself to the Ukraine and the Caucasus. It was very pleasant rolling along in old-fashioned *wagon-lits*, with glasses of tea constantly available, and with the possibility of halting conversation with Party officials and other dignitaries who alone were permitted to travel first-class. Once, an ordinary peasant, rather drunk, lurched into the restaurant car. I have never in my life seen anyone ejected so quickly and so expertly.

The railway carriage was a haven of rest and good cheer. Without, there were unspeakable horrors. One left the train with dread, and caught another with relief. Khrushchev (and he, if anyone, ought to know because he was a high official in the Ukraine at the time) has provided an authoritative account of the appalling consequences of the forced collectivisation of agriculture. To me, even in an age that has overflowed with horrors, it all stands out as particularly horrible—the deserted villages, without any living creature, animal or human, left in them, and the groaning train in a siding packed with peasant families who were being deported; and, by contrast, Bernard Shaw saying in Moscow that there was no food shortage, the lush articles on Soviet plenty by Duranty and others, the bogus supporting statistics naïvely accepted in learned journals.

I finished up at a German agricultural concession near Rostov. It was a little oasis of plenty and prosperity set in the sad wilderness which collectivisation had brought to pass in the surrounding countryside. The Germans in their green suits showed me their fields and granaries, their livestock and poultry, with immense satisfaction. They were friendly and jovial. In the evening we sat and talked and smoked. Their self-conscious efficiency was somewhat irritating, but it was impossible not to agree with them when they dwelt upon how prosperous this vast country might be, and to what a fearful plight it had been reduced. At nine o'clock they turned on their radio set to get the German news, and we heard that Hitler had that day become Chancellor. I expected them to be downcast. After all, they were agronomes, fond of music, kindly in their ways—or so it seemed. 'But this is terrible,' I said, assuming their agreement. Actually, they were delighted by the news, and made no effort to hide their satisfaction. They clustered eagerly round the large map of Southern Russia that hung on the wall, and scarcely bothered to answer when I asked what Hitler and his Nazis could possibly have to offer the likes of them. I knew then that another war was certain.

I came out of the U.S.S.R. by way of Latvia, stopping off at Leningrad. While there I went out to the cemetery to look at Dostoievsky's grave. It was difficult to find, and quite untended. While I stood beside it, a Communist funeral was in progress. The hearse was red instead of black, but otherwise it seemed like any other funeral. There were the same tears, the same consigning of dust to dust, the same embarrassed expressions on the faces of the less involved mourners. What a turn-out there must have been for Dostoievsky's interment! What orations! What an assembling of (to use the precious phrase we owe to Sir William Haley) Top People.

There were not many passengers on the train, but when we crossed the Soviet frontier all of us went into the corridor. We looked back at the small white stakes which marked the end of Soviet territory, and at the G.P.U. guards in their long, grey greatcoats; and suddenly, quite ridiculously, we all began to shake our fists and shout and jeer. It was quite spontaneous, and drew us together. Up to then we had not exchanged a word. Thenceforth, we chattered together, with slight undertones of hysteria, like old and intimate friends. The buffet at Riga station seemed like paradise, and all the open, well-fed and unfrightened faces round us were wonderful to behold. This ecstasy soon passed. Man cannot live by buffets alone, and as things got into focus one realised that all these seemingly radiant visages were only fat, pasty, bourgeois, clutching their brief-cases and counting out their money. The anger, however, remained.

Now I feel it no longer. Anger is a product of a hurt ego rather than of others' wrongs or sufferings. What one was angry about was one's own capacity to be beguiled. This is the fallacy of anti-Communism, or anti-anything. There cannot be darkness at noon—only darkened minds which make the bright noon seem dark. At the time I expressed my anger in the usual ways, arguing, talking, writing. Doubt-less, in a sense, it was a just anger, but now that I am older I distrust anger altogether. The end of *Lear* appeals to me more than *Timon of Athens,* and Saint Paul's Epistles and the Book of Common Prayer more than Marx or Cobbett or Carlyle or any of the vast army of the enraged and indignant.

In a mood of anger I wrote *Winter in Moscow,* which still enjoys a certain repute among old Moscow hands because of some fairly recognisable portraits of local characters, Russians, foreign, and Intourist. I was flattered to find that Mr. Bohlen, lately United States Ambassador in Moscow and Paris, regarded it as a collector's item. Also, I wrote numerous magazine and newspaper articles. One that remained unprinted because at that time it was considered too fantastic was called 'Red Imperialism,' and pointed out that a mission to free the toiling masses in countries adjoining the U.S.S.R. could easily get translated into what would be in effect the old familiar Pan-Slavism. When I read an account in the German Foreign Office archives of Molotov's conversations with Hitler in Berlin at the time of the Nazi-Soviet Pact, I chuckled over this. Most journalistic prophecies are mercifully forgotten, but it is gratifying once in a while to make one which is borne out by events.

When I think of Russia now I remember, not the grey, cruel, set faces of its masters, but rather how kindly and humorous those subjected to them managed to remain despite the physical and moral suffering they had to endure. I remember a little painted church standing in the moonlight like an exquisite jewel. Someone had managed, in inconceivably difficult circumstances, to keep its bright colours fresh and triumphant. I remember, too, going to see a superb production of *The Cherry Orchard* at the Stanislavsky Theatre in company with a Russian lady who had been through the Civil War and the appalling famine which followed, and how she remarked of the play: 'I can't understand what they're all bothering about. They've got plenty to eat.' I remember going to an Easter service in Kiev—the crowded cathedral, the overwhelmingly beautiful music, the intense sense which, as they worshipped, the congregation conveyed of eternity sweeping in like great breakers on the crumbling shores of time. Religion, wisely, assumes misfortune, and so survives, when earthly Utopian hopes, which must inevitably be disappointed, soon perish.

No one but a fool will contend that the Revolution might better not have happened, or, for that matter, that its occurrence was blessed. The point is that it happened, and the miracle is, not what it has destroyed, but what it has failed to destroy. I hear Podolsky laughing at Habeas Cadaver, and his laughter engulfs the Sputnik's bleep. In Boris Pasternak's novel *Doctor Zhivago* his hero feels a pygmy before the Revolution—'the monstrous machine of the future,' but, at the same time, he cannot but reflect: 'What a master operation. To seize . . . cut out . . . so magnificently and at one stroke all the old suppurating wounds.' As Marvell put it:

> To ruin the great work of time,
> And cast the Kingdoms old
> Into another mould.

It is very much how I feel myself. Yet how remarkable that Pasternak should have outlived Stalin and still have been able so to feel! How ominous for the grisly band who have inherited the 'monstrous machine' to which the Revolution gave rise!

Ghosh!

Almost the only Englishmen left in the world to-day are Indians. Who cares about the Boat Race outside Calcutta or Bombay? Where is regimental silver polished as assiduously as in Indian Army messes? If there are any Bertie Woosters still around, they are called, we may be sure, Sen Gupta or Abdul Rahman. Indian parliamentary eloquence retains Gladstonian echoes, unheard in Westminster for many a long day; Indian editorialists thunder and fulminate in a style which vanished, over here, with Garvin.

The fact is that, in expiring, the British Raj perpetuated itself in the persons of its successors. Nehru was the last viceroy; Kipling's ghost walks along the Mall in Simla, not in s.w.1, and those who follow the full Somerset Maugham ritual, and put on dinner-jackets in remote places, are likely to be Indian political officers posted to tribal areas. England's green and pleasant land has been washed up on India's coral strand. In Lucknow not long ago, it seems, a statue of Queen Victoria (these atrocious monuments which litter Indian cities have, alas, also survived; even Edwin Montagu in Calcutta) was found one morning to have been garlanded, I like to think by a painstaking minor government official struggling to marry off a string of daughters. The floral tribute which he thus, greatly daring, laid on the podgy bronze Empress, was, I am sure, heartfelt, and more symbolic than perhaps he realised.

This Victorian afterglow is nowhere more apparent than in the field of academic letters. Our professors have a restless taste for television, semantics and sociology. They no longer browse in their libraries, or notice the flowers that bloom in the spring. The clock at Grantchester may, for all they care, stand at any hour it pleases, or even go. They greatly prefer a good expense account meal in the Caprice to one of those edifying get-togethers in Soho, with plenty of *vin ordinaire* and good, rambling talk. Bloomsbury is as outmoded as Quiller-Couch, and literary whimsicality went out with A. A. Milne, Sir James Barrie and E. V. (or, for that matter, F. L.) Lucas. Even Logan Pearsall Smith, who had the merit of being American and rich, will scarcely do nowadays.

Not so Indian professors. Witness Professor Ghosh, who, in his *My English Journey,* has recorded his impressions of a visit he recently paid to this country under the auspices of the British Council. Professor Ghosh will browse with anyone. Bloomsbury is hallowed ground to him, and even a cup of instant coffee can be ambrosial. In the Café Royal he remembers an earlier bohemian clientele, and, visiting the premises of the National Book League, he pines for the *London Mercury* and the *Bookman*. The P.E.N. headquarters in Glebe Place strike him as 'quite a clearing-house of contemporary culture,' and the Garrick Club as 'a little overwhelming at first, in its magnitude and magnificence.' Calling at 31 Egerton Crescent, the residence of John Lehmann, he notices 'a little laburnum right over the front door-steps' which induces him to hum, sotto voce, as he enters the house:

Bring orchis, bring the fox-glove spire
The little speedwell's darling blue
Deep tulips ringed with dew
Laburnums dropping-wells of fire.

'He must be dull of soul,' Professor Ghosh writes, 'who is not induced to a mood of exalted, romantic reverie by the belfries of Oxford, the pinnacled vistas of Cambridge. Cambridge took me by the throat . . .' The professor, I confess, had a like effect on me. Some forty years ago I taught at an Indian college in what was then Travancore. We were affiliated to Madras University. My subject was English literature. One would take a phrase culled from what we called 'Little Dowden' (to distinguish it from Dowden's larger *Studies in Literature*), such as : 'Dryden found English brick and left it marble,' and expatiate upon it, in the certainty that one's words would be taken down by the attendant students, and regurgitated on all suitable, and even conceivable, occasions in essays and answers to examination questions. This weird rigmarole took place in a lecture-hall open at the sides, so that one looked out on an expanse of paddy-fields where men were treading round bamboo irrigation wheels, and emitting shrill cries as they did so. They looked like grotesquely enlarged daddy-long-legs. The sun beat down, and the moist, enervating heat suffused everyone and everything. It all gave an extra touch of fantasy to the process of education, always, to me, among the more bizarre of human activities.

Professor Ghosh's book recalled the scene with poignant vividness. 'Little Dowden,' one realised, had gone marching on. Dryden was still finding English brick and leaving it marble. Some of the passages ('The essay was born when Montagu began to take stock of himself and all human experience. It is one of the late-comers to the banquet of literature. It pre-supposes security and a civilised outlook on life. Seneca—particularly in his Epistles to Lucius—and Plutarch have been claimed as classical prototypes . . .') were almost unbearably evocative. One heard them being spoken, in that lilting accent, due, it has been suggested, to the fact that Welsh missionaries were among the first purveyors of English education in India. One saw the crowd of students in their white dhotis, as they waited to sit one of their innumerable examinations, frenziedly repeating them in the fond expectation that a question on the essay would come up.

The decay of the essay is a source of deep distress to Professor Ghosh. He 'sensed that something was very seriously amiss when Stephen Spender came to Calcutta a few years ago.' Taxed with neglecting the essay, 'Spender, who is a very good-natured man, said he thought no one wrote essays nowadays.' The professor then pointed out that Ivor Brown, William Sansom and Richard Church, to name no others, wrote them. 'It struck me as odd,' he sternly remarks, 'that the editor of *Encounter* was unaware that three writers, all of whom were his friends or acquaintances, wrote essays at all.' In London, when he brought the matter up again, 'Spender was rather at a loss,' as well as he might be. Professor Ghosh himself, in any case, is doing his valiant best to make good our essay deficiency. Among his four published works, two volumes of essays (*Tragedy and Other Essays* and *Nostalgia and Other Essays*) are listed as being 'in press.'

The most woeful consequence of imposing alien rule on a people is what sticks. Amritsar can be forgotten, and the Black Hole of Calcutta become a dim and legendary memory, but Eng. Lit., once implanted, echoes through the ages. History soon abolishes imperial pomp and circumstance, but not, alas, the *Oxford Book of English Verse*. The captains and the kings depart, the B.A.s remain; the White Man's Burden, when it grows too heavy and unrewarding, is easily shed, but there is Professor Ghosh to pick it up again, and, what is worse, lay it back at our feet. Tagorean Bengal twilight, honourable and right-honourable swamis, William Morris ashrams, a whole bastard culture, and the derelict hopes and fancies that go therewith—this survives, when the Raj itself is one with Nineveh and Tyre.

Thus Professor Ghosh rises up like an old issue of *The Times Literary Supplement*. Of Dr. Johnson: 'Like Charles Lamb, he is made one with London, and is a portion of the loveliness he once made more lovely.' Of Max Beerbohm's letters: 'The dainty, fastidious handwriting revealed the perfectionist who was always looking for the *mot juste*.' H. M. Tomlinson 'had the East End in his bones.' 'Sir Arthur Barker told me at Oxford—we were walking down Turl Street, after some book-shop browsing . . .' 'A faint aroma of leisure and of the academic life—something smacking of the port and Madeira in an Oxford common room hang about Bernard Darwin.' 'After all, it is because of the farewells and the sadnesses that the world is so infinitely sweet to us.' 'Not all the money of the Birlas or the Tatas can purchase the sanctities of Time.'

I could go on quoting for ever, like an old dotard thumbing over the banal relics of his first love affair. God bless you, Professor, I never thought to read such sentences again. God bless, too, the British Council that brought you here, and Sir Maurice Bowra who contributes a Foreword to your *English Journey* ('The friend from an ancient land, which has for centuries cultivated the fine art of words, knows what he is talking about'), and Frank Swinnerton who provides an Introduction ('Professor Ghosh came, saw and conquered'), and Macaulay whose famous Minute began it all, and the many willing hands and minds which have toiled in the Indian vineyard of Eng. Lit. Apart from 'Oliver Edwards' in *The Times,* nothing like it has been seen this many a year. Incidentally, how if 'Oliver Edwards,' hitherto assumed to have been Sir William Haley, were, after all, Professor Ghosh? It strikes me as quite a possibility.

Down with sex

In Racine, Wisconsin, on a Sunday morning the late autumn sun was shining, and the little lakeside town had a sleepy, tranquil air. A wide variety of religious services were available, ranging between a synagogue, a Roman Catholic mass, and some of the more exotic and peculiar of the Protestant sects. As far as I could judge, Racine's population divided themselves fairly evenly among these different edifices, and then emerged to stand about in little groups preparatory to dispersing for a midday meal.

Thus far everything was in accordance with the standard notion of a Mid-Western Sabbath as laid down by Sinclair

Lewis three decades and more ago. It was only when I dropped into a drug-store for a cup of coffee and a sandwich that I noticed a change which would have scandalised Babbits, and doubtless Lewis himself. Among the paper-back books and magazines displayed for sale was enough pornography to have made any under-the-counter Paris dealer in my young days green with envy. Not just the old familiar 'classics' in the genre—Frank Harris's *My Life and Loves*, *Fanny Hill* and so on; not merely the *Playboy*-style near nudes in what are known as provocative postures out of which schoolboys and adult solitaries weave their erotic fantasies. One-handed literature, as it used to be called in the days of the Weimar Republic in Germany. As well, the really vicious stuff about flagellation, wife-changing, every sort of kinky practice and perversion. As I ate my sandwich and drank my coffee I glanced through some of the advertisements. Old gentlemen could apply to a box number and be accommodated with a Lolita. Old ladies likewise with a gigolo. Contraptions were offered for sale for strapping on to substitute for a waning or spent organ. Likewise a long-playing record of a couple fornicating, recommended as providing sound-effects to enhance the delights of masturbation. All the squalor and filth underlying a sex-ridden society was on display and available.

A feeling of infinite melancholy afflicted me. How sad, how infinitely sad, all this was! In the Racine drug-store, it seemed to me, I was at the end of a long road. Havelock Ellis, D. H. Lawrence, H. G. Wells and many another pointed the way. Old Freud threw in his blessing, Kraft-Ebbing had a word to say. Wilhelm Reich was standing by with his orgone box. We were all to be happy as crickets in our freedom from past inhibitions and frustrations. Freedom broadening down from orgasm to orgasm; girls resolved to live their own lives by their own gas-fires, and easily persuaded to undress in its dim glow. On sun-drenched beach, in mountain hut, through dewy meadow and by winding stream —hey, ho! there's wind on the heath, sister, and an eiderdown on the bed.

And now it had all ended in this sordid display of printed matter; not in Sodom or Gomorrah, but in Racine, Wisconsin; not in Byzantine scenes of debauchery, but in a drug-store; no vine leaves to put in the hair, but only hamburgers and

42

ice-cream sundaes to swallow; no nymphs and satyrs, but only cheesecake, and the sad dreams of forlorn lovers, solitary playboys, whose mistresses come to them through the camera lens, that most ubiquitous of pandars.

What, then, has happened to sex which, according to the gospel of D. H. Lawrence, was to re-fertilise a spent civilisation, re-animate the wilting bodies of an unduly cerebral generation of men, and generally restore to our mid-twentieth-century lives the joyous fulfilment of happier and more innocent times?

The simple answer is that sex has been over-played. It has become an obsession, a mania, a sickness—as it was, incidentally, for poor Lawrence himself; like most of the prophets of this cult, a near, if not an actual, impotent. In America particularly, but to a greater or lesser extent throughout the western world, we have all got sex on the brain, which, apart from any other considerations, is a most unseemly place to have it. Every poster yells it at us, every popular song is about it, every dance enacts it; motion pictures and the television drench us with it, novels make it their interminable theme; it permeates every corner and cranny of life, from birth to the grave. Dating begins at nine years old, and even earlier; tiny tots who ought to be reading about Peter Rabbit and the Seven Dwarfs wear padded bras, paint their faces, and howl like randy hyenas at the Beatles. Young lovers arm themselves with birth pills and the *Kama Sutra,* and engage in erotic exercises which might have seemed excessive in the pages of *Les Liaisons Dangereuses*; middle-aged couples swap partners and bone up on *soixante-neuf*. The elderly, male and female, with dentures gleaming, look lecherously round; doze in their bath-chairs over *Candy* and *The Tropic of Cancer,* and with gibbering eagerness inform themselves on sex customs among Polynesian Aboriginals. Even the dead are curled and pomaded and scented for a tumble in the grave should any such possibility arise. The very worms must swoon at the perfumed morsels their cadavers offer. Nor is dedication to sex restricted to this world; the angels and the archangels, one is given to understand, have corporeal as well as heavenly blisses to confer. The bodies we resume on the Last Day will be in good shape thanks to Elizabeth Arden and Helena

43

Rubinstein; the trumpet will sound in the manner of some beatific Satchmo, and we shall twist and belly-dance our way into eternity.

Never, it is safe to say, in the history of the world has a country been as sex-ridden as America is to-day. And the rest of us, all eagerly emulating the American Way of Life, are going the same way. Sex has become the religion of the most civilised portions of the earth. The orgasm has replaced the Cross as the focus of longing and the image of fulfilment; the old pagan admonition, Do What Thou Wilt, has superseded the Pauline teaching that, since spirit and flesh lust contrary to one another, Ye Cannot Do the Things that Ye Would Do. In the beginning was the Flesh, and the Flesh became Word. Sex is the mysticism of materialism. We are to die in the spirit to be re-born in the flesh, rather than the other way round. Instead of the cult of the Virgin Mary we have the cult of the sex symbol—the busts, the thighs, the buttocks, of a Jean Harlow, a Marilyn Monroe, a Carrol Baker displayed in glossy photographs, on cinema and television screens, to be feasted upon by countless hungry eyes, the physical tensions thereby set up being subsequently relieved in auto-eroticism or in squirmings and couplings with an available partner. Eyes which launched, not a thousand ships, but a vast sea of seminal fluid; mistresses, not of kings and great ones, but of the Common Man, who clasps them to him and enjoys their wanton favours in his secret dreams.

The commercial possibilities of so overwhelming and omnipresent an obsession have naturally not been overlooked. Sex is very big business indeed. In a society whose most pressing need is to create wants and desires, sexual appetite is obviously a valuable adjunct to salesmanship. All that has to be done is to relate this particular appetite to the one needing to be stimulated. Nothing could be easier. A man smoking a particular brand of cigarette, or wearing a particular brand of shirt, is shown with a pretty girl. Both are smiling happily. They are by a waterfall or in a boat together. The implication is that shortly, in these delectable surroundings, they will be more intimately engaged. Thenceforth, puffing at the cigarette in question, or wearing the shirt, will be calculated to give a pleasurable sense of amorous anticipation. The same technique is applied to the most unlikely commodities, like bulldozers and computers. One imagines hot eyes feasting on a display of these ostensibly not very sensually alluring objects in the expectation that their erotic possibilities will become manifest. A rather more plausible association is provided by a television advertisement of a brand of coffee. One sees a married couple glumly at their breakfast table. Hubby irritably sips his coffee; then, as he appreciates its excellence, a beatific look spreads over his face. He decides after all not to go to the office that day; telephones to say he has a bad back, and one sees him disappearing into the bedroom with his spouse. Moral—wives who give their husbands that brand of coffee may expect a bonus matrimonial tumble in the mornings.

In the case of motor cars the sexual connotation is more flagrant. American motor cars are specially designed for sex-play. They are themselves sex-symbols; shining with chromium lust, redolent of aphrodisiacal leather, or, in the cheaper models, plastic. Mechanical ingenuity has removed the gears which might impede sex-play, and designed the seating arrangement in such a way as to facilitate every form of amorous indulgence except straight fornication. This can, admittedly, be undertaken in the back seat, but only with discomfort and some frustration.

Here we have something very characteristic of the American sex-obsession, which is ostensibly highly moral, and even respectable, in its manifestations. Its language is of love, not lechery; its intentions are honourable, not licentious. The bunnies in the Playboy Clubs are not for touching. That would be improper. Private eyes patrol the premises, and a poor bunny who just takes a tiny bite at one of her customers is fired out of hand. Everything short of war, President Roosevelt promised the English by way of help in the dark days of the blitz; in the same way, American girls are liable to promise their beaux everything short of fornication.

Visiting a Fraternity House on an American campus recently, I was shown with pride the Dating Room. Its lights were dim; musak was gently playing; a television set's unblinking eye stared at me. There were four or five divans discreetly arranged not to be too near together. What happened on them when they were in use? On the whole, I decided, it was better not to inquire or speculate. The scene, as I surveyed it, suggested a sterilised, homogenised, air-conditioned, centrally heated orgy of a kind which would assuredly have astonished, and maybe disgusted, the Emperor Tiberius.

Never, I should suppose, have human beings been so bombarded with sex as they are to-day on our side of the Iron Curtain. It lurks at every street corner, it glares from every page. Vast lips come pouting out to unite in inexorable suction with the other vast lips. From highbrow films moving at leaden pace, Curzon Street, Mon Amour, to strip-tease joints where expense-account lunchers, shreds of smoked salmon still about their mouths, work off their ultimate brandies in hyena yells as the last diaphanous covering on the female form divine is reached. Ah! Simone de Beauvoir, ah! Diana Dors, and, thanks to Sir Stanley Unwin's enterprise, welcome good old *Kama Sutra,* Big Ben of erotica, blue-chip offering from the mysterious East, steadfast over the years. Sex falls, like dark atomic rain, on the just and unjust alike. Ah! *dolce, dolce vita!*

An exposed, perhaps the most exposed, position in this downpour is pin-pointed by a letter, which appeared in the *New Statesman,* signed 'Mother of Two.' 'Sex,' she writes, 'is something to keep off until you are sure of the regular supply which only marriage ensures.' A husband's absence for a week, she goes on, after years of marriage, frustrates more than years of virginity. One would like to make the acquaintance of 'Father of Two' and silently shake his hand. He deserves a long-service medal, and perhaps danger money. *Erotica domestica* on so exalted and exacting a standard is something that not even William Burroughs has cared to tackle. *Les Liaisons Légitimes, Lady Chatterley's Husband*—what a terrific theme of ravening, quenchless and familiar lust between lawful sheets! What a tumble, valiantly and ingeniously protracted over the arduous years of regular supply, in a marital bed!

There are not wanting amiable guides to this jungle, red in denture and bra, of whom the late Marie Stopes was a forerunner. One remembers, breathlessly and secretly, turning over the pages of *Married Love* long before one had loved or been married. A toiler to-day in the same vineyard is Dr. Rebecca Liswood; founder and Executive Director of the Marriage Counselling Service of Greater New York. Dr. Liswood is an enthusiast for marital intercourse. At her lectures on the subject, she tells us, she exhorts her audience to keep at it, every day if possible, three times a week for moderate performers and, in the case of the handicapped, at any rate once a month.

They should, she insists, 'go right home and practise. Because practice makes perfect.' One imagines them making their way homewards from her lecture, two by two, a look of resolution in their faces, a sense of purpose in their step. The little woman, following Dr. Liswood's guidance, has her diaphragm 'washed and dried and dusted with cornstarch, ready to insert.' Hubby, with true gallantry, is ready, if need be, to 'make believe he is out with a mistress, and bring her flowers and chocolates.' He will even go to the expense of a baby-sitter and spend the night in a hotel (with his wife, not the baby-sitter) if thereby a more dazzling and effective performance is procured.

The case for monogamous marriage is strongly reinforced by such an attitude. A retired policeman in Darwin, Australia, described to me once how a large, blond German had arrived there and conceived a passion for an aboriginal girl, in other eyes squat and ill-favoured. As sexual relations with aboriginals are illegal for Europeans in Australia, he went off with her into the bush. In a week or so, the girl, though half his size, carried her German back into town on her back and handed him over to the authorities, politely explaining that she had done with him. Now, had they been married, a sagacious marriage counsellor might have groomed and induced him to stick it out sturdily and patiently.

When it is necessary Dr. Liswood can be severe. To a wife who complains that her husband has come bounding into the house and 'announced rather unromantically, "To-night, darling, wear the diaphragm," ' the doctor sharply remarks: 'Be complimented! Have intercourse with him! Enjoy it!' Her specification for the perfect wifely routine is as follows:

As a married woman you expect to have intercourse with your husband. Every night I want you to prepare yourself for this intimate occasion. You take your bath. You brush your hair. You brush your teeth. You put on a deodorant. You put on a pretty nightgown. And you insert your diaphragm. You will look pretty and fresh and sweet to him, and he will respond lovingly to you. It is not too much trouble to look your best and be your most appealing. Because you will be richly rewarded for your pains.

In the light of these careful conjugal instructions, the mass self-inflicted castrations which took place in the first years of the Christian era, so elegantly described by Gibbon, become comprehensible at last. One feels, as Gibbon suggests Origen did, that it might, after all, be more prudent to disarm the tempter.

A couple who might expect to receive an award from Dr. Liswood as model matrimonialists ran into an unexpected snag. So well, dutifully and cheerfully did they go to it each morning that the wife was induced to 'let out a great big whoop of pleasure,' which rang through the apartment building in which they lived, penetrating its thin walls and awakening their slothful and less amorous neighbours. The facetious comments thereby induced led the husband to desist in his efforts. Dr. Liswood, however assured him that the facetiousness was due to jealousy, and that 'he should have been glad that his wife enjoyed their relationship so much.' Thenceforth he continued with the good work unabashed. One likes to think of that chanticleer cry punctually sounding, to announce each morning that the day has dawned and the noise of life begun again.

Dr. Liswood's requirements are really quite exacting: 'Once or twice a day I'd like you to tighten the sphincter muscle that controls the bladder opening, for at the same time you will be pulling up the muscle at the entrance to the vaginal canal . . .' What with thus toning up the muscles of the vaginal canal, washing, drying and dusting the diaphragm, and so on, there is plenty to do. Nor need the coming of the menopause, the passage of years, the dropping out of hair or teeth, or any other intimation of physical decay, be admitted to impede the marriage of true bodies. In sickness and in health, till death them do part, they may continue, Dr. Liswood eloquently insists, to pursue happiness in one another's arms.

Even the outcasts are catered for. The great, and growing, spectator sex industry exists for their delectation. One sees them dotted about the auditorium in cinemas where erotic films are showing, staring hungrily at the photographs and posters advertising strip-tease joints, furtively turning over the pages of girlie magazines or perusing the outside covers of pornographic books. Forlorn figures, grey with years and hopelessness, unable or unwilling to find some partner with whom to share their sexual stirrings, such as they are; preferring their solitary fantasies and reveries—they, too, are admitted to America's great sex-feast, if only to pick up the crumbs which more favoured participants have let fall.

The doctrine behind the great dedication to sex is that sexual indulgence, being part of the pursuit of happiness, is part of the American heritage. Fortunate citizens of the Land of the Free are as entitled to sex as they are to the vote. Sex is an intrinsic element in the American Way of Life, and can no more be dispensed with than a refrigerator, or an automobile, or a broad highway to drive it along.

The sort of intellectual fervour which in the Thirties was dedicated to the Spanish Civil War and other leftish causes, trailing off into espionage for the U.S.S.R., now looks Kinseywards, and beyond. In the mid-twentieth century, it would seem, the workers of the world have nothing to lose but their orgasms. Anti-communism has suffocated the American Left, whose devotees, coughing and reeling, turn hopefully to a new dawn of sexual liberation. Many illustrious prophets and teachers have pointed the way, from Wilhelm Reich to Wayland Young. Reich, inventor of the orgone box (in which, in times past, distinguished writers like Saul Bellow and Norman Mailer have taken their seats with a view to charging their batteries), and a prolific theorist and evangelist, ended up a martyr to the cause, while Dr. Kinsey, a Mr. Greatheart of the sexual urge, if ever there was one, himself came to an early grave as a result of his earnest endeavours on its behalf. The work the doctor initiated is being carried on at Indiana State University, supported by the royalties on his books and the munificence of Colgate's toothpaste. In England, characteristically, the sexual revolution has been ushered in by more romantic and incoherent figures like D. H. Lawrence. *Lady Chatterley's Lover* may, in this sense, be compared with William Morris's *News from Nowhere* or Wilde's *Soul of Man Under Socialism,* the English text-book for an earlier social revolution.

In any case, the sexual revolution, unlike the social one, has actually happened. What is more, it has had the tacit approval of the powers-that-be. Clownish efforts have been made, admittedly, to censor particular books, and even to persecute particular individuals, but by and large established authority and big business have been solidly acquiescent. The great advertising industry, for instance, has helped by producing a quenchless flow of effective, if sometimes crude, propaganda in the form of cheesecake and erotica of various kinds. Likewise the publishers and the entertainment moguls. Even television has now joined in, with *Peyton Place* at the top of the Neilson Ratings, and shown twice a week in prime time. Faced with so formidable an array of forces, pockets of resistance like the Roman Catholic Church have been forced on to the defensive, and even to retreat.

It is not difficult to see why vested interests are liable to favour a sexual revolution. Nothing is more calculated to induce acceptance of the social and economic *status quo* than erotic obsessions when they are divorced from love or pro-creation. These, especially the former, can prove subversive forces in that they stimulate individual and particular emo-tions and loyalties, whereas eroticism is generalised and there-fore conducive to a conformist state of mind. Bread and circuses have to be paid for by the State; pornography is cheap and in plentiful supply. Marx said that religion was the opium of the people. Sex is better. It is their purple heart, their barbiturate; neatly capsuled, coloured, easy to swallow, inexpensive, or, better, on the National Health for nothing.

Religion, in any case, cannot evade posing certain moral propositions, however hypocritically and in however muffled a form, which tend to promote subversion. Thus Christianity has the disadvantage, from this point of view, of containing in its scriptures references to, for instance, the unsavouri-ness of riches, which are calculated to bring millionaires into disrepute. Sex has no such disadvantage. It challenges nothing, questions nothing. Unfolding the month's playmate in *Play-boy* magazine, any tendency to think and question things is automatically extinguished. Vietnam seems far, far away, and Alabama a song, not a place. It is interesting, in this connection, that whereas the Un-American Activities Committee assiduously hunted down every kind of political subversive, however obscure or crazy, it never seriously bothered about sexual subversives. Sex is American, and therefore O.K.

Even the most ardent advocates of the sexual revolution are inclined to feel that it is not working out quite as it should. Instead of sex-happy citizens of all ages blissfully coupling, psychiatrists and sexologists are besieged by patients eager to pour out their sexual woes. Orgasms have been too little and too late; despite bodies duly sealed and pasteurised, and recommended positions duly taken, the promised delight has failed to materialise. Happiness pursued in accordance with the book hast proved elusive. Something must be wrong.

Nonetheless, the concept of sex as pleasure primarily is pursued ever more fervidly and relentlessly. The function it has hitherto been thought to have—procreation—can be circumvented by contraceptives, rubber or pill; its emotional implications and undertones can be minimised to the point that the word 'love' is drained of all meaning and significance. I saw scrawled on a wall in Santa Monica in California: 'Lie down! I think I love you.' Thus stripped, sex becomes an orgasm merely. To the self-evident Rights in the famous Declaration there should be added this new essential one—the Right to Orgasm.

And, in the last resort (as has been brilliantly argued by Dr. Leslie H. Faber, a distinguished Washington, D.C., psychoanalyst), an orgasm is most conveniently, most hygienically and most inexpensively procured, not by love's transports, nor even in some casual sexual encounter, but in solitary masturbation. This, Dr. Faber plausibly contends, is the apogee of American sex:

According to the lesson of the laboratory there is only one perfect orgasm, if by 'perfect' we mean one wholly subject to its owner's will, wholly indifferent to human contingency or context. Clearly, the perfect orgasm is the orgasm achieved on one's own. No other consummation offers such certainty and moreover avoids the messiness that attends most human affairs. . . . Nor should we be too surprised if such solitary pleasure becomes the ideal by which all mutual sex is measured.

A similar view is expounded in more down-to-earth terms by Dr. Albert Ellis, one of the numerous popular sex evangelists of the day, in his *Sex and the Single Man*. He adduces the following formidable list of advantages offered by masturbation; that it

is most easily available; interferes not a whit with the sex rights or desires of others; is free from the dangers of venereal infection, pregnancy and abortion; serves as a fine apprenticeship in erotic fantasy; has a most calming effect on the sex urges and emotional excitation of millions of people who require relief quickly, and who are not likely to get it in non-masturbatory ways; involves a minimum of expense; requires much less expenditure of time and energy than do most forms of sexual activity; can be practised in many circumstances where heterosexual activity is impractical; can easily be interspersed with various nonsexual occupations that the individual is required to perform; ordinarily requires no preliminary steps; involves no apparatus or hygienic precautions; can be engaged in when one is sick, lying in bed, or living under conditions which normally preclude other forms of sex relations; and has various other advantages.

A strong recommendation indeed! Dr. Farber's interesting reflections on the subject were stimulated by a Sex Research Project to which his attention was drawn, directed by Dr. William H. Masters at the Washington University School of Medicine. This involves no less than, in the doctor's own words, the use of 'coloured motion-picture photography to record in absolute detail all phases of the human response cycle.' Dr. Farber's account of the resultant silent movie ('wisely, I think, the director has omitted a sound track, for the tiny events of the flesh he wishes to depict are not audible') is both diverting and perceptive. Its theme has already been imaginatively presented by Ingmar Bergman in his film, *The Silence,* and in ribald terms in the Dr. Krankheit sequence in *Candy.*

Dr. Master's movie, as Dr. Farber describes it, 'opens quite abruptly with a middle-distance shot of a standing naked woman, her head and lower legs deliberately outside the movie frame.' One arm, we learn from Dr. Farber, hangs at her side, 'the other is stretched towards her genitals in an Eve-like posture, except that it is apparent she is caressing rather than covering her parts.' More in the service of decorum than silence, Dr. Farber adds, 'There are no close-ups of her hand.' He goes on:

The naked, yet faceless, body informs us that this is a human female we are observing. The subsequent bodies which will appear in the film will also be faceless: as cuts are made from one body to another, the viewer may momentarily wonder if it is the same body he is looking at until he becomes used to distinguishing one body from another by differences in shape of breasts, distribution of pubic hair, etc.

In the first part of the movie 'all that occurs could take place on that lonely, upright body which appeared in the opening scene.' Then, 'quite suddenly and without preparation that body is no longer upright but supine, and the scene is a brilliantly lighted close-up of the opening of the vagina.' We may spare ourselves what follows, and hurry on to Dr. Farber's final Swiftian sentence: 'With some shrewdness, the director has withstood the tempting aesthetic impulse to conclude his movie with a final shot of the upright naked body with both arms now hanging limply down.'

This is Kinsey with a vengeance. The Indiana sexologist, as we must all hope, has gone to a better place where there is neither orgasm nor the giving of orgasm, but his spirit goes marching on in the person of Dr. Masters. Now, it would seem, the *reductio ad absurdum* really has been reached in this latest and most bizarre of all sex-symbols; the Lady of the Laboratory, as Dr. Farber felicitously calls her. Like the Unknown Soldier, she deserves a monument. She is the ultimate cover-girl; Bunny of Bunnies, a broiler-house Bardot; a Marilyn who has been transported into transcendental regions of orgasm pure and undefiled, a Carrol Baker observed, not by libidinous dreamers, but by scientists in white coats going about their lawful laboratory occasions.

Love's mysteries in souls do grow, but yet the body is his book, Donne wrote. Dr. Masters's movie is the book itself; a torso and a hand, presented in colour. No need now to date and strive. Lay aside potions, unguents, creams and colours and pencils; all the multitudinous and so often and so sweetly recommended resources of the great Beauty Industry. They are needed no longer. Let the musak cease from troubling, the diaphragm stay undusted, and the birth pill rest in its box. Hush! Peace! Our Lady of the Laboratory is at work. Her orgasm is dedicated to science, not pleasure; to knowledge, not love. It is for all of us, presented in colour, silently. Oh, what rapture!

It would seem that the cycle is now complete. Sex begins in ecstasy, momentarily fusing two separate egos into union with one another and with all life; it ends in the total separation of one ego exclusively preoccupied with its own orgasm. Sex begins as a window on to eternity, and it ends in a dark cellar self-enclosed and boarded up with time. Sex begins as the sap rising in a tree to make buds and blossoms and leaves and fruit; it ends in Dr. Masters's movie. Sex begins as a mystery out of which has come the art, the poetry, the religion, the delight of successive civilisations; it ends in a laboratory. Sex begins in passion which comprehends the concepts of both suffering and joy; it ends in a trivial dream of pleasure which itself soon dissolves into the solitude and despair of self-gratification.

The legend of Max

Considering that Max Beerbohm resolutely refused to put pen to paper, either to write or draw, in the last decades of his life, the growth of his reputation during those years was quite remarkable. As with E. M. Forster, his fame waxed with every book he did not write. Round the Mediterranean coast from Rapallo, where Beerbohm lived, lies Cap Ferrat on the French Riviera, where another English writer, Somerset Maugham, as diligent as Beerbohm was indolent, lived out his last days. *His* reputation, he would sometimes wryly reflect, unlike Beerbohm's, dwindled as volume succeeded volume and edition edition, until, by the time *Of Human Bondage* touched the million mark, there was no critic so lowly of brow as to pay him homage.

I remember once at luncheon at Maugham's Villa Mauresque (a good deal more stately, it goes without saying, than the Rapallo establishment) someone remarking that T. S. Eliot had made himself responsible for raising a small sum to buy Beerbohm a wireless set. Our host looked fussed, and his stutter became more compulsive. There was something preposterous, as he seemed to feel, about the whole project —Eliot, a wireless set, Beerbohm's penury! No poet bothered his head about whether or not he, Maugham, had a wireless set; least of all Eliot. It was Sir Max, but not Sir Somerset. Life is so very unjust. After all, *Cakes and Ale* is an incomparably better piece of writing than anything Beerbohm did, or could have done. Yet no ponderous Behrman arrived at Cap Ferrat to produce one of those interminably detailed *New Yorker* series, afterwards published as a fat volume, on life at the Villa Mauresque.

Beerbohm never was a popular writer, and remained to the end of his life in relatively straitened financial circumstances. His books had a small but steady sale in a collected edition, and, of course, the drawings in their originals were deservedly much sought after, though a project I once vaguely put up to Beerbohm's publisher for a portfolio of reproductions was not considered feasible. His only contact with the larger public outside his relatively restricted circle of devotees was through radio. During the 1939-45 war years, when he was perforce settled in England, he gave some talks in the form of personal reminiscences. Probably no one has ever used radio in this particular genre to better effect. The voice, faltering a little, was precise and kindly. the style elegant, with an agreeably old-fashioned flavour, particularly appreciated in that time of Churchillian rhetoric, boys' paper Montgomery slang, and one of the war's more lamentable consequences—Forces humour. I had occasion to listen to a tape of one of the talks—on George Moore—and found it quite excellent. Beerbohm, I may add, resolutely refused to have anything to do with television. An American crew once actually arrived in Rapallo, and tried to lure him in front of the cameras. No persuasion, financial or other, would induce him to yield. All he had to do, he was told, was to smile and say: 'Good evening, I'm happy to be with you.' 'But that wouldn't be true,' Beerbohm sweetly riposted.

It was as a person rather than as a writer or cartoonist or very occasional broadcaster that Beerbohm was famous. Consciously and deliberately, in his ways, attire, idiom and attitude of mind, he modelled himself on a figure of the eighties, and never ostensibly put so much as a toe into the twentieth century. His conversational gifts and charm were much exaggerated by admirers who in reality were more attracted by the period flavour he conveyed than by any intrinsic excellence in his writings or pleasure in his company. The world has proved a decidedly sombre place in recent years for the consciously cultivated classes. They have been forced either to make idiots of themselves by joining inherently unsympathetic Leftist causes, or to isolate themselves in an unfashionable æstheticism, drivelling away their lives in university lecture-halls or the editorial offices of high-brow journals. In the circumstances, any occasion for indulgence in nostalgia is welcome. Beerbohm provided such an occasion, deriving, as he did, directly from the Wilde-Beardsley circle, with no intervening contamination as a Friend of the Soviet Union, or of Berenson.

The more's the pity, then, that Beerbohm's official biographer (rather significantly, his own choice) should have been Lord David Cecil; precisely the sort of person to fix his gaze on the legendary, period Beerbohm, and to ignore the little, nervous, greatly talented and very likeable man, who, after all, did exist, however discreetly and skilfully camouflaged. Cecil's book really tells one nothing about Beerbohm that was not known before. He just, as it were, nicely mounts and hangs the official portrait—which, I fear, is exactly what his subject wanted. His biography is skilful, tired, wan, considerate, and quite unmemorable. It will stand on the shelves of every decent library unread through the years— the definitive Max.

There was a steady stream of visitors to the Rapallo shrine, carefully controlled by successive *gouvernantes*—first, the actress Florence Kahn, and then Elizabeth Jungmann, a German lady. As it happened, I paid visits under both régimes. the villa itself was singularly unattractive, formed by amalgamating two adjoining residences into one. When Beerbohm first went there, it may well have been pleasant enough, but subsequently a main road just outside the front door brought a noisy and unending stream of traffic, with accompanying petrol fumes. The din was terrible. It would have been perfectly possible to dispose of the villa reasonably advantageously, and to buy another quieter one with the money, but Beerbohm resolutely refused to move. He said he did not mind the noise; in fact, positively liked it. On one of my visits we were left alone together for a few moments on the roof, the reigning *gouvernante,* Miss Kahn, having been called to the telephone. Beerbohm whispered to me confidentially that he spent a lot of time standing in the sun. To prove his point he took off the straw boater he habitually wore at a rakish angle, revealing the nut-brown dome of his head. There was something splendid about that tanned old head exposed to the Italian sun during long standing sessions. Sitting, I reflected, might have implied the possibility of addressing himself to work at a desk. In that sense, standing was an act of defiance, which I applauded.

The first time I went to see Beerbohm, not knowing the way I took one of the broken-down, fly-blown horse carriages which still ply for hire in Rapallo. It was a lamentable equipage, whose horse creaked as rustily as the springs. Beerbohm himself came to the door to let me in, and, seeing how I had arrived, murmured: 'Carriage folk, I see.' It struck the right note, and greatly pleased me. Inside there was Miss Kahn, Beerbohm's first wife, a powdery, quavery American lady, very fussy and tiresome. Such ladies combine the contralto petulance of Kensington and Park Avenue; a dread combination. If there is one thing worse than a bad actress it is a good one; better Bardot than Bernhardt any day. By chance I once had seen Miss Kahn act in some infinitely tedious Pirandello play at a repertory theatre somewhere in the north of England. As I had forgotten the name of the play and where I had seen it, I did not try to curry favour with my hostess by mentioning it.

Beerbohm was wearing a carefully pressed linen suit, cream coloured and double-breasted, a stiff collar and tie, and the already mentioned straw boater. We sat down to a delicate tea of wafer-thin cucumber sandwiches, tiny cakes, and weak china tea and lemon dispensed by Miss Kahn. Beerbohm's eyes were red-rimmed and watery, and, I thought, very forlorn. He was such a sad, sad little man, really.

Over tea, prodded by Miss Kahn, he regaled me with anecdotes; rather automatically, as it seemed to me, as though he had told them many times before and was sick to death of them. He was like a poor old performing dog at a circus, wearing its little faded skirt, and still able to get on its hind legs—just; then looking round in the apologetic, melancholy way old animals do. 'Tell him about Hilaire Belloc's washing,' Miss Kahn rapped, and he obediently embarked on a long story about how Belloc ('dear Belloc,' he called him) left his laundry in some great house, with endless complications over recovering it.

This routine of telling anecdotes under the reigning *gouvernante*'s supervision became a sort of ritual which precluded authentic conversation. When I mentioned with admiration his brilliant cartoon of Edward VII, that gross, despicable figure, he just murmured something about the dear Queen Mother. It is generally believed that the caricature in question delayed his knighthood for some twenty years. I calculate that, on the same basis, I might reasonably expect to join the Beatles as an M.B.E. in my late eighties or early nineties. Again, I spoke of Beerbohm's harsh treatment of Kipling in the drawing he did of him. He just shook his head sadly. It was something, he said, which he regretted because Kipling had been kind to him when he first started writing. Yet again, on the subject of *Punch* Beerbohm was evasive. Yes, it was true that his drawings had been rejected by the then editor, Owen Seaman (a portentous ass, if ever there was one), and that he and Belloc had worked for a while on a rival magazine, *Judy*. The venture soon fizzled out. As *Judy*'s political cartoonist, Beerbohm was not a great success, being little interested in day-by-day politics, and lacking the capacity of a Partridge or a Low to reduce public issues to some simple, vivid proposition.

After Miss Kahn's death in 1951, Miss Jungmann took up her residence in the Rapallo Villa. Her régime did not differ greatly from the Kahn one, though she gave an impression of being more robust and less consciously refined than her predecessor. Before coming to Beerbohm she had looked after an ailing German writer, Gerhardt Hauptmann. Obviously, she specialised in caring for elderly, frail men-of-letters, and I rather earmarked her in my mind for Eliot after Beerbohm. As things turned out, she married Beerbohm more or less on his death-bed, and then shortly afterwards died tragically in her bath in the Rapallo Villa. Under Miss Jungmann, the tea, provender and anecdotes were more or less the same. Her hand on the reins was clumsier, but perhaps kindlier; Beerbohm looked at her out of the corner of his rheumy eye with, I thought, less apprehension than in Miss Kahn's case. It was like the difference between a torrid sirocco wind and a gusty north-easter.

The impression Beerbohm left on me was of someone in whom the instinct to run for cover had become second nature. But what was he scared of? What was he running away from? Needless to say, no light is shed on the question in Lord David Cecil's biography. Fortunately, the Letters to Reggie Turner, Beerbohm's closest friend at Oxford, edited by Rupert Hart-Davis, and Professor Weintraub's excellent Life of Turner, are, at any rate by implication, more informative. Beerbohm, it seems to me to emerge, was in panic flight through most of his life from two things—his Jewishness and his homosexuality. Turner, by contrast, was an admitted, almost a stage Jew; the illegitimate offspring of a wealthy Jewish family, the Levi-Lawsons (the double-barrelled name represented a half-way house on a journey from Levi to Lawson, where they came to rest until the head of the family was raised to the peerage as Viscount Burnham), who owned the *Daily Telegraph*. He was also a more or less open homosexual, who went in for 'renters,' male prostitutes of the kind who brought about Wilde's downfall. It was, as I see it, Turner's courageous acceptance of these two, in Beerbohm's eyes, appalling disabilities which induced him to be so devoted to Turner, almost to the point of hero-worship, despite his hideous appearance, his obscure birth and dubious social position, which in the ordinary way would have offended so fastidious and snobbish an observer of the English social scene.

When Hesketh Pearson was writing his biography of Beerbohm's half-brother, the actor and impresario Beerbohm-Tree, he exchanged letters with Beerbohm. In the course of one of them, which he showed me, Beerbohm mentioned whimsically that, unfortunately, the family was not Jewish, as had often been suggested, but pure German. Cecil accepts this at its face value. Other members of the family, including Beerbohm-Tree, as I understood from Pearson, took a different view. The only interest in the matter is why Beerbohm should have been so insistent upon not being a Jew. Doubtless the explanation was his passion to emerge into the English upper-class social landscape. The upper-class English are not, like their American equivalents, overtly anti-semitic, but they create a milieu in which Jews seem outlandish, and therefore feel alien and ill-at-ease. The worst thing we do to well-off Jews in England is to make them as stupid, snobbish and philistine as the well-off natives. This is our version of Dachau. It took a Disraeli to break into the English upper-classes on his own terms, and triumph over them. Beerbohm was by no means a Disraeli, and desperately wanted to substitute Burke's *Landed Gentry* for the family Talmud. The English upper-classes do not persecute Jews; they ruin them. A Mailer or a Bellow over here, at any rate in Beerbohm's time, would be sporting a Guards' tie, and, like a Siegfried Sassoon, wearing himself out riding to hounds. Behind Beerbohm's façade of a Yellow Book æsthete there lurked a frightened Rabbi.

Beerbohm's homosexuality is obvious even in Lord David Cecil's biography, despite a categorical denial that Beerbohm was homosexual at all. His actress passions—for Cissy Loftus, Grace Canover (Kilseen), Constance Collier; all prototypes for his Zuleika Dobson—are quite unconvincing. Like many another, the Wilde trial troubled and distressed him. By comparison, Turner was both more candid and more courageous. Beerbohm was the famous and successful one, and Turner only a writer of indifferent, and now hopelessly dated, novels, and the originator of that last infirmity of ignoble gossip-writers, 'London Day by Day' in the *Daily Telegraph*. Yet, one feels, Turner with his india-rubber face, blue complexion, huge nose, blinking eyes and endlessly repeated reminiscences of Wilde, so well portrayed as Constable in D. H. Lawrence's novel, *Aaron's Rod*, was the more real, and in a way the nobler, character of the two of them.

Though Turner was living in Florence when Beerbohm was at Rapallo, they saw each other only very occasionally. Beerbohm's affection for Turner remained undiminished, but in the presence of grander visitors he was probably a little ashamed of him. Turner, for his part, seems to have found his visits to Beerbohm flat and tedious. There was really no point in either of them telling stories which both knew only too well, and obligatory abstemious practices like retiring to bed at ten o'clock were little to Turner's taste. All the same, I should very much have liked to see the two of them together—the little, sad, faded dandy, and his gargoyle; the dearest Reggie of other modes and days.

The eye-witness fallacy

The darkest of Dark Ages is surely upon us, not owing to a paucity of documentation, but to a superabundance. So many participants and ostensible eye-witnesses have had their say, often at unconscionable length. The fat Memoirs, Journals, Biographies, and Autobiographies accumulate, as do the mountainous, yellowing files of newspapers and magazines. There was a hope that in half a century or so they might disintegrate into dust. Now, the invention of microfilm ensures their indefinite preservation. Trying to reconstruct the recent past from them, one finds oneself trapped, like Jonah in his whale, in a dark, cavernous stomach of print. The record of our times is plenteously and minutely available, but so confused, so contradictory, so tainted with conscious and unconscious deception, prejudice, and self-justification, as to produce, in its final effect, only a blur. There is a thronging cast; all concerned to speak their lines with maximum effect. But where's the play? Only a crazy spectacular without sequence or plot.

One is the more grateful, therefore, for any attempt to package and cellophane-wrap selected portions of this vast documentation. What gives acute indigestion taken as a meal can be painlessly consumed in cereal form, as a breakfast food. Two volumes in this genre have lately come into my hands—*They Saw It Happen*, compiled by Professor Asa Briggs, and *Eye-Witness*, selected and edited by Mr. John Fisher. The former is sub-titled 'An Anthology of Eye-

Witnesses' Accounts of Events in British History 1897-1940,'
and the latter 'An Anthology of British Reporting.' Professor Briggs begins with an account by H. W. Lucy, the
famous Toby M.P. of *Punch,* of the moving of the Royal
Address on the occasion of Queen Victoria's Diamond Jubilee.
He ends with Sir Winston Churchill's first appearance in the
House of Commons as Prime Minister, on 13th May, 1940,
as described by Harry Boardman, for many years the writer
of the *Guardian*'s Parliamentary Sketch. Mr. Fisher's collection ranges from *The Times*'s report of Napoleon's departure for St. Helena after his defeat at Waterloo, to the *Daily
Telegraph*'s of Khrushchev's huge turbulent press conference
in Paris, when the Summit Conference failed to take place.
Where Professor Briggs's sources are varied, Mr. Fisher's are
exclusively journalistic.

For one who, like myself, has been professionally engaged
for the last four decades in reporting and commenting upon
the contemporary scene, compilations like these have a more
than passing interest. How far, one asks oneself, can eye-
witness reports of the kind chosen by Professor Briggs and
Mr. Fisher be accepted as objectively true? Considered as
historical evidence, what degree of credibility may be accorded
them? At some of the scenes described I was myself present.
Quite a number of the eye-witnesses adduced, more particularly
in Mr. Fisher's volume, I have known and liked; trailed round
with them from Abadan to Little Rock, from Nairobi to
Singapore; sat in bars gossiping, laughing, speculating on
how the day's hard-won story will fare at the hands of sub-
editors. To consider whether these jovial companions may be
regarded as witnesses of truth implies no reflection on them.
Reporters, like players in an orchestra, must keep a wary eye
on the conductor. Moreover, there is some basis for the
distinction, constantly made in Soviet apologetics, between
subjective and objective truth. Take, for instance, Rousseau,
who was convinced that his *Confessions* were, as he claimed,
entirely truthful. In fact, for the most part, they consisted
of fabrications, often to his own discredit. Nonetheless,
the *Confessions* remain an enchanting exercise in self-revela-
tion. Again, Harold Laski was one of the most elaborate
and audacious liars I have ever known. He is still, however,
and I dare say rightly, regarded as an accomplished and

perceptive scholar, whose testimony about his times deserves consideration, and sometimes quotation.

Professor Briggs includes an extract from George Orwell's *Homage to Catalonia* by way of covering the Spanish Civil War. The book is a fine one, perhaps, apart from *Animal Farm,* Orwell's finest, and Orwell himself was considered by his friends and admirers (among whom I count myself) as being ardently truthful, to the point of awkwardness. Yet a closer examination of his writings discloses grotesque inaccuracies in what purport to be objective descriptions. For example, his account of Kentish hop-pickers and hop-picking in *A Clergyman's Daughter.* Or his account of working-class life in *The Road to Wigan Pier* (also quoted by Professor Briggs), which is simply the fruit of an Etonian's reading of Dickens, Gissing, and other late-Victorian novelists, reinforced by the *News of the World*—one of Orwell's favourite newspapers. Or, for that matter, his account in *Down and Out in Paris* of being a waiter. This, according to a professional I consulted, is quite ludicrously inexact. Orwell, in fact, was neither Down nor Out, in any true sense of the terms. Like all who have strong convictions and creative imaginations, he saw what he wanted to see, and became what he wanted to be. His own authentic being was abolished when he changed his name from Blair to Orwell. They ever must believe a lie who see with, not through, the eye, Blake wrote. Orwell saw with the glass eye he had fixed into Blair's skull. And he believed what this glass eye registered with all the deep, dry fervour of a passionately truthful nature.

Another of Professor Briggs's eye-witnesses who has, for me, a particular interest, is Beatrice Webb. Her *Journal,* so elegantly written and diverting, so full of 'inside information' and undertones of malice, may well be regarded by posterity as a basic document of this age. As one who knew her, and was present at some of the occasions described in the *Journal,* I should be hesitant about thus accepting her testimony at its face value. She was a woman with strong and fluctuating sentiments, especially where people were concerned, and adjusted her account of encounters and conversations with them accordingly. The melancholic disposition of an insomniac and frustrated mystic (especially operative in the small hours of the morning, when she was accustomed to write up her *Journal*) coloured and distorted her impressions. In her earlier anti-communist days, she found Marxists, in particular Soviet ones, personally repugnant and politically derisory. When she decided, with her consort, Sidney, to abase herself before the Soviet régime, they became creatures of light and virtue. Her fine intelligence was dedicated, in the closing years of her life, to upholding the monstrous false-hoods of Soviet propaganda, and to justifying the monstrous cruelties of Stalin's rule. All this is understandable and tragic in personal terms, but what about the chronicler? Can the *Journal* of the inspirer and part-author of *Soviet Communism: A New Civilisation* be accepted as valid historical evidence?

A Beatrice Webb or George Orwell deceive themselves; journalists are paid to deceive others. To succeed in their profession, they must get on to the front page, the way to which, more often than not, is paved with bad intentions. One is covering, let us say, a G.A.T.T. conference in Geneva for one of Lord Beaverbrook's newspapers in the day when he controlled them, as he did in his lifetime, from day to day, and often from hour to hour, however far away and inaccessible might be his physical presence. Idle, then, if one's story is ever to see the light of day, to make it other than derisory. Lord Beaverbrook did not care for G.A.T.T. Or, again, one is covering for the *Guardian* a revolt against British rule in some colonial territory. Equally idle to file except on the supposition that the revolt is justified. Liberal-ism requires that anyone who murders a British soldier is a hero, and anyone who is murdered by a British soldier is a martyr. Our enemies are always admirable, our friends (a diminishing band) despicable.

The perversions of principle are liable to be more deleterious than those of self-interest and sycophancy. The Rev. C. F. Andrews, in the days of C. P. Scott, used to report on India in the *Manchester Guardian*. He was a bearded, earnest man, of saintly ways, and passionately devoted to Indians and India. His reporting was deeply coloured with his own expectations and hopes; his prognostications, as I recall them, have all been falsified by events. He believed, for instance, that moderates like Shrinivasa Sastri and Jayakar wielded enduring influence; that the Congress leaders were wedded to non-violence, and would be satisfied with Dominion Status, and that Jinnah's Moslem League would readily participate in an All-India Government. Once he told me that he saw a close resemblance between Gandhi's trial by the British and Christ's by Pilate. The very fact that a reporter like Andrews is so sincere, and, in his own estimation, so truthful, makes his falsifications the more acceptable. After all, when Lord Beaverbrook drove his editorial and reporting chain-gang into demonstrating, in the late thirties, that there would be no war, the fraud was too palpable to convince any but the most gullible of his readers. Likewise when he similarly drove them into action to oppose any move to take Britain into the Common Market.

It is sad to reflect that the more reputable the eye-witness, the greater the caution with which his testimony should be received. In the post-war years, *The Times* correspondence from Eastern and Central Europe tended to reflect Communist sympathies, on the same principle, presumably, that induced Geoffrey Dawson, when he was Editor, on his own confession, to strive to keep out of the newspaper's columns anything which would displease the Third Reich's Nazi bosses. Such distortion, just because it appears in *The Times*, is more effective than the ravings of a Northcliffe or Rothermere or Beaverbrook. The accomplished, the opinionated, the reputable writer, liable by virtue of these very qualities to see what he wants to see and hear what he wants to hear, will easily persuade and delude, where the hack's obviously slanted reporting gets disregarded. Out of righteousness and sincerity have come more deception than out of villainy and deliberate deceit. The tabloid Press, with many readers, deludes few: Serious newspapers like *The Times* and *The Guardian*, with fewer readers, delude many.

In 1932-3, when I was a reporter in Moscow, far the most distinguished and famous of the foreign journalists there was Walter Duranty. His dispatches appeared in the esteemed *New York Times*, prominently displayed among All the News That Is Fit to Print. He briefed visiting notabilities; the State Department and the Foreign Office paid heed to his views and account of Soviet conditions. As an eye-witness, he

C

was pre-eminent. The story on which we were all, at that time, mainly engaged was the collectivisation of agriculture, which Stalin had ordered should be carried through whatever the consequences. Duranty reported that, far from there being any famine as a result of collectivisation, the granaries were bursting, the milk-maids were apple-cheeked, the peasants were stuffing themselves with good things. Photographs and documentary films in the same sense were made plenteously available by the Soviet authorities and widely distributed and used. All this was totally untrue. There was an appalling famine. I saw it myself, and a far more eminent eye-witness that I—none other than Mr. Khrushchev—has admitted its existence, and dwelt upon its horrors. Yet Duranty's dispatches exist still, in the *New York Times* files, doubtless one day to be extracted by some future Professor Briggs or Mr. Fisher as eye-witness reports of unimpeachable reliability. As a drinking companion Duranty was delightful. In private conversation, he was cynical, amusing and shrewd. In the respectable and solemn columns of the newspaper he served he planted monstrous falsehoods, capable of misleading posterity as they misled his contemporaries. Like the evil that men do, the falsehoods that they tell live after them; their truths are all too often interred with their hopes.

In assessing the reliability of the reporting of foreign correspondents, it is necessary to consider their circumstances—a corrective which is rarely applied, doubtless because, except among professionals, it is too little understood. Correspondent A is stationed in the capital of a monolithic Communist State. He has, perhaps, a wife or a mistress of the country. On the whole, his life there is congenial. He wants to stay. Black Market currency, at a more advantageous rate than appears in his expense accounts, enables him to be relatively affluent. He knows that, as is the case with all foreigners, especially those not enjoying diplomatic immunity, it would be easy for the authorities to fabricate plausible charges against him to get him expelled, or even arrested. In such countries, normal journalistic activities can be presented as espionage, normal capitalistic 'fiddling' as a crime against the State. Small wonder, then, that he finds it expedient to be on good terms with the authorities, which means, in practice, that his tussles with the censorship are shadow-boxing, and that he is, to a greater or lesser extent, available as a channel for propaganda. Such is his situation inside the country. Outside, even in the discerning eyes of a Professor Briggs or Mr. Fisher, he rates as an eye-witness. Whereas exiles or émigrés are suspect, his *bona fides* are impeccable. He knows because he has seen. His reports are from the horse's mouth. They carry the authentic stamp of a date-line—that treacherous beacon lighting the way to so much falsification, though news-editors have no choice but to chart their course by it.

Correspondent B is stationed in one of the capitals of what we like to call the Free World; let us say Washington. He naturally and necessarily has friends on Capitol Hill, from whom he gets news, and who, in return, deserve consideration in his dispatches. His contacts in the White House and the State Department are no less important to him, and can only be nourished by, to some extent, refraining from treading on their corns or troubling their ulcers. No exclusives fall to the awkward squad. His own Embassy is an important source of news. The Ambassador will scarcely be available for one of those cosy, private chats, so helpful in making a good appearance in to-morrow's paper, if yesterday's contained matter displeasing to him. The pressures are more subtle and gentle than in the monolithic Communist State; the brain-washing is done with rose water and delicately scented soap. But still there are pressures, there is brain-washing.

Correspondent C is a rover. He moves from trouble-spot to trouble-spot, arriving in Baghdad or Laos or Vietnam with the necessity upon him to file an authoritative story within twenty-four hours. It is a challenge, an opportunity. He sees his by-line in large black type; observes in his mind's eye the cross-heads and slabs of solid print in which his story is set forth. Who will fill him in before it is too late for the first edition? There is always a bar where others similarly bent congregate; there are always stringers, thank God for them —underlings in the trade, whose meagre earnings are often supplemented from government, or other public or private funds in return for services rendered. No matter. How do you spell it, old boy—'BOUMEDIENNE'—'BOUNOUM.' Thanks, old boy. The story is duly confectioned. It duly appears. Once more Our Special Correspondent is on the spot, and first with the news.

Either A or B or C, especially if he happens to write as elegantly as an Alistair Cooke, as vividly as a Hershley, or as forcefully as a Joseph Alsop, can provide precious pabulum for a Professor Briggs or Mr. Fisher. After all, they are indubitably eye-witnesses.

Mr. Fisher includes in *Eye-Witness* an account by Maurice Fagence of the *Daily Herald*, of the sentencing of the Nuremberg War Criminals. Had he turned to the late *News Chronicle* for the subsequent scenes at the scaffold, he would have found an equally vivid report of Goering's execution, his demeanour and last words being faithfully recorded. In fact, of course, as Goering took his own life he never was executed. So what? It is a fine piece of writing by an eye-witness. Take, again, another of Mr. Fisher's choices, A. J. Cummings's report, also in the *News Chronicle,* of the close of the Metro-Vickers Trial in Moscow. As Cummings saw it, the opening stages of the trial were a 'model of calmness and correctitude.' Vishinsky, who was to become famous as the bullying prosecutor of Old Bolshevik comrades when they were at his mercy, was 'a man of great culture,' and the Judge, Ulrich, a toady so obsequiously disposed towards the shifting ferocity of Stalin's terrorism that he managed to survive the purges, 'might be mistaken in England for a middle-class stockbroker with a benevolent outlook on the world at large.' Cummings was an intelligent, likeable man, who prided himself on his journalistic integrity. I have no wish to malign his memory. Even so, as a Moscow eyewitness he seems to me, to put it mildly, of doubtful validity. From conversations with him towards the end of his life, I would deduce that he would then have agreed with this judgment. Mr. Fisher, however, deems otherwise, and who shall blame him? Cummings is a reputable name, and the *News Chronicle* was a reputable newspaper.

After the Nuremberg and Metro-Vickers trials, it is interesting to turn to J. E. Dillon's report, in the *Daily Telegraph,* of Dreyfus's second trial in 1899. Whether or not Dillon over-dramatised the scene, I have no means of knowing, but at least his reaction to Dreyfus's conviction was one of honest indignation. He resented the perversion of law in order to cover up the obnoxious racialism of a military élite, and saw that this perversion was a much graver matter than the trial itself. No such reaction is apparent in the case of the reports of the Nuremberg and Moscow trials. Cummings found no difficulty in accepting a grotesque parody of judicial procedure as the genuine article. At Nuremberg, as far as I know, no eye-witness pointed out that for Western judges to sit side by side with Soviet ones, and convict Germans of using forced labour and partitioning Poland, was itself a monstrous crime against our civilisation, or, at any rate, a manifestation of its advanced stage of decay.

When Napoleon was dispatched to St. Helena, according to the already mentioned *Times* report, he was treated coldly, but not subjected to moral exhortations; not adjudged guilty of war-crimes. It sufficed that he had been defeated. If there is any crime in war, it lies, surely, in waging war at all. Criminality cannot be only on the side of the vanquished. To pretend that it can is to connive at the destruction of law itself. In Professor Briggs's and Mr. Fisher's parade of eye-witnesses, one may detect, indeed, a progressive deterioration in their moral, if not in their literary or journalistic calibre. Thus Grey's account of the outbreak of the 1914-18 War:

> The real reason for going into the war was that, if we did not stand by France and stand up for Belgium against this aggression, we should be isolated, discredited, and hated: and there would be before us nothing but a miserable and ignoble future,

is greatly to be preferred to Churchill's more rhetorical version:

> Once more now in the march of centuries Old England was to stand forth in battle against the mightiest thrones and dominations. Once more in defence of the liberties of Europe and the common right must she enter upon a voyage of great toil and hazard across waters uncharted, towards coasts unknown, guided only by the stars. Once more 'the far-off line of storm-beaten ships' was to stand between The Continental Tyrants and the dominion of the world.

For myself, I find it difficult to see how truth could ever

be extracted from this plethora of eye-witnesses, whose ostensible credentials are so impressive, but whose testimony is so dubious. The rugged, honest David Kirkwood said in the House of Commons that, during the economic depression, the Clydeside unemployed never tasted meat. Bertrand Russell has recounted how, during the McCarthy period in the United States, all books about Russia were removed from public and university libraries and destroyed. 'They are queueing up in Gorky Street to buy cars,' a *Times* Special Correspondent began a dispatch from Moscow. 'Bread,' Mrs. Naomi Mitchison wrote in the *Guardian,* 'would assuredly soon be free in the Soviet Union.' Such absurdities abound, relating to all countries, all régimes, all the desiderata of our time, and all bearing the eye-witness hallmark. It is not surprising that Pilate did not wait for an answer when he asked his famous question: 'What is truth?' He, too, had doubtless been studying eye-witnesses' reports, including, of course, that of Judas Iscariot.

Forgotten in tranquillity

The first school I went to was kept by a Miss Monday. It was round the corner from where I lived, and in a semi-detached suburban house like ours. This type of school has, I imagine, now ceased to exist. There were about a dozen pupils, and we used slates to practise making letters and figures. Of Miss Monday herself I have only the vaguest memory. As I dimly recall her, she was plump and grey and kindly, with a billowing skirt and blouse, beneath which there was a whalebone structure to hold her in shape. She had a sister living with her. They were, presumably, two maiden ladies with some education and scanty means, which they augmented by the minute fees the school brought them. The establishment had a faint aura of respectability and represented a slightly superior alternative to the infants' department of the local elementary school. From my parents' point of view, the convenience was its nearness. There was only one road to cross from our house to hers, and that a cul-de-sac.

This was in 1910. We were living in Sanderstead, a village which was in process of being absorbed in the rapidly growing dormitory suburb of Croydon. It still, however, had a few relics of its former village status, such as an ancient horse-trough, and one or two old-style country houses. Against the occupants of these my father constantly fulminated, keeping a watchful and suspicious eye on rights-of-way through their grounds to ensure that they were kept open. I was proud to be allowed to accompany him on one of his nocturnal expeditions to overturn what he considered to be an impermissible 'Trespassers Will Be Prosecuted' notice.

From Sanderstead we moved into Croydon, to a rather larger, detached house, which had been built in accordance with my father's specifications. It had one large room, running from the front to the back, whose most striking piece of furniture was an enormous inappropriate cosy corner which once, I should suppose, graced some ancient pub parlour. It looked, I dare say, infinitely silly in our twentieth-century living-room, but was very characteristic of my father, and therefore, to me, dear. I often sat in it. During the move I was sent away to the country for a year because of threatened tuberculosis. I stayed in a village near Stroud with family friends—a mother and a, then, unmarried daughter, from whom I received occasional instruction, and who caned me once or twice for 'answering back.' This offence, I may add, dogged me through my schooldays and, indeed, subsequently. I cannot recall then, or on any other occasions, feeling resentment at being physically chastised. Thus the indignation which infused a short leader I wrote on the subject years later in the *Manchester Guardian* was decidedly synthetic. As I was a new-comer, before starting to write I put my head in through the door of a colleague's room to get the 'line' on corporal punishment. Without looking up from his typewriter, he said: 'The same as capital, only more so.'

During the semi-invalid year, my education, at best, but limped along. Only in one direction did it make a great leap forward. Near where I was living there was a Tolstoyan colony, in whose foundation my father had been vaguely

71

concerned, and to which I was taken on periodical visits. Among other enlightened practices, such as holding all property in common and eschewing the use of money, the colonists were in the habit of bathing in the nude in a stream which ran conveniently through their land. This interesting spectacle provided me with biological instruction by the direct method. I was spared the tedium of pollen and stamens, and went straight to the heart of the matter, gazing curiously at the unclothed bodies of the matrons of the colony and with rapture at their slimmer, more shapely daughters.

When I returned to my family I was sent to a co-education, or, in the then jargon, 'mixed' State elementary school. This was housed in one of those solid, ungainly edifices which successive Education Acts spread over the country. There was an asphalt playground into which we charged at playtime, setting up a curious animal din, still to be heard whenever the inmates of State primary schools are briefly released for recreation. The classrooms were divided by wooden partitions, which could be opened to provide an assembly hall. Here we gathered in the morning after the roll-call had been carefully recorded in a register—a red stroke for those present and a black nought for the absent. Attendance, in those days, was one of the staff's chief preoccupations. On it was based the amount of money made available for running the school. Those of us who failed to turn up impoverished the education of all. We began with a hymn and a prayer. Any irregularities in pronouncing the aspirates were corrected by the head-master while the prayer was in progress. He might make us repeat 'Our Father which art in heaven' as many as three or four times before he was satisfied with our diction. For the hymn he used a tuning-fork to get us off on the right note. One of the female teachers provided piano accompaniment.

With our morning devotions over, the partitions were closed, and we began our studies. Classes were fifty or sixty strong, but usually included some who withdrew themselves from the proceedings and remained in a condition of blessed and total illiteracy. I learnt to read and write and add without any great difficulty, and developed a faculty which has often subsequently held me in good stead, particularly in the army, and at press conferences, for seeming to be eagerly engaged when actually my thoughts and attentions were elsewhere.

The only teacher I remember was a Miss Helen Corke—
a short, eager woman in a gathered smock. I was interested
to discover, later, that she was an intimate of D. H. Lawrence,
at that time also an elementary school teacher in Croydon,
at the Davidson Road School. She makes a somewhat lurid
appearance in one of his novels—I think *The Trespasser*—and,
in a small volume, has added her gentle and moderate testimony to the numerous other accounts of him which Lawrence's associates have provided. The picture of Miss Corke,
after grappling with us, her turbulent and unsatisfactory
charges, laying aside her gathered smock and proceeding to
grapple with Lawrence's turbulent and unsatisfactory Dark
Unconscious is surprising and rather comical. Only on
Fridays were there afternoon devotions. Then, the partitions
were again drawn back and we assembled to sing 'Now the
day is over.' The strains of this otherwise banal hymn have
still a magical quality for me. They signified release for two
whole days.

At the age of twelve I gained a scholarship to the local
Borough Secondary School. The examination for this included
an interview with the local Inspector of Schools, a portentous
Scotsman with a mop of white hair whom I held in great
awe. My enemies, to my indignation, hinted that my success
in the scholarship examination was due to the Inspector's
desire to ingratiate himself with my father, who was an active
and vociferous Labour councillor and member of the Education Committee. I hope their malignant suggestion was base-
less, but honesty compels me to admit that this was the
only examination in which I ever achieved any success.

The Borough Secondary School was temporarily housed in
a Polytechnic building. We used it during the day, but its true
purpose was for evening classes. Later, our school was
transferred to a building of its own. Its organisation was
vaguely derived from that of public schools. There were four
'houses'—Alpha, Beta, Gamma and Delta—which, in practice, had little more than a nominal existence, as well as
prefects, colours and other trappings reminiscent of *Tom
Brown's Schooldays,* not to mention the *Magnet* and the *Gem.*
We had a Latin motto, *'Ludum Ludite,'* or 'Play the game,'
invented, I suppose, by one of the masters.

Such schools as these, paid for by the State and ardently

promoted by Socialists like my father, limped along after the older-established grammar and public schools, cordially despised by them, but aiming at turning out a similar product. During a brief period of respectability when first I was editor of *Punch,* I was asked to address my old school on its annual speech day. I found that the process had been carried much further. Its name had been changed to 'Grammar' instead of 'Secondary' school. There was even a school song, sturdily intoned. Waterloo may have been won on the playing fields of Eton, but the class war was assuredly lost on the playgrounds and in the classrooms of State Secondary Schools. Social reform provides the safest, strongest, surest foundation of the *status quo.* The old *Morning Post,* which long ago disappeared, romantically tried to defend privilege; *The Guardian* and *The Times* continue to devote their energies to the more profitable task of adjusting its camouflage to suit changes in the social climate.

These were the years of the 1914-18 war. Most of the staff had been called up and were away, fighting and dying in Flanders mud. Their replacements were a curious collection of oddities—among others, an Indian with an imperfect command of English who instructed us in chemistry, a lady with a shrill, genteel voice for whom we wrote compositions, an elderly mathematics master with rather obviously dyed hair and frenzied moustache who desperately flung chalk at us when, as frequently happened, we failed to get his point. I can remember them all, in their tattered gowns—this one genial, that one erudite, and this other seemingly malignant as he sat, dark and glowering, while one stumbled over French irregular verbs.

I rode to and from school on my bicycle. The very air was full of the hysteria of war. Recruits were marched off to the railway station behind military bands. There were old boys who appeared, resplendent in their uniforms. We ourselves had a school cadet corps which we were compelled to join. I attained the rank of C.S.M., a success which should have warned me of pitfalls to come. The headmaster was in charge of the corps with the rank of major, and shambled along at the head of us when we had occasion to march through the streets, his uniform, as even my ignorant eye could detect, in strange disarray.

When, later, at Cambridge and elsewhere, I got to know the products of public schools, the thing that struck me about them was their passionate entanglement in their schooldays. At first I rather envied them this, and wished that I, too, had memories of famous cricket matches, a private, exclusive slang, and all the other outward and visible manifestations of belonging to an inward and invisible élite, self-contained and economically and socially advantageous. On further consideration, however, I changed my attitude. It seemed to me that the great advantage of the sort of education I had was precisely that it made practically no mark upon those subjected to it. Scholastic and other deficiencies were more than compensated for by the fact that one's first vivid impressions of life were provided, not by a closed and essentially homosexual community of schoolboys under the direction of masters who had themselves been through the same process, but by men and women actually living and earning their livings. How much I preferred the ribald, noisy, dangerous world to any walled garden, however elegantly arranged and full of summer fragrance! No one ever seems to forget Eton. I easily forgot my Borough Secondary School.

In our spare time we roamed the Croydon streets, gazed wistfully at dazzling girls playing tennis in public recreation grounds and otherwise disporting themselves, and hoped that the war would stretch on until we, too, could participate in its glories and adventures. I even, on one occasion, went so far as to present myself at a recruiting office, tremulously insisting that I was in my nineteenth year. The N.C.O. in charge was sympathetic, but sceptical. He told me to return with a birth certificate.

Games were voluntary. I have practically never played football or cricket, for which I am profoundly thankful. Even to watch these games is for me an anguish of boredom. The first conversational exchange I had at a *Punch* lunch occurred when one of the staff asked me whether I was interested in cricket. I replied briefly: 'No.' This total absence of a games *mystique* eliminated hero-worship. There was no Steerforth in my life. My days have not been haunted by any lingering adoration of some god-like athlete, compared with which adult fleshly love seems coarse and demeaning. Plato did not arise in those days at Borough Secondary Schools. Our adolescent sensuality was directed exclusively towards girls, whose persons, as we grew older, we ventured to explore, in scented cinema darkness, or beside blackberry bushes under the August sun. I had never even heard of homosexuality until I went to Cambridge. The idea of embracing, or being embraced by, persons of one's own sex when females were available seemed to me highly bizarre.

School, to us, was a place to get away from as soon as possible and for as long as possible. Everything exciting, mysterious, adventurous happened outside its confines, not within them. We were poorly taught, admittedly, and lacked utterly the team spirit. Our South London Cockney grated sharply on the ear. No group photographs of us were taken. We had no blazers or gilded caps. We were urchins of the suburbs. Looking back, I feel grateful that it should have been so. On the whole, the more boring and flat education is, the better. Glamorising it constitutes a kind of brain-washing. It fixes the victim neatly into ways of behaviour and of thought from which escape is difficult, and seems a kind of treason. When I embarked upon the arduous, but infinitely exhilarating, pursuit of the meaning of things, it was from the bottom of a stony hillside, with no golden memories of lost innocence about my head, no nostalgia for a vanished schooldays world about my heart.

I like Dwight

I have for years been a Dwight Macdonald fan. His one-man magazine, *Politics,* used to delight me when I was fortunate enough to lay hands on a copy. He did a dissection of Henry Wallace at the time of his foreign policy row with President Truman in a masterly manner just when the usual claque were setting Wallace up as the definitive Good Guy in the Washington Western. His *New Yorker* pieces ('The Book-of-the-Millennium Club,' fo instance, reprinted in *Against the American Grain*) are among the very best in what has become, by and large, a rather dreary publication. He and Mary McCarthy before ever I knew them in the flesh were my two favourite Americans. Now that I do know them in the flesh, they remain so.

I note that nowadays Dwight gets knocked around a bit on both sides of the Atlantic. That weird Playboy of the Eastern World, sometime Congo Kid and subsequently Redeemer Nkrumah's Man of Learning in Accra, Conor Cruise O'Brien, had a go at him in the columns of the *New Statesman*. Even Cyril Connolly (who paid me the delightful compliment, and Dwight the dubious one, of saying that he, Dwight, reminded him, Cyril, of me) was a good deal less than whole-hearted in his appreciation of *Against the American Grain*.

Part of the trouble probably is Dwight's being on the staff of *The New Yorker*. It is a magazine that somehow manages to look, and perhaps is, too rich to be true. All those ads about Men of Distinction, Rolls-Royces and Commander Whitehead are unnerving, and when you read in small type that some piece which has threaded its way through wodges and wodges of them is the first of five articles on someone or other, you cannot but feel dispirited. The thought of Dwight in so inappropriate a milieu is distressing. Besides, we none of us can bear the notion of anyone we like and admire being other than impecunious. If Jesus Christ had worked for *The New Yorker* Christianity would never have got started.

When I was editor of *Punch* I used to drop into *The New Yorker* office whenever I was in New York and see the editor, Mr. William Shawn. He couldn't have been nicer and kinder. Several times he took me to a meal at that fabulously expensive restaurant, the Pavillon (so expensive that on one of the occasions the taxi-driver taking me there, noting, as I assume, my English accent and down-at-heel appearance, remarked in the kindest possible manner, but with great emphasis: 'You can't go in there, mister'). Shawn's nervousness was such that it intimidated me. He is a minimomaniac. In his company one's mouth goes dry, one reaches round desperately in one's mind for words. He and his office, and the corridor outside, take on the character of a Kafkaesque nightmare. One wants to flee but is rooted to the spot.

Once, after managing to tear myself away, I found that I needed to visit a lavatory, and after wandering around for a while rather desperately, found one. Then, relieved and cheerful, I began, as I thought, to make my way towards the main entrance and the street outside, when to my horror I found I was back at Shawn's office, with him still standing at the open door where he had lately, as he supposed, seen me off. The thought of his anguish at seeing me appear again so afflicted me that I took to my heels and actually ran. This eerie experience gave me a certain sympathy with the spirit of Mr. Tom Wolfe's strictures on *The New Yorker* and its editor in his now notorious *Herald-Tribune* articles. Mr. Wolfe's style, in any case, was a decided relief after the dreadful solemnity which, as I well know from my *Punch* experience, afflicts the staff and premises where allegedly humorous magazines are produced; not least *The New Yorker*'s.

Yet, after all, if we are to be incriminated on the strength of the character of the publications which we have appeared in or worked for, where would any of us be? I can only say that, in the course of a long and arduous career in journalism, involving clawing my way up from the *Manchester Guardian* to the *Sunday Pictorial* (one is now the plain *Guardian* and the other the *Sunday Mirror*), I have had to write for publications like *Punch* and the *New York Times* Sunday Magazine, the thought of which even now brings a blush to my old cheeks.

Dwight is a tallish man with a pointed beard who is liable (or was the last time I saw him in New York) to deck himself out of an evening in a coloured velvet jacket. One of the things I like about him is that he is a scholar; but a comic one, which is the only honourable kind. He reminds me of the sort of mad professor who used to appear years ago in boys' comics with a butterfly net and an air of poetic absent-mindedness. Alas, nowadays, all the professors are sane and serious; protagonists of the Two Cultures and equally turgid whether they are writing about thermodynamics, *The Ancient Mariner* or *Moby Dick*. Our only hope in England is the so-called brain-drain, down which one or other of them (fortunately, more often than not, the most vociferous) is liable to disappear. Every time this happens I make a little holiday in my heart.

What Dwight does to perfection is to take something like the Third Edition of Webster's New International Dictionary

and tear it apart with gusto and derision. ('The String
Untuned,' also included in *Against the American Grain*.)
When he has finished, there are not even any pieces to sweep
up; only one tome less in the world. Or again, he will make
an analysis of the reviews of Colin Wilson's *The Outsider*
('Inside the Outsider'), a prize collection of imbecility if ever
there was one, and leave the field strewn with portentous
corpses; Edith Sitwell, Philip Toynbee, Elizabeth Bowen,
Maurice Cranston, etc. Incidentally, Dwight should have
added a postscript on the strange contortions whereby admirers of *The Outsider* tried to extricate themselves from the
position they had taken up when its sequel appeared. That,
too, is a fascinating and even more despicable, story.

Dwight used to be one of those vehemently anti-European
Americans who are such a relief to visiting English lecturers
afflicted by American anglophilia, a disease endemic in
college campuses, ladies' clubs, and wherever two or more
sometime visitors to the Edinburgh or Salzburg Festival are
gathered together. One gets to know the signs—pipe-smoking,
wine-drinking, uncomfortable small foreign car, trophies of
foreign travel; words of praise for draught beer, the Shakespeare Memorial Theatre, and the B.B.C. One is liable to
have piled on one's back such unwelcome and unsuitable
burdens as T. S. Eliot and the Queen Mother. One may even,
unless one is wary, find oneself autographing old copies of
Punch, or endorsing the treasured sayings of Lord Snow.

Though a spell in Europe, and specifically in London s.w.,
has sullied the purity of Dwight's anti-European sentiments,
he remains just as much a relief as ever after one has been
making one's way, like some Hindu fakir, across the red-hot
cinders of small-time American culture. So at least I found
him when I arrived hot-foot from addressing a Forum in
up-State New York, the last of a lecture series which had
carried me, as it seemed, interminably up and down the North
American continent and to and fro in it. Dwight refused
to be side-tracked into considering the sorrows, the ardours, or
the mitigations of this experience. He only wanted to know the
fee and the size of the audiences. When I told him he was
aghast, and let off a kind of whinnying 'No, no, no, no,'
which is very characteristic of him. He greets with this liquid,

babbling negative any statement one may make which is displeasing to him; as that Oxford dons will do anything to get on television, or that *The Times Literary Supplement* is the very mouthpiece and unburnt offering of his abhorred Midcult.

Dwight's mental pilgrimage is clearly enough marked. It began inevitably on the Left, but led him rather along pacifist-anarchist-Trotskyist courses than into Party Line commitments. At each of our generation's Stations of the Cross —the Depression, the October Revolution, the Purges, the Spanish Civil War, Munich—he paused to mutter a prayer and lightly beat his breast. All this may be gathered from *Memoirs of a Revolutionist,* an earlier collection of his pieces which appeared in 1957. What is greatly to his credit is that he did not go in for any of the resorts of eggheads at bay, refraining from becoming an editor of the *Reader's Digest,* or serving in the O.S.S., or taking to radio or television. There was, it is true, a brief spell with Luce's *Fortune,* followed by that heroic one-man effort with *Politics,* after which, whatever the sometime Sage of Ghana may say, he need not be grudged his *New Yorker* perch, though I have to admit that seeing him in *The New Yorker* office, as I once did, with all that female fiction screaming along the corridors, he seemed like someone who had strayed in by accident, thinking it was a dental surgery, rather than an inmate.

A more serious matter is the, to me, awkward point of Dwight's present advocacy of re-creating 'a cultural—as against a social, political or economic—élite as a countermovement to both Masscult and Midcult.' That odious expression, the *avant-garde,* recurs with ominous frequency in his more recent writings. In an often quoted sentence, he writes that our aim should be 'to restore the cultural distinctions that have become increasingly blurred since the Industrial Revolution,' adding that 'out of such attempts to do this as the 1890-1930 *avant-garde* movement of Joyce-Eliot-Picasso-Stravinsky has come whatever is alive in our culture to-day.' What, one asks onself, is alive in our culture to-day (assuming that anything is) that derives from that grisly quarter? Nothing that I know of.

Dwight does, it is true, in *Against the American Grain,* rustle up some affectionate approbation for James Agee (whose work, I regret to say, is little known to me), beginning with the admirable and characteristic sentence: 'The late James Agee's *A Death in the Family* is an odd book to be written by a serious writer in this country and century, for it is about death (not violence) and love (not sex).' Even here, however, one has the feeling that it is Dwight's heart rather than his head which is operative. 'Like Keats,' he writes, 'Agee died just when he was beginning to mature as an artist. That Keats was twenty-five and Agee forty-five doesn't alter the point. Agee was an American, of a race that matures slowly, if ever.' It is a good example of the one-way resemblances which nowadays are growing increasingly common and never fail to delight me. Agee was like Keats, but Keats was not like Agee. Likewise, Mandy Rice-Davies may have been, as she claimed, like Emma Hamilton, but Rachman, her property-dealer protector, was not like Nelson.

Dwight, clearly, has become so fed up with Masscult and Midcult that he feels bound to invent, in the teeth of all his own instinctive predilections, an Elitecult before which he may prostrate himself. It is, for him of all people, a ludicrous posture, especially when, as in *Amateur Journalism,* his veneration is directed to such essentially Midcult publications as *The Listener, The Observer,* the *Spectator,* the *New Statesman,* and *The Sunday Times.* He must just get up off his knees and recognise that the *avant-garde* in question is neither forward nor guarding anything at all except its own chances of getting photographed in *Life* magazine, or cashing in on an X certificate and a part for a Marienbad Bardot. Take, for instance, Eliot, that old carved skeleton, as Frieda Lawrence felicitously called him in one of her letters. Midcult flocked to those atrociously flat and commonplace plays of his, not, as Dwight suggests, out of a vicious passion to lower their cult-rating from Elite to Mid- or Mass-, but because the plays themselves were Midcult *in excelsis*; mother's milk to the Midcult Edinburgh Festival or London West End audience. In Midcult are many temples, temples of Eng. Lit. and Third Programme, and in every one of them *'The Waste Land'* is a sacred book, providing texts for countless sermons delivered to cowering congregations of Midculters in classrooms, before radio sets, or turning over the leaden pages of literary magazines and 'quality' Sunday newspapers.

Then again, E. M. Forster. Does anyone *read* those dated novels of his in which the thin homosexual blood of dusty dons is stirred by a visitation of the Great God Pan while on long vacation in the Italian Alps? I doubt it very much. The Midcult appreciation of them derives, I like to think, from unillumined words squeezed into the pages of literary magazines and discharged into the air on waveband 194 and 91.3 Mc/s, with dear Oliver Edwards (back in print, I'm delighted to see, on Holiday Reading. Stick to old friends, is his advice. Well, he's one of mine) to throw in his blessing. Dwight does his best with *Finnegans Wake* in his study of Joyce, but all he has to say in the end is that Joyce dedicated himself to writing incomprehensibly, and heroically persevered in this gallant endeavour to the end. About Hemingway, Dwight is excellent; a Walt Whitman of the twentieth century, Midcult's one and only Papa.

I can hear Dwight whinnying 'No! No! No! No!' But it's 'Yes! Yes! Yes! Yes!' It really is. Midcult is not a perversion of Elitecult. It exists in its own right. When *Time* magazine quotes Eliot, or reproduces Picasso, or serialises Hemingway, or lucifies Joyce, it is but flowering. One day the *Reader's Digest* will surely condense *Finnegans Wake,* and Orson Welles produce a film version of it. For all I know, this has already happened.

Masscult and Midcult, that is to say, are not, as Dwight suggests, a perversion of Elitecult; any more than mass-production is a perversion of craftsmanship. Television was not invented to make human beings vacuous, but in an emanation of their vacuity. The genius of Man in our time has gone into jet-propulsion, atom-splitting, penicillin-curing, etc. There is none over for works of imagination; of spiritual insight or mystical enlightenment. I asked for bread and was given a tranquilliser. It is important to recognise that in our time man has not written one word, thought one thought, put two notes or two bricks together, splashed colour on to canvas or concrete into space, in a manner which will be of any conceivable *imaginative* interest to posterity. Minds like Orwell's and Dwight's, which have so insistently and valiantly proclaimed that words have a sanctity of their own deserving of respect, provide an *avant-garde* in reverse. They defend the rear. Let Dwight continue from there to lob over his admirable hand grenades at Mid- and Masscult hordes as they advance on their own automated, and, as it may in the end prove, cindered wilderness.

The Wodehouse affair

The strange episode of P. G. Wodehouse's wartime disgrace is now, one is happy to note, largely forgotten, or seen in retrospect as the squalid outburst of mass hysteria that it was. From having been greatly adulated, particularly among the socially respectable and eminent, he became overnight the object of a gibbering, hysterical campaign of obloquy and calumny. Nothing enrages people more than to feel that they have engaged in unprofitable adulation. Those who were most sycophantically disposed towards the Duke of Windsor when he was Prince of Wales were the most venomous when he abdicated in order to marry Mrs. Simpson. The strongest supporters of Neville Chamberlain's policy of appeasing Hitler became the most inveterate anti-Germans. So with Wodehouse. Fellow-writers who had paid fulsome tribute to his literary distinction turned on him with particular fury, as did dons who had eagerly promoted the conferment of an honorary doctorate on him by Oxford University. The Beefsteak Club, once so proud of his membership, expelled him. Even Dulwich College, his old school, expunged him from some roll or other. Characteristically, Wodehouse minded this most.

As it happened, through a chance of war, I found myself involved in this Wodehouse affair. In 1944 I was a liaison officer with the French *Services Speciaux,* and in this capacity went to Paris at the time of the Liberation, flying in with two French officers, one named Paiolle and the other Pelabon. We were given a little plane piloted by a Canadian, and, as Orly and Le Bourget were out of action, had to land at an air-strip some sixty miles from Paris. We completed our journey in an army truck, being greeted everywhere with hilarious cheers, flowers and embraces. As the bottles of brandy which kindly patriots threw to us began to take effect, we responded to the public enthusiasm with mounting ardour. In Paris things were pretty confused, and a certain amount of street fighting was still going on. In the circumstances, there seemed little liaising to be done, and I abandoned myself to the prevailing celebrations. One woke up from time to time in unexpected circumstances, and with unexpected companions, with only a vague notion of the happenings in between.

Finally surfacing, I established contact with two fellow-officers, Victor Rothschild and Trevor Wilson, and we all three lunched together. As long as their supplies lasted, the better French restaurateurs fell over themselves to purge their collaborationist past by lavishing attention on Allied clients. We benefited from this. It was the one and only time, I should suppose in French history, when it was difficult to pay. After a stupendous meal, we mellowly decided that it behoved us to make contact with some sort of military command. Trevor Wilson had heard that a G.O.C. British troops existed somewhere along the Rue St. Honoré, and thither we repaired. Actually, there were very few British troops in Paris at that time, the theory being that the French loathed us, and loved the Americans because of Lafayette. I myself found little evidence of either sentiment. Liberators, of whatever nationality and ideology, always seem to be detested by those they liberate.

We located the office of a brigadier who, for the moment, was our commanding officer, and sat waiting there for his return in that somewhat moody state of mind which follows a post-luncheon project, joyously undertaken, but delayed in execution. When at last the brigadier arrived, he failed, I thought, to kindle at the spectacle of the three of us. He was a rather smart-looking officer in the Blues or some stylish regiment of the sort. It occurred to me that, with our Intelligence Corps badges, we presented, from his point of view, a somewhat lamentable appearance. Trevor Wilson had acquired from somewhere or other a French other-rank's great-coat, which swept the ground in massive shapeless folds. He kept between his lips a fragment of stained cigarette, which, when he spoke, added to the indistinctness of his, in any case, spasmodic utterances. I perhaps bore traces of my Liberation celebrations. Rothschild was a massive, but scarcely a soldierly figure.

Trevor Wilson explained to the brigadier that we were, roughly speaking, cloak and dagger men, which considerably mollified him. He probably thought that we were going about, for reasons of our own, in some ingenious and carefully thought out disguise. Also, he was relieved to know that we had merely come to report; not in search of billets and rations. Trevor Wilson had already moved into an elegant apartment off the Rue de Rivoli, formerly occupied by an Abwehr officer. Rothschild and I later took up residence in the Avenue Marigny, in one of his family's mansions. It was spacious, if chilly, and in excellent condition. According to M. Félix, the major-domo, a Luftwaffe general who resided there during the German occupation had been a careful custodian, doubtless with an eye to the future. Emperors and Führers come and go, but Rothschilds go on for ever.

By the time we got up to go our relations with the brigadier were positively jovial. If there was anything at any time that we could do, I said, he had but to mention it. At this he looked suddenly thoughtful. Yes, there was one thing, he said, over which we might be able to help. He had been asked to procure a white Rolls-Royce for an Air Marshal's wife. Could we possible lay hands on one?

Trevor Wilson had the air of a man with a whole string of white Rolls-Royces at his disposal. It was just a question of picking the right one. I murmured rather feebly that we would keep our eyes open. Rothschild looked, I thought, a little surly. He, after all, might well have had a white Rolls-Royce.

It was when walking away from this curious encounter that Trevor Wilson muttered to me that P. G. Wodehouse was in Paris, and that he had received instructions to keep an eye on him. Would I, perhaps, undertake this duty. I agreed with alacrity. I should add that, beneath a seeming vagueness of manner, Trevor Wilson had an acute mind, and a remarkable capacity for quick, audacious action. Though his eccentric temperament could be disconcerting, no one who worked with him could fail to find the experience enthralling. We never, by the way, did find a white Rolls-Royce, or, indeed, ever again set eyes on the brigadier.

I went to see Wodehouse that very evening at the Bristol Hotel, where he and his wife were staying. Of the details of his alleged misdemeanour I knew then very little, beyond a vague memory of some broadcasts from Berlin, followed by one of those nauseating outbursts of public wrath, when the ecclesiastical, literary and administrative performing seals find an occasion to outdo the monkey-house in the grimaces they put on and the yells they emit. It had all happened while I was engaged in military duties at G.H.Q. Home Forces, which, though not exacting, were sufficiently unfamiliar to require my undivided attention.

At the Bristol Hotel reception desk, a sleek individual in a black cutaway coat and striped trousers gave me the number of Wodehouse's suite without displaying the slightest embarrassment or curiosity about my visit. An odd and little publicised feature of war is how much goes on unchanged despite it. Thus Paris, which we all expected to be quite different after the years of German occupation, and now the Liberation, was a bit battered, but, essentially, just the same. The tall shuttered houses seemed oddly inviolate; as quiet and inscrutable as the hotel receptionist, who judged so much more sagely than we did. He knew that when all the excitement had died down, and all the arm-bands and cartridges had been handed in, there would still be expensive hotels, and their clients, to whom politeness was due.

The receptionist must have telephoned to Wodehouse's suite while I made my way up there because he seemed to be expecting me. 'Oh, hallo' he said when I opened the door and stepped inside. He was standing by the window, a bald, amiable-looking, large man. The encounter seemed so natural that it only occurred to me afterwards that Wodehouse, confronted with a British officer in uniform, may have thought that I had come to arrest him or something. He was wearing grey flannel trousers and a loose sports jacket, and smoking a pipe; a sort of schoolmaster's rig. I asked him long afterwards what sort of person he had expected to come into his room. 'Oh, I don't know,' he said, 'but not you.'

I had made no sort of preparation for my visit, and had

no plan as to how I should approach Wodehouse. It was difficult to know where to begin. I attempted the banal observation that his books had given me great pleasure. Even this was not strictly true. With my strict socialist childhood, Bertie Wooster and Jeeves had about them a flavour of forbidden fruit; like Sade or Casanova in the eyes of a Methodist. To me, Wodehouse was just a distinguished and highly original writer, and, as such, entitled to be kept clear of the atrocious buffooneries of power maniacs and their wars. Otherwise, I had no feeling about the matter at all.

There was still a lot of stamping and shouting in the street outside, and even an occasional pistol shot. Wodehouse turned away from the window and we both sat down. Then, after a short period of silence, I made a hesitant approach to the business in hand. I had no idea, I said, to what extent he had been able to follow what was going on in England, but there had, in fact, been quite a row about his broadcasts—a row which I personally considered to be ludicrous. All the same, in order to clear matters up, questions would have to be asked, and the legal position would have to be gone into. I slipped in the reference to the legal position (about which, of course, I knew nothing) in order to stress the gravity of Wodehouse's situation. In the circumstances then prevailing it was decidedly serious. William Joyce (Lord Haw-Haw) was hanged as a result of a grotesque and shameful perversion of law, whereby the fraudulent acquisition of a British passport was held to involve acceptance of all the obligations of British citizenship. This was like prosecuting a bogus doctor for infringing the B.M.A.'s code of behaviour. Who knows what would have happened to Wodehouse if he had come before a British court at that time? Judges know better than most which side their bread is buttered, and can be relied on to follow, if not to anticipate, the wishes of their paymasters.

In the course of the ensuing, and many subsequent conversations Wodehouse told me exactly what happened to him from the arrival of the Germans at Le Touquet, where he had a house in which he continued to reside until the collapse and occupation of France. There is also what he calls his 'Camp' book, so far unpublished, which I have read, and which contains a full, and characteristically amusing account of his wartime experiences. Then there are the broadcasts themselves. They describe truthfully and most divertingly Wodehouse's journey from Le Touquet to Tost, in Poland, where he was interned in what, he was happy to discover, had formerly been a lunatic asylum. Finally, there is a large M.I.5 file, I assume still extant, which presents the whole 'case,' with all the relevant documentation and evidence.

When the Pétain Government surrendered, Wodehouse, like all other enemy aliens in France, was taken into custody by the Germans. The normal procedure is to release civilian internees when they are sixty. Wodehouse was released some months before his sixtieth birthday as a result of well-meant representations by American friends resident in Berlin, America not being then at war with Germany. He made for Berlin where his wife, Ethel (who had not been interned) was awaiting him. The Berlin representative of the Columbia Broadcasting System, an American named Flaherty, asked him if he would like to broadcast to his American readers, and, foolishly, he agreed, not realising that the broadcasts would have to go over the German network, and were bound to be exploited in the interest of Nazi propaganda. Such a use of enemy communications in time of war was technically a treasonable offence, though a minor one, of which prisoners-of-war sending radio messages to their families were likewise guilty. It has been alleged that there was a bargain whereby Wodehouse agreed to broadcast in return for being released from Tost. This has frequently been denied, and is, in fact, quite untrue, but nonetheless still widely believed. Lies, particularly in an age of mass communications like ours, seem to have much greater staying power than truth.

In the broadcasts there is not one phrase or word which can possibly be regarded as treasonable. Naturally, they were gone through minutely to confirm that this was so. Ironically enough, they were subsequently used at an American political warfare school as an example of how anti-German propaganda could subtly be put across by a skilful writer in the form of seemingly innocuous, light-hearted descriptive material.

The broadcasts, in actual fact, were neither pro- nor anti-German. Wodehouse is ill-fitted to live in an age of ideological conflict. He just does not react to human beings in that sort of way, and never seems to hate anyone—not even old friends who turned on him. The furthest he will go is to admit, like Charles Lamb, to imperfect sympathies, and to express the hope that this or that public personage might be induced to return to his padded cell. Such a temperament unfits him to be a good citizen in the mid-twentieth century.

As we went on talking the evening shadows began to fill the room. There was no electricity, and so no possibility of turning on a light. I have always loved sitting in a darkening room and talking. It takes the sharp edge off the exigencies of time. In Paris on that particular evening the moment was particularly exquisite, if only because of the contrast between the tranquillity where we were and the mounting confusion outside. I was happy to be spending it with Wodehouse. He sent down for a bottle of wine, which we consumed as we talked. Royalties on Spanish and other translations of his books provided him with adequate funds during the war years. Our conversation soon moved on from his Berlin misdemeanour. Were things still ticking along? Did clubs go on? And *The Times Literary Supplement*? And A. A. Milne? And *Punch*? Wodehouse wanted to know what books had been published and how they were selling; what plays had been put on, and how long they had run; who was still alive, and who was dead. I satisfied him as best I might on these points, hampered by a tendency, reaching morbid proportions in the war years, to suppose I have read the obituaries of practically everyone, especially women novelists, eminent Quakers and popular clergymen. Bernard Shaw, I told him, was certainly still alive. The news, I fancy, fell rather flat. 'And Wells?' he asked eagerly. 'He might be dead,' I said, leaving him to extract whatever grief or satisfaction he might from my uncertainty. This last theme pulled me up sharply. I remembered having read in the newspapers that his stepdaughter, Leonora, had died, and felt I ought to tell him. 'I'm afraid,' I said, 'that your stepdaughter is dead.' I never knew her, but from what I have heard she seems to have been one of those women everyone adores. Certainly, Wodehouse adored her. After a longish pause he said: 'I thought she was immortal.' He got up to go and tell Ethel, and I made off, promising to come again the next day.

Thenceforth I saw a lot of Wodehouse and Ethel. She is a spirited energetic woman, who tries as hard to be worldly-wise as Wodehouse does to be innocent; a bad sleeper, who wanders about during the night polishing tables, and planning to pull down whatever house she is living in and rebuild it nearer to her heart's desire; a mixture of Mistress Quickly and Florence Nightingale, with a bit of Lady Macbeth thrown in. I grew to love her.

Fortunately, the Wodehouse 'case' was taken out of my hands (in so far as it had ever been in them) by a friendly and capable barrister named Cusden, who was sent over from England for the purpose. He went into everything in the way barristers do, treading purposively along the paths I had so cursorily explored, and arriving, I was relieved to learn, at the same conclusion—namely, that there was nothing Wodehouse had done or said which could be regarded, in any real sense, as treasonable or dishonourable. Blowing down his nose in a legal way, like a judge (which I hope he now is, or will soon be) he delivered himself of the opinion that Wodehouse 'should be kept out of the Jurisdiction.' It reminded me of Mr. Jagger's advice about Pip's benefactor in *Great Expectations*—to secure the portable property.

One morning, before Cusden's arrival, I received a message from Jacqueline de Broglie to the effect that the Wodehouses had been arrested the evening before by the French police. It seemed that, at a dinner party given by the then Prefect, Luiset, an English guest had remarked on how scandalous it was that two such notorious traitors should be at large in Paris. Luiset thereupon gave orders that the Wodehouses should be apprehended, and four men with sub-machine-guns, and wearing black leather jackets, duly appeared in their bedroom and took them off.

I located the Wodehouses at a police station on the Quai d'Orléans. No one seemed to know why M. and Mme. Wodehouse (as they appeared on the warrant) were there, and I had no difficulty in arranging for Ethel's immediate release. As far as I could gather, in her highly individual French she had reduced the whole *Sûreté* to a condition of prostration and panic. Also, she had her peke, Wonder, with her, and, by the time I arrived on the scene, the police were desperately anxious to get both Ethel and Wonder off

the premises. More difficult was to get permission for Wodehouse to have his razor returned to him. This involved
filling in an enormous form, whose items I only imperfectly
understood. I went out and got some food, and we all
lunched together. What with everyone accusing everyone else
of collaboration, and the Palais de Justice itself being in a
state of total confusion, the administration of justice, as may
be imagined, proceeded even more lamely and imprecisely
than usual.

It appeared that the only way to ameliorate Wodehouse's lot
was for him to be ill. This presented difficulties. His equanimity had not been disturbed by his arrest, and he looked pink
and well. However, an amiable prison doctor felt his pulse,
shook his head, and decided that he should be transferred to
a clinic. The only one available was a maternity home, and
there Wodehouse stayed for some weeks, with ladies having
babies all round him. Each day the doctor took his tem-
perature, which was normal. Two guards were posted at his
door. He used to play cards with them in the evenings. His
mornings were spent, as always, in writing. Between being
taken into custody at Le Touquet and his spell in the
maternity home he wrote six novels, as well as the 'Camp'
book. Incidentally, during the period of his disgrace more
copies of his books were sold in England than ever before,
which provides yet another illustration of how public obloquy
is as much a myth as public adulation. The cheers and hisses
are taped as in radio shows.

After his release from the maternity home, I took Wodehouse and Ethel out to a hotel near Fontainebleau. With
the ending of the war things eased up for them, and they were
able to go to America, where they are now living. Ethel has
been back to England several times, but Wodehouse never,
though he is always theoretically planning to come. I doubt
if he ever will. His attitude is like that of a man who has
parted, in painful circumstances, from someone he loves,
and whom he both longs and dreads to see again.

Wodehouse's true offence was to have disinterested himself
in the war. When I discussed his 'case' with Duff Cooper, then
British Ambassador in Paris, this was the line he took. Wodehouse, he said, had always evaded reality and his responsibilities as a citizen. Yet, after all, as I tried to indicate, there

are different sorts of reality. Can we be so sure, for instance, that Hitler's ranting and Churchill's rhetoric and Roosevelt's Four Freedoms will seem more real to posterity than Jeeves and Bertie Wooster? I rather doubt it.

As Evelyn Waugh pointed out in his elegant broadcast tribute to Wodehouse on his eightieth birthday:

For Mr. Wodehouse there has been no fall of Man, no 'aboriginal calamity.' His characters have never tasted the forbidden fruit. They are still in Eden. The gardens of Blanding's Castle are that original garden from which we are all exiled. The chef Anatole prepares the ambrosia for the immortals of high Olympus. Mr. Wodehouse's world can never stale. He will continue to release future generations from captivity that may be more irksome than our own. He has made a world for us to live in and delight in.

It could not be better put. Is the creation of such a world an evasion of reality? Does it represent (to use the current jargon) a lack of 'commitment'? I do not think so, any more than, when the founder of the Christian religion said that his kingdom was not of this world, that represented a lack of commitment. There are commitments and commitments. It is perfectly true that Wodehouse provided upper- and middle-class readers with a means of retreating from reality—which was why they made such a fetish of his works, and were so infuriated by his Berlin broadcasts. This, however, is a reflection on them, not on Wodehouse.

Duff Cooper, as Minister of Information, led the pack against Wodehouse. In Paris, to his credit, he showed no inclination to follow up the attack with a kill. I was able to produce to him one instance of an authentic contribution by Wodehouse to the war effort. The Germans, in their literal way, took his works as a guide to English manners, and actually dropped an agent in the Fen country wearing spats. This unaccustomed article of attire led to his speedy apprehension. Had he not been caught, he would, presumably, have gone on to London in search of the Drones Club, and have thought to escape notice in restaurants by throwing bread about in the manner of Bertie.

When I am in New York I always go out to Long Island to see Wodehouse and Ethel, whose architectural and rebuilding activities continue unabated. He, too, lives in his accustomed way—the typewriter in the morning, a stroll to the post office with the dog in the afternoon, and a couple of benign cocktails in the evening. The last time I saw him he complained that a television serial he always watches at noon had failed to appear that day. Instead, an oafish figure named Khrushchev had occupied the screen. On another occasion, a young, earnest American was present, who brought up the subject of nuclear warfare, which, he said, might well destroy the whole human race. 'I can't wait,' Wodehouse murmured. His eightieth birthday was celebrated in England with great fervour; a successful B.B.C. television series has been made of his stories, and no doubt Oxford University, the Beefsteak Club and Dulwich College would like to undo his expulsion and bask once more in his glory. I dare say they have found a way.

As with all imaginative people there is an area of inner reserve in Wodehouse which one never penetrates. The scars of his time in the stocks are hidden there. In one of his rare references to the experience he said to me that it had made him feel like a music hall comedian, accustomed to applause, who suddenly gets the bird. This, I think, is what it signified to him, and, perhaps, indeed, what it signifies.

Christ!

The late Lord Beaverbrook, searching round for another subject for his busy pen, hit, in *The Divine Propagandist,* upon Jesus Christ. It might seem, at first glance, a curious choice. The founder of the Christian religion scarcely measures up to the heroes of the City and of politics who have previously attracted Lord Beaverbrook's attention. Nor, one might suppose, would his teaching be calculated to make a strong prima facie appeal to one who, throughout his public career, always insisted on worldly success as the reward and measure of all human endeavour. The Empire Crusader can surely have found little to his taste in a gospel of renunciation. Was a millionaire to applaud the sentiment that the poor are blessed? Could the so assiduous familiar of prime ministers assent to the proposition that the meek inherit the earth?

Anyone who has worked, as I have, for a Beaverbrook newspaper will know that there was a strong strain of religiosity in the proprietorial directives with which editorial underlings were ceaselessly bombarded. Mixed up with the log-rolling, the endless reiteration of some lunatic proposition, as in the thirties that there would be no war, the relentless pursuit of private vendettas and crusades, were fragments of scripture and echoes of Presbyterian earnestness. Into that crafty, resounding voice there came from time to time what another former employee, Tom Delmer, has aptly described as a 'magnificent diapason of deep sincerity.'

Lord Beaverbrook was, indeed, a spoilt evangelist. He had strong biblical predilections. The faith he imbibed as a son of the manse in New Brunswick left its mark upon the style and idiom of his utterances, if not upon his conduct. He fought the bad fight with all the exuberance and fervour of old-style revivalists like Moody and Sankey. In my day, the *Evening Standard* vans carried a bill: 'IS THERE AN AFTER LIFE? SEE TO-MORROW'S EVENING STANDARD.' It was made abundantly clear to us that the answer offered must be emphatically in the affirmative. Anyone who was a believer when he picked up a Beaverbrook newspaper must be a believer when he laid it down.

It is true that Lord Beaverbrook's own course, from youthful speculative triumphs in Canada, to newspaper proprietorship, and somewhat furtive shuffling along Lord Snow's corridors of power, could only with difficulty be equated with that of Bunyan's pilgrim. This, however, did not deter him from seeing himself as a Mr. Great-Heart. In his entourage of sycophants, buffoons and tame celebrities he liked to include someone who could provide organ accompaniment for nocturnal hymn-singing sessions. Any tendency to carry mockery into the realm of Christian apologetics was liable to receive a sharp rebuke.

Jesus Christ, in any case, is a Name Which Makes News. During his lifetime he would not, perhaps, have rated the attention of William Hickey, but his subsequent fame, and the wealth and eminence of many of those associated with it, qualified him for a place in any gossip-column. From Lord

Beaverbrook's point of view, his was essentially a success story. From humble origins (though, as the Son of God, he might be considered to have exalted connections) he achieved a position of outstanding power and influence. The Crucifixion was a set-back, certainly, but the Resurrection more than compensated for it. Thenceforth, the movement he founded progressed almost as fast as the circulation of the *Daily Express*. Though his earthly estate was negligible, and far below the level at which death duties become payable, his posthumous circumstances put him in the multi-millionaire class. This astonishing career, from carpenter's son to an accepted position on God's right hand, exemplified Lord Beaverbrook's favourite proposition that dazzling opportunities await whoever has the shrewdness, energy and pertinacity to see and seize them. Not even the sky was the limit.

It was as a successful propagandist that Jesus Christ won Lord Beaverbrook's particular admiration. Without the advantages of a chain of newspapers, lacking financial resources and powerful earthly connections, he still managed to put across his ideas so effectively that nearly two thousand years later they are still ringing in mankind's ears. Is it surprising that so outstanding a feat should have impressed another operator in the field of propaganda who, with so many additional advantages, saw every cause he espoused founder, every individual he attacked thrive, and most of those he praised fall in public esteem?

No doubt, too, Jesus Christ would have made, in Lord Beaverbrook's estimation, an admirable columnist: a sort of super-Godfrey Winn, felicitously reminding his readers of life's deeper purposes and truer values. His evangel might well have been advanced by editorial support such as the *Express* newspapers could have afforded, but the fact remains that, by mere word of mouth, he did surprisingly well. Lord Beaverbrook attributes this success, in the first place, to his choice of disciples. He eschewed 'intellectuals who would have spread the doctrine quickly,' and went 'for simple men of tenacious character who will obey and bear witness.' 'Almost any twelve honest men selected at random,' Lord Beaverbrook considers, would have been as serviceable as the actual apostles. It was not for them to 'theorise and embroider on the teaching as men of greater intellectual force would certainly have done,' but just to report what they saw and heard. Like good *Daily Express* correspondents, their function was to be on the spot, and first with the news.

After the Sermon on the Mount, Lord Beaverbrook tells us, Jesus Christ embarked upon his 'great campaign,' in the conduct of which he appears 'simply and nakedly as the greatest propagandist the world has ever known.' The main propagandist weapons he used were 'personality, example and oratory.' It is significant that so old a hand at the game as Lord Beaverbrook should have omitted any reference to the truth of what was being propagated as a factor in its successful propagation. Here, he was following his own practice. In his own essays as a propagandist he always concentrated on presentation rather than content, and assumed that Jesus Christ would necessarily have done likewise. The skill of this earlier practitioner was such, moreover, that he needed no Christiansen to devise the make-up and the headlines. Christ was his own Christiansen.

As for the teaching itself, Lord Beaverbrook is inclined to accept its validity as originally propounded, but to deplore subsequent glosses upon it. St. Paul, for instance, falls under his displeasure as importing

> into the pure ethic of the word as preached by Our Lord a vast amount of extraneous matter whether out of Neo-Platonism or Mithraism or the Osiris cult which formed the substratum of the vast superstructure of Catholic doctrinal Theology.

He was 'a citizen of the world,' 'a highly educated man,' 'an intellectual,' and, as such, divorced from 'the simple folk' to whom Jesus Christ addressed himself. In Lord Beaverbrook's eyes, one feels, St. Paul might almost have been a contributor to *The Observer*.

Lord Beaverbrook has to take account of certain seeming discrepancies between Christian teaching, as propounded in the Gospels, and his own, as propounded in the *Daily Express*. Take, for instance, the awkward question of riches. If there is one point on which the *Express* newspapers, under Lord Beaverbrook's direction, were consistently emphatic, it was in recommending as laudable and beneficial, the assiduous laying up of treasure on earth. Against the ostensibly harsh observation about the eye of a needle, and the difficulty a rich man has in entering the kingdom of heaven, Lord Beaverbrook sets the parable of the talents, which, as he sees it, amounts to a clear recommendation to study the stock market, and invest boldly and profitably. His conclusion is that Jesus Christ considered the habit of acquisition 'laudable enough in the first instance,' but disapproved when it grew 'until the victim becomes a slave to his money.' Here he can derive comfort from the thought that, as his own career amply showed, in becoming rich and important it is the first instance which counts.

Again, the *Express* newspapers reckon, in all circumstances, to strike a note of optimism. A boom is always with us, or round the corner. Dangers which seem to threaten never will materialise. Old men live for ever, trade is always brisk, and stock-market prices are always rising. Any suggestion that Jesus Christ was inclined to take a poor view of man's earthly circumstances is, in Lord Beaverbrook's opinion, another of the deplorable falsifications of his teaching by intellectuals and theologians. On the contrary, he was an advocate of 'social cheerfulness' here and now.

Nor will Lord Beaverbrook countenance what he calls the 'Gentle Jesus' view of the founder of the Christian religion. Paintings like 'The Lost Sheep,' and phrases like the 'Lamb of God' have been 'pressed into service' to propagate this fallacious view. So have 'those parts of the Sermon on the Mount which deal with non-resistance, the suffering of a persecution gladly, and the doctrine of turning the other cheek.' 'Extraordinary vigilance,' he insists, 'has to be exercised against accepting an absolutely literal interpretation of such sayings.'

Jesus Christ, that is to say, was no 'Man of Sorrows,' but rather a 'happy warrior,' whose robust teaching 'has been conquering the world ever since Calvary, and continues every year by year its victorious advance.' So considered, he can take his place in the *Daily Express* pantheon, along with Bonar Law, Sir James Dunn, Sir Winston Churchill, Bernard Baruch, and other worthies who deserved and enjoyed Lord Beaverbrook's esteem. So interpreted, his teaching can be appropriately included in the *Daily Express* Opinion Column, which, as directed by Lord Beaverbrook, day by day enthused four-million-odd readers.

'The desire for the spiritual Kingdom,' Lord Beaverbrook writes, 'is apt to belong to later years.' Volumes of belated piety like *The Divine Propagandist* are not uncommon among ageing captains of industry and of the press. Normally they are privately printed, and circulated gratis among relatives and unresisting employees. This particular one, projected and promoted by the publicity machine Lord Beaverbrook created, has to be paid for, and is likely to enjoy a wider circulation.

Lord Beaverbrook's mental processes may have been some-what rudimentary and confused, to the point of, at times, baffling the best efforts of the performing seals he maintained to expound them. Yet they were undeniably spirited, and self-propelled on a majestic scale. Thus his views on the life and teaching of Jesus Christ, though not, in themselves, either profound or illuminating, have a certain piquancy precisely because they are his. To students of the contemporary scene, *The Divine Propagandist* is by way of being a collector's piece. It would be absurd to suggest that Lord Beaverbrook's motive in writing it was to allay stirrings of conscience which may have afflicted him in old age. A more likely explana-tion, I should have thought, is that *The Divine Propagandist* was intended to provide what the French police call a *pièce justificative* for use, as and when required, in the hereafter. 'Have we a sure hope of immortality?' Lord Beaverbrook asks, and goes on: 'The answer is "Yes." ' In the light of this certainty he must have expected to appear, in the not too distant future, at the pearly gates, where the circulation and advertising revenue of his newspapers, and the cause of Empire which they have so stoutly upheld, might, alas, make little impression. In this contingency, a presentation copy of his latest work, he doubtless calculated, might come in handy. Did it? I wonder.

In defence of Randolph Churchill

It is by no means true that the major figures of history are the most interesting. Indeed, in a sense, the opposite is the case. Those who take the leading roles in the world of action are often so obvious that there is really nothing to say about them, and vice versa. Thus, for instance, Benjamin Constant is (as Sir Harold Nicolson has so admirably shown) inherently more interesting than Napoleon; and I myself, if I had to choose between undertaking a biography of Sir Winston or of Mr. Randolph Churchill, would unhesitatingly choose the latter.

To some this may seem a whimsical judgment. Sir Winston, they will contend, belongs to history, and will be remembered as long as the English-speaking peoples, etc., etc.: whereas his son has been, in politics, a non-starter, in letters, no more than a privateer journalist, in society, a turbulent nuisance —an embarrassment to his friends, a gift to his enemies, and a brawling bore to neutralist or uncommitted associates.

At first sight, he might seem something of an anachronism —a pinchbeck Marlborough in the century of the common man, who for a consideration is prepared to allow the public to look round his views and prejudices in much the same way that his distinguished kinsman allows them to look round Blenheim; an ageing *enfant terrible* whose pranks and teases become ever more dated. This, however, would, in my opinion, be a very superficial view. Mr. Churchill belongs essentially to this age, and his clowning and outrageous sallies are the measure, not of his obsolescence, but rather of his contemporaneousness. Like Cyrano de Bergerac, the secret of his appeal lies in the fact that everything about him, including his appearance, is somehow out of focus. The edges are blurred. He puts into the causes he champions (for instance, his crusade against newspaper pornography) more than they can rightly contain. It is a case of old wine in new bottles. Considered as a political warship, he carries a lot of antique artillery, but the shells fall in unexpected places—here, there and everywhere, but rarely on the enemy. And quite often the guns misfire or backfire, to the great disconcertment of any who have been foolhardy enough to associate themselves with him.

At the same time, how preferable this is to the sort of career which seemed to offer so surely when he was young, handsome, eloquent, and in the full enjoyment of the *réclame* which his name effortlessly bestowed. Surely, one thought in those days, he will soon be in parliament, soon on the Treasury Bench. It was the first Lord Rothermere, I think, who called him England's young man of destiny—a scarcely original epithet which would, admittedly, have been more impressive from another source, but still heady enough for someone in Mr. Churchill's situation.

Who would have thought in those days that Conservative Party constituency selection committees thirsting for knighthoods would one day turn palely away when his name was put forward as a possible candidate? That even Bournemouth, which had meekly, if coldly, taken Brendan Bracken to its bosom, would indicate unmistakably that it did not want him? That the vast wash of Churchillian influence, capable, among other extraordinary feats, of translating a Professor Lindemann into a Lord Cherwell, would quite fail to translate its most natural, its most obvious, beneficiary into anything at all?

Dealt an incomparable hand, that is to say, Mr. Churchill has scarcely taken a single trick. Why? The answer doubtless lies embedded in his curious and contradictory temperament; in some farouche strain which induces him to kick over the table just at the moment when he seems to be about to play his aces, or (what really amounts to the same thing), in a propensity to self-pity which can dissolve away in a moment his seeming resolution and pugnacity, leaving him to be counted out before anything in the nature of a knock-out blow has been delivered.

Nonetheless, it would be quite mistaken to regard him as a total failure. If one of his brothers-in-law managed to hold his ministerial position even after Sir Winston's retirement, and another to plant his foot firmly on the ladder of preferment, Mr. Churchill has made far more noise in the world than they have, or are ever likely to make. Hostesses on both sides of the Atlantic may grow pale at the prospect of one of his visitations, but they know that, as a topic of conversation, he is inexhaustibly diverting. Everyone has an anecdote to contribute, wounds to display, bizarre episodes to recount. As a conversationalist himself he is often as devastating as one of those hurricanes which sweep away whole towns in their train; as a stimulant, *in absentia,* of other conversationalists, he is the very top class.

It is, of course, true that his lack of success in conventional (as distinct from nuclear) politics has been a bitter disappointment to him; but there is always White's bar, whose proceedings, like those of the House of Commons, quite often get reported in the Press, and whose frequenters (particularly as the afternoon wears on) provide on the whole a more lively and appreciative audience than Members of Parliament. There is also the telephone—an instrument peculiarly suited to Mr. Churchill's particular brand of declamation. Night and day, it is always available, and the receiving end is liable, as the pips sound with monotonous regularity, to accept, rather than reject or question, spirited polemics, whether impromptu or read from a prepared manuscript.

As a journalist Mr. Churchill has enjoyed a kind of Indian summer. By concentrating his fire on press lords and fellow-conservatives like Sir Anthony Eden, he has overcome the faults of diffuseness and imprecision which marred many of his previous productions. His most persistent detractors cannot but admit that his latter-day denunciations of newspapers and their proprietors have been, by comparison with the feeble and meandering efforts of the Press Council, as red biddy is to ginger ale.

In this connection, it may seem a little disappointing that one press lord, and he not the least vulnerable—I mean, of course, the late Lord Beaverbrook—should have become, as it were, immunised to the Randolph Churchill virus. However, one has to write somewhere and be paid by someone. And anyway it must be counted to Mr. Churchill for virtue that he often used the platform Lord Beaverbrook provided to assail his favourite public figures and lambast his favourite propositions. To judge from past experience, it is also probably true that, by employing Mr. Churchill, Lord Beaverbrook was preparing a rod for his own back. Other newspaper proprietors have likewise employed him, and look what has happened to them!

For myself, I would not have him otherwise. Like the sirens in the blitz, his arrival at any social gathering sends everyone scampering for cover; produces that slight shiver and tautening of the nerves which presages danger and excitement. When the 'all clear' sounds and he departs, there is a corresponding sense of relief, but the intervening experience (as long as one has not been personally involved in the explosion) is exhilarating, or at any rate memorable. Society needs its scourges. What more suitable one in this strange, twilit time than a displaced Churchill—uproarious, unexpected; above all, uninhibited?

Mr. Churchill's recently published fragment of autobiography (*Twenty-one Years*) only serves to confirm one's former impressions. As its name implies, it covers his life up to his majority. More is promised. So slight an effort would not, we may be sure, have been accorded publication at all but for his illustrious name. It is not merely that the length amounts to little more than a longish essay; the treatment is superficial and the tone facetious; in the manner and style of a superior gossip-columnist. Some run-of-the-mill childhood reminiscences are laced with anecdotage about famous figures like F. E. Smith, and the whole washed down with draughts of rather ponderous old-style drollery paternally matured.

All the same, it has to be admitted that, like practically everything Mr. Churchill does, *Twenty-one Years* holds one's attention throughout in excess of its intrinsic interest. In this, the book is the man. He, too, manages somehow to continue to be interesting despite conversational fatuities and *longueurs*; bluster, bad manners and bombast. Were I at this moment, as I write these words, to see that so massive figure looming up before me, that grey, battered and oddly woebegone visage staring in at me, there would be, mixed with agonised dread of boredom and rows to be endured or circumvented, a kind of anticipatory pleasure, and even affection.

The common judgment is to marvel that so remarkable a sire should have had so disappointing an offspring. I see it the other way round. How could so unusual and often endearing a misfit issue from loins so ardently adjusted to the atrocious banalities and buffooneries of power? Worldly success has no surprises, and supreme success is always supremely commonplace. Witness Napoleon, or for that matter Hitler. Sir Winston is no exception. Failure, on the other hand, is incalculable, and therefore entertaining. The Devil is successful and a bore. He speaks rhetoric and wears gold braid.

It is touching now to think of Mr. Churchill in his curmudgeonly East Anglian retreat, engaged, with ample assistance, in laying the keel and launching a great Cunarder (let us hope she will prove sea-worthy) in the shape of his father's biography, volumes and volumes of it, one supposes; then momentarily breaking off to survey the so promised political journey he never took, the seemingly so accessible summit he never scaled.

What went wrong? This is his own account of it:

My father, who was F. E. (Smith)'s greatest friend, had brought me up on all the famous anecdotes illustrating his wit, brilliance and arrogance. Without F.E.'s learning or his majestic command of language, I sought to emulate his style of polished repartee. It didn't work in my case. I did not have my godfather's shining abilities and could not aspire to his brilliant gift of repartee. Nor did I have his industry or fit myself for a profession to earn my living. I, therefore, took up the calling for which no credentials or examinations are required—journalism. This was to lead me to a chequered career—sometimes up and sometimes down, but in which I now think, at the age of fifty-three, I am beginning to prevail. At the time I was twenty-one we were already moving into a softer world where rough talk was much discouraged and deprecated. However clever and facile I was, I lost friends and failed to influence people. But I boxed on. . . .

His explanation is for once unduly modest, surely. It was not that he failed to measure up to F. E. Smith. Rather, the social and political climate changed so drastically that a comparable performance inevitably fell flat. After all, Smith himself would probably not fare too well to-day. The arrogance and superciliousness which so delighted his contemporaries would seem merely offensive; on television in a Gilbert Harding-style role, it might pass muster, but not on the Woolsack.

Thus Mr. Churchill was emulating something already obsolescent. The fact that he could not pull it off may have been personally frustrating, but was a point for survival rather than extinction. It has enabled him, instead of being drowned along with the doomed class into which he was born, to bob to the surface; puffing and spluttering, certainly, and not in particularly good shape, but indubitably alive.

In the last section of *Twenty-one Years* he describes (or rather quotes the descriptions which appeared in the *Evening Standard* and *Sunday Times*) his twenty-first birthday celebration, on 28th May, 1932. It was a glittering occasion, 'more suited,' he writes, I am sure justly, 'to my pretensions than to my achievements or abilities.' The idea was for distinguished fathers to accompany their sons (Winston Churchill with Randolph, Lord Rothermere with Esmond Harmsworth, Lord Reading with Lord Erleigh, Lord Hailsham with Quintin Hogg, etc.), who might reasonably be expected in due course to achieve fame and distinction in their own right.

Of them all only Mr. Hogg and Mr. Churchill himself remain in the public eye, these two being, in their different ways, gladiators capable of standing up to the *Zeitgeist* itself. The footprints of the others in the sands of time have been but faintly, if at all, stamped.

I see Mr. Churchill as like a sea-lion I once observed washed up on the beach at Margate. The creature was thrashing about, an object of curiosity and some derision, but yet with something majestic in its spirited efforts to disport itself in circumstances so unfavourable. Suppose, I say to myself, he had achieved what seemed to be promised—the Cabinet, Downing Street, even two columns of obituary in *The Times* and a paragraph in the history books. What then, compared with the consequent impoverishment of what Dr. Johnson felicitously called the public stock of harmless pleasure?

Recollected in sanity, the vast outpouring of Kennedyana, reaching a scarcely credible crescendo at the time of the late President's assassination, cannot but give any balanced mind a feeling of distaste, if not disgust. Graveyard, or memorial, prose is among the least edifying and least pleasing forms of human composition. There is a prevailing flavour of syrupy insincerity, an affection of whole-hearted truthfulness, amounting to the worst kind of deception, which sickens as it surfeits. I can only say with all possible respect that if the late President really was as his admirers and posthumous adulators would have us believe; so dedicated a public servant, so faithful a husband and devoted a father, so witty, learned and profound an orator, writer and thinker, so genial a friend, prayerful a Christian and enlightened a statesman, he is better off in Heaven, where, according to an electoral oration in Ohio by Vice-President Hubert Humphrey, we may now confidently assume him to be.

The Vice-President pointed out (and I refer to the matter only as indicating how someone as normally sensible as Mr. Humphrey can be drawn into this obituary morass of sentimentality and chicanery) that next to his beloved State of Massachusetts the late President cherished the State of Ohio, which had deeply distressed him in the previous presidential contest by voting Republican. Now was an opportunity, Mr. Humphrey went on, to make the late President happy in heaven by reversing this black record and voting Democrat. I must say, speaking for myself, that if, as Mr. Humphrey would seem to envisage, election results are tabulated in heaven I have no wish to go there. A glimpse on arrival of Huntley or Brinkley, not to mention the portentous Cronkite, a sniff of a Gallup Poll, would convince me that I had found my way to the other place, and, if so permitted, I should hurriedly make off.

A good deal of the grisly material relating to the late President's life, virtues and achievements had already been

published before the Dallas tragedy, and to an experienced
journalistic eye bears unmistakable signs of external direction. From within the turgid prose the handouts shine forth
with a yellow light, like street lamps in a fog. Thus certain
episodes recur, narrated in almost identical words, in a manner
which suggests the existence of a master-version. For instance,
this from *Young John Kennedy* by Gene Schoor:

'Big party to-night, Jack. Pretty girls, too,' said Torb.

'Everyone will be there,' said Ben Smith.

'Sorry,' said Jack, 'I've got this work to finish before
morning. . . .'

When Torb and Ben finally got home, there was Jack
working away under the lamp on some small-print clip-
ping, some lengthy report by a member of Parliament . . .
[sic].

Finally:

'It's finished!' announced Jack.

'Finished!' echoed Torb.

'All done,' said Jack.

Torb's immediate reaction was to call for a celebration,
but the words died in his mouth. This was serious work;
Torb knew how serious and what it meant to Jack.

'Let's see it,' he said.

They read page after page that night, and late into the
night, throwing one quote after another at each other.

'You've got something, Jack.'

'This is great, Jack.'

The study on which the late President was so ardently
engaged dealt with the Munich Pact and the events which
led up to it, and was subsequently published as *Why England
Slept*. At some point a copy came into my hands. An Introduction by Mr. Henry Luce did not particularly recommend it,
and I remember reflecting that though we English may have
slept, at least we did not, like Ambassador Joseph Kennedy,
the late President's father, sleep-walk—in his case across the
Atlantic to inform President Roosevelt that our cause was
lost, and there was no point in helping us with weapons or
in any other way.

Here is another quotation in a style and idiom which, I must
say, I never thought to come across outside Crawfie:

'I want a piggyback ride, Daddy,' said Caroline.

He may have been President-elect to the whole world; he was simply 'Daddy' to Caroline.

'Sure,' said the man just elected to the most responsible post in the American Government. 'Up you go!'

And up went Caroline on her Daddy's back; and behind him the cameras went 'Click! Click! Click!'

You bet they did. To an American well-wisher like myself it is deeply distressing and disturbing to find the worst kind of fatuity dredged up by upholders of our Monarchy applied now to a President of the United States. One longs for some authentic American voice—a Mark Twain, an H. L. Menken, even a Will Rogers—to send the whole ghastly performance up, not only in the interest of a great American tradition of human equality and the self-respect that goes therewith, but also of the late President himself, whose undoubted qualities and capacities cannot but be submerged under this mountain of sycophancy; fantasy and hypocrisy.

The same unhappy parallel with our degraded monarchy-worship is apparent in *The Kennedy Wit,* a lavishly illustrated paper-back which has already run through numerous editions. The Duke of Edinburgh himself could scarcely be expected to improve on:

Question: Senator, you were promised military intelligence briefing from the President. Have you received that?

Mr. Kennedy: Yes. I talked on Thursday morning to General Wheeler from the Defence Department.

Question: What was his first name?'

Mr. Kennedy: He didn't brief me on that.

Or:

President Kennedy enlivened the ceremony for signing of a housing bill with a touch of Shakespeare. Noting the absence of two Alabama Democrats, Representative Albert Rains and Senator John J. Sparkman, who had manœuvred the bill through Congress, the President declared:

'Having this bill signed without them is somewhat like having *Hamlet* played without the Prince.'

Even an ex-editor of *Punch* winces at such an exercise in wit, more mayoral than Voltairean, surely. Years ago when I was a gossip-writer on a London newspaper, and as such expected to retail the witticisms of the great, I used to toy with the idea of producing an anthology of Royal

Humour. As a basic anecdote I treasured one about King Alphonso of Spain which actually appeared in a gossip-column. One hot summer day the King was out walking in Madrid, and happened to notice a workman engaged in digging a hole in the road. 'Hot work, eh!' our gossip-columnist quotes His Majesty as remarking, to which observation, the columnist goes on, 'the workman laughingly assented.' Now, having thumbed through *The Kennedy Wit*, I feel that I should have to extend the range of my anthology to take in Heads of State.

Of the poetic compositions in honour of the late President I feel less competent to speak. They have been collected together in a volume (*Of Poetry and Power*) with a foreword, alas, by Arthur Schlesinger, Jr. There may, for all I know, be some hidden excellence and profundity in:

The talk is of Johnson and a Congress
Which has done nothing. The accents are
Of Virginia, Maryland, the whining
South. I sit in the back booth of a Chinese restaurant,
Washington, 1963. Before me lie
The *New York Times* . . .

Or:

He sort
of embodied
the air he sort
of embodied the
air where democracy
stood tall, Jefferson
and Robert Frost were
his advisers, he sort
of clearly gave evidence of
wit and democracy . . .

If so, it eludes me. It is only fair to add that obituary verse on public figures rarely attains excellence. Perhaps Tennyson's Ode on the Death of the Duke of Wellington is about the best that can be done, and even then the poet, unlike Mr. Schlesinger's songsters, enjoyed the advantage that Wellington as a politician had been cordially detested, so that he was under no necessity to dwell unduly on his public or private virtues. Poetry and power, in any case, I should have thought, are antipathetic, and the late President's efforts to bring the two together doomed to failure. There seemed to me at the time something tragi-comic in the spectacle of poor old Robert Frost reading inaudibly from a manuscript in an icy wind at the Kennedy Inauguration, though the *New York Times* saw the matter differently. As it wrote in its inimitable way:

The palpable love affair between the White House and a jade called culture shows signs of reaching an impassioned peak this year. With Robert Frost's participation in the inaugural ceremony heralding the romance and three command performances at the Executive Mansion cementing it in recent months, the extraordinary liaison between politics and art has been attracting comment abroad and speculation at home.

I had half hoped that Mr. Harold Wilson, with his hero-worship of the late President and emulation of his ways, might have somehow brought our Poet Laureate, John Masefield, into the State Opening of Parliament when he became Prime Minister. On consideration, however, I realised that it would have been an act of supererogation. With Snow in the Government, the new Prime Minister needed no Frost. Sir Charles (now Lord) Snow may not be a poet, but is he not an indubitable writer of prose?

Anyone acquainted with the late President, or even with one or other of his intimates, knows perfectly well that the legendary image of him so assiduously propagated bears little or no relation to his true self, and that the gap between the two is steadily widening. A small effort to close the gap by Mr. Tom Wicker, *New York Times* White House reporter, in his book *Kennedy Without Tears, the Man Beneath the Myth,* does not, I fear, get us very far. Despite valiant intentions, there is a good deal more myth than man. To demonstrate the late President's humanity Mr. Wicker leans heavily on his wit, which, as I have already indicated, is but a frail prop.

Meanwhile some guidance at least is offered by a fascinating study of Kennedy Senior by Mr. Richard J. Whalen, now an associate editor of *Fortune* in his *The Founding Father: the Story of Joseph P. Kennedy.* Most of the work on the book was done before the Dallas tragedy, and, in any case, since Mr. Whalen's main subject is Joseph Kennedy, incidental references to the late President do not require an organ accompaniment. Thanks to Mr. Whalen, one is able to observe at close quarters the formidable electoral effort put out by Kennedy Senior on behalf of his son in Massachusetts, and later on a national scale. It was not merely that he spent a lot of money; though he did spend a lot; more, it is safe to assert, than has ever been spent on elections before. He operated, as well, a parallel political machine of his own, using all the old-time graft and pressures, stratagems and knavish tricks, in the traditional Boston-Irish style. It was as though St. George's father should have thoughtfully put some knock-out drops in the dragon's supper on the night of the fateful contest.

Mr. Whalen shows how the two machines—the egghead, do-gooding, New Frontier one and the old-style Bostonian-Tammany one—were carefully separated, and functioned independently of one another. There were very occasional moments when they impinged; as, for instance, the unexpected appearance of John F. Fitzgerald (Honey Fitz), the late President's maternal grandfather, in the junior headquarters which had just been fitted with a campaign slogan and theme: 'The New Generation Offers a Leader.' Kennedy Senior's representative there, a man of the name of Kane, Mr. Whalen tells us, spotted Honey Fitz and shouted to a henchman: 'Get that son-of-a-bitch out of here!' Not surprisingly, 'Young Jack looked startled. "Who? Granpa?" ' Yes, it was Grandpa, but the old gentleman knew who was in charge and quickly made himself scarce.

Another point of contention between the two machines during the late President's senatorial contest in Massachusetts was Senator Joe McCarthy, who was well, and even affectionately, regarded by Kennedy Senior, but who was not likely to be much help in offering a leader to a new generation. The best solution, it was felt, was just to keep the Wisconsin Senator away for the duration of the contest. To assure his absence, it seems, Kennedy Senior turned to the ultimate source of all his power—his pocket. Appropriate financial arrangements were made, and the Senator campaigned elsewhere. As for any consequences the other way round; of liberals being shocked by the operations of Kennedy Senior's *apparat*—the danger was negligible. I well remember, when I was a journalist in Moscow, a man in the Soviet Foreign Office opening a conversation by observing that the U.S.S.R. owed an immense debt of gratitude to the Webbs and other Western liberal intellectuals. I rather wearily asked why, expecting the usual claptrap. He surprised me by replying: 'Because they've convinced us that whatever we may be impelled to do in the way of dictatorial and terrorist practices, we never need fear their disapprobation.' In the same sort of way, nothing in the Kennedy record or campaigning ways could mar the effulgence of the New Frontier in liberal eyes. They remain worshippers, and have even extended their worship to the succession régime of Lyndon Johnson.

In the light of all these machinations on the part of Kennedy Senior, it might, one almost feels, be said that he invented, beside begetting, the late President. Certainly, with incredible thoroughness and attention to detail, he created his son's legend. To take but one example from Mr. Whalen's book:

> Distributed across the state were nine hundred thousand copies of an eight-page tabloid featuring drawings of Lieutenant Kennedy rescuing his shipmates in the Pacific. On the facing page was a photograph of young Joe Kennedy, whose fatal war mission was described under this headline: 'John Fulfils Dream of Brother Joe Who Met Death in the Sky Over the English Channel.' Inserted in each paper was a *Readers' Digest* reprint of John Hersey's article on the saga of PT 109, which originally appeared in *The New Yorker*.

Later, the same episode was made into a book, and then a film (which I am happy to say I have not seen), under the careful supervision of Kennedy Senior. It is kinder and more respectful to the late President's memory to attribute such activities to his father's sole initiative. Who, for instance, can doubt where the following originated, taken from a nauseous little volume, *A Day in the Life of President Kennedy* by Jim Bishop:

> The President thinks he would like to have another glass of beer. Mrs. Kennedy puts her work on the arm of her chair and goes through the dining-room into the kitchen and gets it for him. She pours it and puts it on the coffee table

111

before him and suddenly remembers something funny that happened between Caroline and her 'Grand-mère' . . . She asks when his father and mother are coming to visit again. The President is back at his work. He says he doesn't know. Mrs. Kennedy says—impulsively—that she wishes his father lived with them at the White House. 'You know how I feel about him,' she said. It is more than admiration. Sometimes when his name is mentioned in a group, she beams the big open smile she has and says: 'Just love him.'

Comment would be superfluous. In any case, the legend as we have it now, sanctified by blood monstrously shed, was systematically and deliberately created, paid for and propagated as part of an elaborately devised electioneering technique operated by Kennedy Senior, which has proved so strikingly successful that it is likely, in one form or another, to be generally adopted throughout what we like to call the Free World. After the invention of the Australian crawl no one tried to win swimming races with the breast-stroke. The Presidency of the United States and two Senate seats for three brothers not intrinsically of any particular distinction, and, in relation to these offices, exceedingly youthful and inexperienced, must be considered on any showing an outstanding achievement. The highly glamorised reconstruction of the late President's nomination, campaigning and election by Theodore H. White (*The Making of the President* 1960) needs to be supplemented by Mr. Whalen's careful researches. Otherwise, Mr. White's version reads like an account of a successful Woolworth's store in which no mention is made of the till.

Whatever may be history's verdict on the late President's all too brief occupancy of the White House, the arrival of the Kennedy troupe on the public stage, under the direction of their old *maestro* and patriarch, is bound to hold a historian's attention. Those everlastingly smiling visages with, as it were, a neon glow about their mouths as medieval saints had haloes about their heads; the enormous wealth which has mounted the whole performance, and the ferocious paternal egotism which has animated it; the brooding sense of a tragic doom which has already struck mortally three times, hanging

112

over the family's success story—it is a Shakespearian rather than a political or sociological theme.

In the light of this background one can understand why the late President always seemed in his public *persona* to have a certain unreality; as though he belonged to a strip-cartoon rather than to life. He gestures were somehow mechanical; his tone of voice was invariable, whether he was addressing a scout rally or the nation at the time of the Cuban crisis. This robot-like quality, extending even to his charm, enveloped him, as I thought, in a pervasive sadness (references to which, in guarded terms, have crept into the legend itself), noticeable particularly on the rare occasions when the neon smile could be extinguished. It was the sadness, not of failure and frustration, but of their converse (and therefore equivalent)—effortless success and fulfilment. The Casanova sadness (particularly apt in the case of the late President) of the womaniser who moves from seduction to seduction—like an eye passing over a buffet, from the ham to the brawn to the smoked salmon, hand clutching an empty plate; the satiety sadness of the affluent shopper who can buy anything and therefore has nothing to buy; that accidie which so grievously afflicts the children of the rich and the successful as they gather the prizes which fall into their hands and wear the laurels they find about their brows. After all, it is an unhappy fate to be imprisoned, as the late President was, in a legend; whether as avatar or monarch, prelate or president; to hold out bleeding hands for all to shake, to be nailed to an electoral cross, and expire on a universal suffrage Golgotha.

After the late President's death, two of his *apparatchiks*—Theodore C. Sorensen and Arthur Schlesinger Jr.—set about constructing each his own enormous plaster pyramid by way of commemorating the Kennedy presidency. There was a certain amount of unseemly, and even sordid, jockeying for position, but in the end their offerings were unveiled more or less simultaneously, in *Look* and *Life* magazines in the United States and in *The Observer* and *Sunday Times* newspapers on this side of the Atlantic. Subsequently, two massive volumes appeared side by side in the bookshops; the most outstanding literary follies since Beatrice and Sidney Webb produced their *Soviet Communism: a New Civilisation* in the late thirties.

A notable deficiency in Mr. Sorensen's volume—in the circumstances a pretty terrific one—is that it tells one absolutely nothing about the late President. I mean about him as a man; as a breathing, sentient human being. He appears, of course, as an outstanding president; as a loving husband, a doting father, a worthy son, etc., etc. Even—and utterly absurdly—as a distinguished writer. Every aspect of the familiar legend is diligently, and, in the neo-sycophantic style of a *New Yorker* profile or *Time* cover story, skilfully presented. What one looks for in vain is any connection between this lay-figure of a model president, and the easy-going, amorous, rather indolent and snobbish, amiable and agreeable American patrician of whom the late President's intimates used sometimes to speak in private conversation. Mr. Sorensen's Kennedy is entirely based on the lay-figure without so much as a hint of a real man signalling from within to be released. It might just as well have been a study of the Duke of Edinburgh by Garter King of Arms.

Mr. Sorensen was, of course, at the late President's elbow throughout his political career. Not a speech was prepared, not an article written, scarcely a joke made, without his participation. He is thus in the best possible position to survey the late President's record, from his first election to Congress, through the presidential election, the White House set-up, the controversies over civil-rights and steel prices, the Bay of Pigs fiasco, the Vienna meeting with Khrushchev, the Cuba confrontation, to the Dallas tragedy. All is adequately and fairly covered, always remembering that Mr. Sorensen was himself a pillar of the *apparat*. We do not expect a Knight of the Round Table to write dispassionately about King Arthur, or a pious Monsignor to give a wholly unbiased account of Joan of Arc after her canonisation.

He does, it is true, provide details of the late President's attire, diet, relaxations and idiosyncrasies. He favoured two-button suits, it seems, and liked to eat a little often rather than substantial meals at longer intervals. The dummy is dressed, and makes its clockwork movements. We may deduce, indeed, from Mr. Sorensen's narrative how macabre a lot in life is that of the hero in an era of mass communications.

The crutches must be hidden away even when they are desperately needed; the spectacles must never be worn in public however strained the eyesight; a tan must be maintained all the year round lest wrinkles show; the smile must always be summoned up whatever the mood and whatever the circumstances. No actor, or actress even, has been subjected to so inexorable a régime as is required of those who accept the destiny of leadership to-day. Demagogue-divinities, unlike monarchs who ruled by divine right, have to endure being mauled by the sovereign people. The Mikado prudently decreed that his subjects must never lift their eyes to look at him; an American president, on the contrary, must ever be in the public gaze. The ravening crowds wash round him, devouring him with their eyes and lacerating him with their touch. Like Prometheus, he is bound and each day his entrails are plucked out by an adoring multitude. Dusted and caked with make-up, shining beneath the arc-lamps, projected on the waves of sound and light, he provides a sacrificial offering; in the late President's case, all too literally.

In such circumstances, it is, perhaps, absurd to look for a real person. How could one possibly survive when the exigencies of the image are so overwhelming? Probably we shall never know what the late President really said and thought, as distinct from the words and thoughts of others for which he was a vehicle. Nothing in his life, as recounted by Mr. Sorensen, is his own for certain; there is not one single phrase or joke which can be attributed to him with certainty. This is a new development in history; a completely new kind of leadership. The late President was obviously not a moron, but he could have been one. It would not have made the slightest difference in the fabrication and projection of his image. As long as he could smile, and say the words, and wear the clothes, and reach out to shake the multitudinous hands, he could still play his allotted part. If and when computers can smile (and they surely soon will), one may very well be programmed with all the requisite answers and fed with all the requisite speeches, and get elected to the presidency. Why not? Such a computer would doubtless be expensive, but someone as rich as Ambassador Joseph Kennedy would be easily able to buy one and run it for office.

This new development in the character and operation of leadership drastically affects the writing of history and biography. Take Mr. Sorensen's own case. He was an integral part of the Kennedy legend, which he helped to shape and promote—to what precise degree probably he himself is scarcely aware. Thus in writing about the late President and his presidency he is in a sense and to an extent writing about himself. That splendid oration which the late President delivered—after all he, Sorensen, wrote it. In the circumstances he can scarcely be expected to be impartial about it. That Pulitzer Prize for *Profiles in Courage*—his, Sorensen's, contribution was admittedly substantial in winning so notable an award, which therefore must meet with his approval. And so on. We have had in the past plenty of adulatory biographies of public figures, and historians through the ages have displayed great readiness to approve what comes to pass. Since the advent of the speech-writer under Roosevelt, and the subsequent developments in the presentation of contemporary rulers, a new historical era has opened up, in which the legend of what happens is prefabricated, as are the legendary figures who shape the happenings.

'His untimely and violent death,' Mr. Sorensen writes of the late President, 'will affect the judgment of historians, and the danger is that it will relegate his greatness to legend.' In any such process, Mr. Sorensen's own offering will infallibly work in the legendary direction. He writes throughout about the legendary Kennedy; about the dedicated mid-twentieth-century demagogue, with his head in the public opinion polls and his feet firmly planted in ward-precincts, endlessly preoccupied with the shabby, dreary, fraudulent processes of universal suffrage democracy. Surely, one says to oneself, it must be impossible for anyone actually breathing, and normally equipped with human hopes and desires, to fashion a life out of Scotty Reston, Dr. Gallup and the early editions of the *Washington Post* and the *New York Times,* fortified by those indigestible papers which the mills of government endlessly grind. Something, surely, must have happened or been said which could not possibly have been prepared in advance by one or other of the *apparatchiks*. Some joke not in that folder labelled 'humour' which the presidential train carried everywhere. Some spontaneous gesture other than reaching out to that forest of reaching hands. Something unbeknownst to Dean Rusk or McGeorge Bundy.

One looks in vain for anything of the kind in Mr. Sorensen's pages. The legend, as he purveys it, slays the late President as effectually as Oswald's bullets did. That burly figure with the kindly face who captivated so many abroad as well as at home, goes down before his speech-writer's adulation as he did before his assassin's crazy malignancy. With the best of intentions, Mr. Sorensen has created a Frankenstein monster in the shape of a glamorised president. In life, he served the late President assiduously and ably with his pen ; in death, also with his pen, he has obliterated him.

Arthur Schlesinger, when I first met him in 1947, had one of the acutest minds, sharpest wits and readiest pens in the United States. His *Age of Jackson* was already a sort of classic. His pungent comments on the Washington scene were a pleasure to listen to; his circle of friends and acquaintances included most of the Americans one ever wanted to meet. In the academic wasteland of Harvard he was a bright and reassuring light. Through all the turgid controversies of the McCarthy era he kept his head and stood by his friends, without working himself up into an undue lather of self-righteousness. In his own person he provided one with a formidable argument demonstrating that there were American liberals who had seen through the monstrous fraudulence of Stalinism without falling into the sterile error of obsessive anti-communism.

What, then, has happened to turn this luminous and critical intelligence into a slobbering apologist for the late President; an undiscriminating adulator of the whole turn-out, Bobby and Teddy and all, down to the very Hyannis Port dogs? For more than a thousand pages he sustains a tribute to the late President's sagacity, charm, wit, resolution, virtue, erudition and enlightened handling of America's business. His plaster pyramid is even larger than Sorensen's. Looking back on all the literature of obsequiousness through the ages, taking in even the Victorians, and the poetasters of Oriental courts, I find it difficult to match their two efforts in sheer fulsome idiocy. To a brief interlude in American history, to a rather exceptionally light-weight President, they accord honours which a combination of Bismarck, Talleyrand, Metternich,

Gladstone, Disraeli, Lincoln and Cromwell would scarcely have deserved. Whatever has happened to these two men, and to America? I ask myself. Is it, as we must all hope, a passing aberration? Will people wake up and realise the absurdity of it? Or have we got to reckon with the final dissolution of decent critical standards in a land where they have been so excellently and racily maintained. Are Contemporary Americans in a like case with the Romans, who, having lost all their virtue, and all their judgment, actually accepted as deities the ludicrous figures who managed to get themselves robed in purple? Alas, it would seem so.

If anyone had asked me, even a couple of years ago, who wrote the following passage, about the last name to have occurred to me would have been Arthur Schlesinger's.

The frenzy of August had gone, though people stood in quiet clusters at each end of the Kennedy block on Irving Avenue. The compound itself was tranquil and secluded in the drowsy sunlight. The Kennedys were out for a stroll on the dunes. In a moment they returned, Jack in tweed jacket, sweater and slacks, hatless and tieless, swinging a cane and looking fit and jaunty, and Jacqueline, her hair slightly blown in the breeze, glowing in beauty from the walk. One could only think: What a wildly attractive young couple. It took another minute to remember that this was the President-elect of the United States and his wife.

Yet Schlesinger's it is, and one of many in a like vein. There is nothing worse for intellectuals than to attach themselves to authority, other than for money, or for fun at authority's expense; or, as happened in the case of Voltaire and Frederick the Great, for both. Look at Malraux! What has he said or written that would not better be forgotten since he attached himself to de Gaulle? Look at our Snow's performance since he announced that he had found in Harold Wilson a man of destiny! Look, for that matter, at the grisly train of Soviet *illuminati,* from Gorki onwards (standing, as I well remember him, beside Stalin like a poor old derelict bear beside its keeper), all breathlessly racing after the Party Line and denouncing one another along the way. It is difficult to think of a single case of a writer whose talent has not been contaminated to the point of extinction

118

by association with authority on other than hostile or subversive terms.

Schlesinger's study of the Kennedy régime, then, is a long exercise in the *trahison des clercs*. The critical intelligence we all so admired is laid aside; the analytical mind which made him a brilliant historian in his early twenties no longer functions; the pungent style gives place to a sickening emulation of the worst kind of lush descriptive writing suitable to go straight into *Life* magazine without any need for adjustment or processing. At his hands, the late President emerges as a dedicated saint of the White House, with his brother Bobby as his saintly adjutant, and perhaps, in due course, successor. The gleam of the family smile flashes through his pages; youth is at the helm, and hey, ho, for Frontiers New. One reads on with increasing distress, not only at the prevailing atmosphere of sycophancy, but also at the sheer banality of much of the political content.

Not even the pious volumes which appear on our English monarchs after they are dead, describing their idyllic family life, wise statesmanship, piety and enlightened patronage of the arts, quite equal Schlesinger's essay in the same genre. Courtiers in the century of the common man have to be even more obsequious than their like in the days of anointed kings and queens. After all, the toadies of the past—the Saint-Simons, the Harveys and Hickeys—put a little vinegar in the syrup when they came to write up their private diaries. To-day they have to be public relations men who dare not even in their dreams falter in extolling their products. It would be nice to think that Schlesinger had tucked away in one of his drawers his real account of his time in the White House, written with the verve and perceptiveness of his earlier works. I fear not. Regrettably, his Kennedy worship is heartfelt and definitive.

In many respects, the Kennedy régime was more deleterious to its cultural camp-followers than were others more evidently philistine and cold-hearted. Its inherent and devastating second-rateness casts a pall over its adulators. Their faces all look green, as in neon lighting. When, in the 1939-45 war, Churchill wanted two high-grade writers to cover his Atlantic meeting with President Roosevelt, he chose H. V. Morton and Howard Spring—a choice so outrageously naïve as to be rather touching. How much more pernicious if he had chosen, say, T. S. Eliot and David Cecil! Power is by its nature a philistine pursuit; when its practitioners turn to the *Oxford Book of English Verse*, or, more ominously, to Shakespeare and the New Testament, we should beware. Under the Kennedy régime a sort of middle-brow pantheon was constructed large enough to accommodate every cultural cover-story, from Frost to Sinatra, and taking in Hemingway. The resultant set-up has been described as a twentieth-century Versailles; if so, a Hollywood version, surely, in vistavision, with Sorensen and Schlesinger looking after the continuity.

Sometime, I suppose, this miasma will lift, and some young, uncontaminated Schlesinger will get to work, extricating a man from his legend, and subjecting his tragically abbreviated presidency to a proper historical and sociological analysis. Then we shall be able to see how, if at all, the course of American history has been affected, and to answer some of the questions which insistently arise. Not only do the Sorensen and Schlesinger volumes tell one nothing about the late President and the Kennedy régime that one wants to know; they have the negative effect of burying under a mountain of verbiage the clues and leads which might enable one to find out.

It is comforting, even so, to reflect that the plaster monuments they have constructed cannot, in the nature of things, be expected long to withstand the passing of time. They will soon, we may be sure, collapse into a heap of forgotten dust. Let us hope that some other less engaged hand will one day write the Kennedy story; not as a paltry twentieth-century political fantasy, with a golden youth and glamorous girl walking hand-in-hand into the White House, to discover together there that life is real, life is earnest. Rather, in the manner of a Greek Tragedy, in which the rage of the gods is called down on those who smile too often, too concertedly, and too determinedly.

Senator McCarthy McCarthyised
or the biter bit

The following transcript of the proceedings of a Congressional investigating committee was produced by a recent visitor to the United States. It will be noted that the habitual role of Senator McCarthy is reversed. Instead of interrogating he is being interrogated. On the other hand, the questions put to him are so pointed, and the Senator's answers are so fumbling, that the proceedings described are by no means implausible.

In any case, their publication here may serve as an inducement to that alert body, the Un-American Activities Committee, to crown its labours by investigating the possibility of Senator McCarthy being himself an under-cover Communist who has cunningly adopted the pose of the great chastiser of Communism in order the more effectively to promote the Communist cause. It should be added that this is at present no more than a plausible hypothesis. Nothing has been proved one way or the other.

If the Senator is, indeed, a card carrying Communist, the Federal Bureau of Investigation has not so far produced any concrete evidence to that effect. Nor, it is only fair to add, has his name been mentioned by Elizabeth Bentley or Whittaker Chambers; or even by Mr. Budenz. It is, however, an irrefutable fact, supported by a great body of circumstantial evidence, that the effect of the Senator's activities has been notably to serve the cause of Communism both in the United States, and, still more, in Western Europe and Asia.

For those who have not been fortunate enough to witness a public committee hearing on Capitol Hill, some brief account of the scene presented may be helpful. Imagine, then, a smallish room, with the members of the investigating committee seated upon a kind of dais, each with a microphone before him. The Chairman or Acting Chairman is in the centre. At another table are seated the Committee's counsel or legal advisers, among them, perhaps, the watchful Mr. Cohn, the astute Mr. Schine, and for a while the present Democratic Senator for New York, Mr. Robert Kennedy. Then, in front of the main table, sits, or stands, the individual to be interrogated: in this case the Senator from Wisconsin himself.

The rest of the room is filled with the public, including usually a number of fashionably dressed ladies. The front rows of the public seats are reserved for reporters, who scribble busily, and, at dramatic moments, rush in and out with copy in their hands. In the no-man's-land between the Committee and the Press the photographers operate, kneeling, and engaging in other gymnastics, to get good shots, and occasionally performing astonishing feats in the way of hanging from chandeliers, and otherwise disporting themselves.

Soon the floor becomes littered with used bulbs, whose flashes punctuate the proceedings throughout. Broadcasters are speaking into microphones in odd corners; walkie-talkie and peepie-creepie men are on the prowl, and the whole show is being televised, necessitating arc lights and a good deal of complicated apparatus about the place.

CHAIRMAN: Well, Senator, picking up our questioning where we left off yesterday, you will admit, I take it, that when you defeated the late Senator Robert La Follette in the Wisconsin primaries in 1946, you had the support of the Communist and fellow-traveller vote?

SENATOR MCCARTHY: What of it? As I said at the time, Communists have votes, don't they?

CHAIRMAN: Please answer the question, Senator. Did you have the support of the Communist and fellow-traveller vote against La Follette?

SENATOR MCCARTHY: I believe so.

CHAIRMAN: Right. Now would you also agree that La Follette, whom you defeated with the aid of this vote, though holding strong liberal views, was intensely anti-Communist, long before you or most other professed anti-Communists of to-day thought of taking up such a position?

SENATOR MCCARTHY: I'm not familiar with the late Senator's record.

CHAIRMAN: It's not within your knowledge, then, that he was

Not <u>your</u> house – this time!

MAYBE NEVER BUT . . .

Fire Damage takes an increasingly heavy toll every year, and as the value of dwelling-houses and contents increase, so does the cost of replacement.

Have you ever paused to consider how much it would cost to replace your house and its contents ? Have you ever tried to estimate the value of the furnishings, carpets, clothing, personal belongings, and the thousand-and-one things that are acquired over the years ? Few people realise the value of their home or how much it would cost to replace it. The risk is so great yet the remedy is so simple.

The cost of Fire insurance of an average dwelling-house is a mere 1s. 3d. yearly for each £100 of value. The contents can also be insured against the ravages of fire for a very small yearly premium.

PLEASE SEND ME DETAILS ENTIRELY WITHOUT OBLIGATION

MR./MRS. ....

ADDRESS ....

....

CO-OPERATIVE INSURANCE SOCIETY LIMITED, MANCHESTER 4

CFN

BUSINESS REPLY SERVICE
Licence No. 9839

CO-OPERATIVE INSURANCE SOCIETY LTD.

MILLER STREET,

MANCHESTER 4

USHER GALLERY, LINCOLN

I am interested to receive postal information of Gallery Exhibitions

Name (BLOCK LETTERS) ....

Address ....

....

....

In future, advance information will be sent only to those returning this slip to the Secretary, Usher Gallery, Lincoln.

Additional forms available on application.

one of the very few members of the Senate to see, in advance, the appalling dangers of the mood in which President Roosevelt approached the Yalta Conference, to the point that he actually went to see the President before he left for Yalta to plead with him to take a tougher and more realistic attitude towards the Russians?

SENATOR MCCARTHY: No, it's not.

CHAIRMAN: You see what I'm getting at, though, don't you, Senator—that the Communists and fellow-travellers in Wisconsin had very good reasons for wanting to get La Follette out of the Senate and you in, and were delighted when you succeeded?

SENATOR MCCARTHY (*banging the table, thereby stimulating a new burst of energy on the part of the photographers*): If that is so, they've had every reason subsequently to regret it.

CHAIRMAN: Are you so sure?

SENATOR MCCARTHY: I'd like to read into the record a resolution passed by the American Communist Party published in the *Daily Worker* to the effect that Senator Joseph McCarthy is one of the bitterest and most unrelenting foes of Communism . . .

CHAIRMAN: You can read anything you like into the record, Senator, but did you help to draft the resolution?

SENATOR MCCARTHY: Did I help . . . that's ridiculous. We're both grown up, aren't we?

CHAIRMAN: Answer the question.

SENATOR MCCARTHY: No, I didn't.

CHAIRMAN: Now another question. Have you got any present or former Communists on your staff?

SENATOR MCCARTHY: I . . .

CHAIRMAN: The question, Senator.

SENATOR MCCARTHY: My staff has been carefully selected and screened . . .

CHAIRMAN: What we want to know is whether there are any present or former Communists among them.

(*A pause.*)

SENATOR MCCARTHY: Two former Communists who . . .

CHAIRMAN: Good. For the record, the Senator employs two former Communists. He was elected in Wisconsin with Communist and fellow-traveller support. He denies being as of now a member of the Communist Party, but it is a matter of public knowledge that his activities since he became a Senator have greatly benefited the cause of Communism here in the United States and abroad. Furthermore, it can be said with certainty that, if he were an under-cover party member, chosen for that reason to oust La Follette (particularly dangerous, from the Communist point of view, because a progressive himself, and bearing a name famous among progressives, and at the same time intensely and knowledgeably anti-Communist), everything he has done and said subsequently would support such a hypothesis.

(*Senator McCarthy begins to expostulate violently, again lavishly photographed the while.*)

CHAIRMAN: You'll have every opportunity, Senator, to rebut these grave charges. The session is now suspended.

My fair Gentleman

The dust jacket of Mr. F. J. Stopp's study of Evelyn Waugh shows Mr. Waugh, dressed in check tweeds, a large, unlighted cigar in his hand, and leaning over a gate inscribed: '*Entrée Interdite aux Promeneurs.*' This portrait is by Cecil Beaton, who specialises in photographic studies of the Royal Family and other fashionable celebrities. It conveys the whole irony and poignancy of Mr. Waugh's life out of which his writings have come—the notice in French (a language he prides himself, when he is abroad, on being totally unable to speak) on the gate of what is supposed to be an English country house, itself, along with Mr. Waugh's singular fancy dress, serving to draw attention to him when, according to Mr. Stopp's and his own account, one of his major objects in life is to avoid being intruded upon. As a further twist, Mr. Beaton describes in his Autobiography how, as a small, sensitive child, he was bullied by a gross, hearty boy at the same preparatory school who turned out to be Evelyn Waugh. The photographer and his subject had met before.

My own acquaintance with Mr. Waugh is slight. The last time I saw him was at a wedding. I am no expert on wedding attire, but his seemed unusual. A tall black top hat, I thought funereal in character, provided an additional bizarre touch. He made considerable play with an old-fashioned Victorian ear-trumpet, though whether for use or ostentation I cannot say; probably the latter. Mr. Waugh seems to have sharp enough ears when required. Occasionally he seemed to head in my direction, almost to orbit round me, but no trace of recognition appeared on his large, rubicund countenance. I felt no particular desire to be recognised by him, but these strange gyrations struck me as odd. In any case, on the few occasions that I have been on speaking terms with Mr. Waugh, I have formed the impression that he does not like me.

Usually, such antagonisms are mutual. I cannot, however, say that I reciprocate Mr. Waugh's dislike. There is, to me, something oddly sympathetic about this professional eccentric. I admire the bizarre, though none-the-less often highly effective, protests he has made against the times in which we both live. I once saw him at Brighton, on this occasion attired in an enormous overcoat and grey bowler hat. He was making his way alone on to the pier. I was tempted to follow him and see whether it was the machines—'What the Butler Saw'—which attracted him or whether he just went to the end to stare for a while out to sea. Despite his bulk and peculiar accoutrements, he had, I thought, an air almost of sanctity. The fool who persists in his folly becomes wise, Blake wrote. In this sense at least, Mr. Waugh may be accounted wise. Most of us, in the pursuit of folly, at a certain point prudently draw back. Mr. Waugh has persisted to the end. He has fought the good fight, if only with bladders and in the setting of a harlequinade.

Mr. Stopp's study is painstaking, sympathetic and occasionally illuminating. He suffers, however, under the disability that he has only felt able to offer serious criticism in the words of others. His own attitude is too uniformly approving to be interesting. Unfortunately, too, he notably lacks Mr. Waugh's gift for the terse ironical phrase, the sharp, icy comment. He is deeply serious, if not solemn, and has that curious convoluted way of writing which life at a university (in his case, Cambridge) seems so often to inculcate. Mr. Waugh has long passed the time when he needs an apologist. He has, in any case, been most ardently his own.

The Ordeal of Gilbert Pinfold, with its mysterious voices, and the strange suggestions they insinuate of homosexuality and other repellent attitudes and practices, as alien to Pinfold as to his creator, conveys to a discerning reader a great deal more about Mr. Waugh than most authors have disclosed about themselves. Mr. Stopp could scarcely have hoped to add to this.

His *Evelyn Waugh* is divided into two parts, the first biographical, the second an analysis of Mr. Waugh's works. The biographical section takes us rather sketchily from Mr. Waugh's childhood in a prosperous London suburb, Golders Green, the son of Arthur Waugh, for many years head of the publishing firm of Chapman and Hall, to his time at Lancing, where he began to emerge as a 'character,' and distinguished himself at the school debating society. Mr. Stopp adds, rather naïvely, that the Headmaster's House, at which Mr. Waugh was, had special connections with Eton, and that this may account for Mr. Waugh's subsequent large acquaintanceship with Etonians. I can think of other explanations.

Mr. Waugh went on to Hertford College, Oxford, where he obtained a history scholarship, and there became an eminent figure among the group of æsthetes whose leader and chronicler was Harold Acton. A portrait by Henry Lamb belonging to this period bears out Acton's gruesomely dated description of him as

> a prancing faun, thinly disguised by conventional attire.
> His wide-apart eyes, always ready to be startled under raised eyebrows, the curved sensual lips, the hyacinthine locks of hair, I had seen in marble and bronze at Naples, in the Vatican Museum, and on fountainheads all over Italy.

He neglected to take his degree, though he obtained a third class in his finals. After Oxford, he was at a loose end, did a bit of preparatory school teaching (resulting later in *Decline and Fall*), tried his hand at carpentry, and then began to write. His first marriage was a failure. The years before the outbreak of the 1939-45 war were mostly spent in travelling and writing travel books.

With great gallantry and persistence, although by this time thirty-seven, he managed to become a combatant soldier, and was with the Royal Marine Commandos in North Africa. Then he transferred to the Blues (the Royal Horse Guards), and, by one of life's little ironies, was given indefinite leave of absence to write a book—*Brideshead Revisited*. From this compulsory retirement, he was rescued by Mr. Randolph Churchill, with whom he joined Fitzroy Maclean's Military Mission in Yugoslavia. It was during this period that he first elaborated his interesting theory that Marshal Tito is, in fact, a woman. I caught a glimpse of him in the war, in Algiers, at a picnic party given by the Duff Coopers. He seemed, I thought, somewhat bemused and melancholy. His uniform, though exact, somehow gave the impression of not quite belonging to him. He looked, I decided, like a letter delivered to the wrong address.

In 1930, he had been received into the Roman Catholic Church, and subsequently married into a delightful and ancient family of that faith, the Herberts. Thenceforth, he settled down to elaborate his impersonation of a crusty old country gentleman, collecting the requisite properties, both personal and household, and occasionally appearing in London in this role. Mr. J. B. Priestley and others have complained about the impersonation on the ground that the writer has been suffocated by the elaborate superstructure it has required. This seems to me absurd for two reasons—firstly, that Mr. Waugh remains an excellent writer, probably the most accomplished to-day in the English language, and, secondly, that his impersonation of a country gentleman is as integral a part of his writing as was George Orwell's equally absurd converse impersonation of a down-and-out.

An interesting comparison could be made between these two. Whereas Mr. Waugh considers it 'common' to pile plates after a meal, Orwell thought it 'unproletarian' to drink in a saloon bar; whereas Mr. Waugh's wardrobe is based on sporting prints of the late nineteenth century, Orwell's followed the general lines of a workman in *Punch* jokes of the same period. If Orwell had not been able to convince himself that he was once down and out in Paris, and to dress and play the part, however imperfectly, the probability is that he would never have written *Animal Farm* or *1984*. In the same way, Mr. Waugh's masquerade has been essential to his work. Without it we might well have lacked his delightful comedies in the Wodehouse manner (though Wodehouse with a decided dash of vinegar), that little masterpiece, *The Loved One,* as well as *Brideshead Revisited,* his books on the war, and, finally, *Pinfold.*

Precisely the same comment may be made on Mr. Waugh's occasional political attitudes, which some have found offensive. Peppery old gentlemen living in the country, and needing ear-trumpets to hear what is said to them, who hate abroad and can't abide foreigners or speak their lingo, are naturally pretty antediluvian in their ideas. *The Times* is too Red for them, modern Toryism is little better than Bolshevism, and if they have occasionally heard the radio playing in the servants' hall, television is something they just do not know about. So it must be with Mr. Waugh, though, according to Mr. Stopp, acute boredom often induces him to go off to the local cinema in the afternoon. Again, it is an infinitely touching picture—the grey bowler perched on the large head, the defiantly 'loud' country suit, the pony-trap harnessed, the whip cracked. But to go where? To the local Odeon to see Gary Cooper. 'World, World; Oh! World,' as Lear remarked in not wholly dissimilar circumstances.

Mr. Waugh would, in any case, accept what he supposed to be the political attitudes which went with his Roman Catholicism. For instance, he would feel bound to approve of General Franco quite irrespective of any private distaste he might have for the Franco régime. He has laboured hard to make himself into a conformist, though his conformism is a Do It Yourself brand of his own. Thus, as a war-time soldier, his object was to submerge himself in smart regimental life. The novelist and gentleman must give way to the officer and gentleman. This, of course, did not make for popularity in the mess. His fellow-officers wanted to be diverted by the author of *Vile Bodies,* not confronted with a slightly grotesque, ageing version of themselves. They expected him to be funny and unusual, not taciturn and sullenly labouring to be usual. As is clear from his war novels, *Men at Arms* and *Officers and Gentlemen,* the Pinfold voices told Mr. Waugh this at the time—which must have made this suffering all the greater. He bore it, as always, with fortitude.

128

Mr. Stopp is puzzled by the great popularity of Mr. Waugh's novels—especially, of *Brideshead Revisited*—in the United States. This is the only book by Mr. Waugh I have never been able to get through. It seems to me to be tedious and rather foolish. On the other hand, I find no difficulty in understanding why its American edition should have sold 700,000 copies. Its success, surely, is exactly comparable with that of *My Fair Lady*. Indeed, it might well have been called *My Fair Gentleman*. It sustains the illusion, especially dear nowadays to many Americans, that the old familiar social landmarks are still extant in England. Yesterday's *Chicago Tribune* target has become to-day's solace. It is the kind of situation with which Mr. Waugh in his young days would have been particularly fitted to deal. Indeed, up to a point (Lord Copper) he does deal with it in the first part of *The Loved One*. That he should have benefited from it financially is, therefore, right and proper.

The side of Waugh which is most admirable, as Mr. Stopp clearly shows, is his unpretentious dedication to the craft of letters. He has refused to be side-tracked into all those ancillary activities upon which others have, uselessly and often shamefully, expended so much spirit. He decided to be a writer instead of a carpenter, and thenceforth devoted himself wholeheartedly and conscientiously to this pursuit. How few in our time have managed to do this! Even the terrible Pinfold experience (equivalent, in the context of his life, to Scott Fitzgerald's Crack-up) was coolly, neatly, expertly recorded. So rare a devotion deserves at least the Order of Merit. I should love to see it round his neck even though he still looked at me across it with those angry, explosive little eyes of his. Mr. Waugh, I always feel, is an antique in search of a period, a snob in search of a class; perhaps even a mystic in search of a beatific vision. His bad temper and bad behaviour are symptoms rather of an unrealised quest than of any native malignancy in himself. Like all failed saints, he is given to ill-temper and humour; the one absurd, the other delectable.

Mr. Waugh's own autobiography has now begun to appear. Alas, it is scarcely more informative than Mr. Stopp. We are still left with *Pinfold* as the main source-book. As with everything he does, including (perhaps particularly including) his humorous writings, there is a deep undercurrent of melancholy. If he still somehow contrives to extract a certain forlorn, elephantine zest from the remembrance of the pranks and fads of the 'smart' contemporaries to whom he managed to attach himself when he was at Oxford, he is conscious, one feels, of how ineffably silly it all was. Mr. Waugh is a sad man, and his autobiography is a sad book. The fame and success he has enjoyed have brought him, it would seem, little satisfaction. On the earthly level, I should suppose, his dissatisfaction derives from the fact that he was born into the middle-classes instead of into the landed aristocracy as described so ardently, so sycophantically and so fatuously in *Brideshead Revisited*. He would so like to have gone to Eton, ridden to hounds, lost enormous sums of money at gambling without turning a hair, and so on. Instead, his father was a publisher who lived in Golders Green.

From his point of view, fate could scarcely have been un-kinder. His own residence—a massive country mansion with Victorian furnishings and Pre-Raphaelite paintings on the walls—would seem to be as remote from Golders Green as it is possible to get. Yet is it? I very much fear that thanks to those Pinfold voices, the tainted air of N.W.11 may still effect an entry.

While I was casting a last look at these words about Evelyn Waugh came the news of his sudden death. I was deeply distressed, not only because the most accomplished writer of our time was silenced for ever; more, because of the despair which I knew had latterly afflicted him in his self-imposed solitude. I thought of Swift in those last terrible years in his Dublin Deanery, and of the epitaph he wrote for himself—UBI SAEVA INDIGNATIO COR LACERARE NEQUIT. Surely, Evelyn Waugh, as he so well deserves, is now likewise where his furious indignation can no longer lacerate his heart.

Mr. Wayland Young's researches into erotica through the ages have been diligently undertaken, and, one must assume, accurately expounded. They will save those interested in the subject the trouble, and possibly the embarrassment, of procuring access to erotica normally kept from indiscriminate public inspection. Mr. Young, who is a peer of the realm under the style Baron Kennet of the Dene, must be considered a somewhat unlikely individual to display such zeal and dedication in this particular field. A Frank Harris, even a Havelock Ellis, yes; but this earnest Labour scion of true-blue Tory stock whose ambition of being Mr. Harold Wilson's choice for some minor ministerial position, has now been realised—surprising! One should not, however, underestimate his disinterestedness in publishing a book like *Eros Denied*. The Labour Party, with its Nonconformist antecedents, is far more prudish than the Conservatives, as was clearly apparent at the time of the Profumo Affair. The Marquis de Sade is not a name to conjure with in Transport House.

In presenting and explaining his material Mr. Young makes frequent and unrestrained use of words which still come amiss to writers of my generation. We are asterisk men. Such diffidence, I am well aware, would meet with Mr. Young's strong disapproval as signifying life-denying old codgers. So let it be. To get over the difficulty I shall adopt the convention of using 'to Wayland' for the verb which occurs on almost every page of *Eros Denied*, and 'Young (m)' and 'Young (f)' for the almost as frequently referred to male and female organs. Thus, to illustrate the usage, one might say: 'Inserting his Young (m) in her Young (f) he Waylanded her good and proper.'

In addition to making available much out-of-the-way pornography, Mr. Young clearly has some sort of message that he wishes to convey. Alas, it eluded me. He labours under a sense of righteous indignation that some of the higher

131

flights of erotica should be denied, not only to the common people, but even, in certain cases, to peers and acknowledged experts like himself. I cannot personally share his righteous indignation. There would seem to me to be no high principle at stake here; no cause for which men of goodwill should be prepared to sacrifice themselves. Mirabeau appends to his pornographic novel *Ma conversion* ('A first-person account,' Mr. Young tells us, 'of the life of a gigolo, avid for *tartufferies*, for the licence behind the pious façade') the exhortation: '*Eh bien, lis, dévore, et branle-toi*'—'And now read, devour and masturbate.' Though Mirabeau, with characteristic shrewdness, puts his finger (in the most literal sense) on the point of all pornography, from *Fanny Hill* to *Lady Chatterley*, *branle-toi* scarcely seems a cry, like *liberté, egalité fraternité*, which one would wish to hear ringing through the world. Or is it, in Mr. Young's estimation? Waylanders of the world unite! You have nothing to lose but your Youngs.

The same difficulty arises, I may add, in other writings by Mr. Young that I have read. He is, for instance, considered something of an authority in defence matters; in this case, fighting rather than Waylanding being his theme. As in *Eros Denied* there is an impressive array of information, but one looks in vain for a cogent conclusion. Likewise, his recent volume on the Profumo Affair was supposed, one gathered, to point some moral about the Conservative Party, but apart from the rather obvious suggestion that Conservative Ministers are liable to be keen, and sometimes indiscriminate, Waylanders, no particular conclusion seemed to be reached about the Party's present circumstances and future prospects. Mr. Young reminds me of a hydro-electric scheme in which the massively dammed waters and the elaborately installed turbines just never get together to generate any electricity.

One chapter in *Eros Denied* I had previously read when it appeared in the magazine *Encounter* with the title 'Sitting on a Fortune.' It is about prostitutes and their lives, the information on which it is based having been collected in person by Mr. Young. One imagines him, notebook in hand, zealously questioning the girls, who, I suspect, pulled his leg a little. If they did, who shall blame them? Like all enthusiasts for erotica, Mr. Young is deeply, if not abysmally, serious—a state of mind which invites a certain amount of ridicule among the naturally ribald. Some of the stories the girls fed him are old chestnuts which, to my certain knowledge, have been circulating this last half-century and more. A prostitute, D, whom I got to know well (for Waylanding, not documentary, purposes) told me that the worst part of being a prostitute was not drunken sailors, nor even kinky clients who might want to jump on you from the top of a chest of drawers, or perform other weird capers. No, the hardest to bear were clergymen and other earnest persons who would insist on telling you how they loved their wives, showing you snapshots of their children, and probing the alleged miseries of a prostitute's life. D was accustomed to charge such clients time-and-a-half quite irrespective of their, often insignificant, Waylanding requirements. She would, I feel sure, have put Mr. Young in this bracket, and, at the same time, have taken an impish delight in filling his notebook with nonsensical anecdotes. Her own view, incidentally, was that most prostitutes were, like herself, congenitally lazy, and took to prostitution because it enabled them to get up late, loll about through most of the day, and earn good money with a minimum of effort. D, I may add, married a police officer, and, as far as I know, lived happily ever after.

Pornography has always, of course, been popular, and enjoyed a wide, if usually under-the-counter, circulation, though without arousing in most people the sort of obsessive interest displayed by Mr. Young. Its avowed purpose is to excite sexual desire, which, I should have thought, is unnecessary in the case of the young, inconvenient in the case of the middle-aged, and unseemly in the case of the old. Such obsessive concern with what Dr. Johnson (when he declined Garrick's invitation to go behind the scenes at Drury Lane) called his 'amorous propensities,' can be fostered equally by impotence (as with D. H. Lawrence) and revulsion against fleshly necessities (as with Swift and Aldous Huxley). Neither attitude is conducive to mirth. Laughter serves to neutralise pornography, and is therefore anathema to most pornographers. A man I know was thrown out of a Marseilles brothel for laughing at a pornographic film which was being shown there to stimulate business. I quite see the point. His laughter was liable to reveal the film's absurdity, and therefore to defeat its purpose.

In this connection, it is interesting that Rabelais is unmentioned in *Eros Denied,* though, as far as vocabulary is concerned, Waylanding and the two Youngs occur with a frequency which might have been expected to win our author's warm approval, or at any rate arouse his interest. Rabelais, however, is neither erotic nor pornographic (Are they to be distinguished? According to the Oxford Dictionary, not very markedly), but merely funny. His indecencies do not arise out of sexual desire, or out of its Janus-face revulsion. Rather, they convey a sense of the sublimely grotesque disparity between human aspiration and human performance. They cannot, therefore, stimulate sexual desire; the juveniles, young and old, who retire to dark corners with their *Kama,* their *Chatterley,* or their *Cancer,* henceforth, perhaps, with their *Eros Denied,* there to follow the Mirabeau routine (*lire, dévorer, branler*) would find Rabelais not at all to their purpose. He would break into their secret lechery with the same devastating force as a beam of sunlight into the murky, strip-teasing afternoon of businessmen on a spree.

Mr. Young's attitude is very different. His very solemnity makes even the highest flights of erotica as tedious as an address by a prep-school headmaster to his charges on the facts of life, beginning with stamens and pollen and working up to Waylanding. 'The Christian concept of God,' Mr. Young writes with singular asininity, 'as a single creator who loves us would founder altogether if it were to attempt to take on board the intractable biological fact of orgasm.' Considering what that fantastic old bark has managed to stow under its hatches—mortality, for instance—without foundering, one cannot but smile at naïveté like Mr. Young's which can suppose so trivial an additional cargo would sink the ship.

In another passage Mr. Young looks forward to 'a time of perfect sexual freedom,' when everyone will be able to live 'in the manner he has been conditioned to by chance and society, or has chosen by introspection and will.' They 'will find their own way into the right life for them in accordance with those forces in society and themselves which cause them to seek that way and not another, and the individual-causing factors will be stronger than the social ones.' I am not at all certain what this sentence means, if anything, but it appears to envisage a sort of erotic paradise whose sacred texts Mr. Young has collected; a drive-in Elysium with a shining screen dedicated to the promotion of orgasm pure and undefiled; Eros for ever undenied. For my own part, I should be happy to avoid any such paradise, especially those sacred texts, that mirthless screen. If this be Eros, then better denied, say I. St. Paul's Epistles are preferable, and anyway incomparably better written.

Boring for England

Leadership is always apt, even under universal suffrage. Government is seldom imposed, except for brief periods, and in politics there are never any Guilty Men. It is not by chance that a Baldwin or a Neville Chamberlain, an Attlee or a Roosevelt, or for that matter a Hitler or a Mussolini or a Stalin, emerge. Governors and governed seek and find a *modus vivendi*; the collectivity expect those set in authority over them to manifest, in a recognisable manner, the *zeitgeist* to which they belong. Otherwise they get rid of them.

Thus, Anthony Eden was an eminently suitable prime minister, conveying, as he did so exactly in appearance and in personality, the benevolent intentions and earnest purposes whereby an almost extinct ruling class seeks to protract itself a little longer. His somehow slightly seedy good looks and attire, his ingratiating smile and gestures, the utter nothingness of what he had to say—did it not all provide an outward and visible manifestation of an inward and invisible loss of authority and self-confidence? Yes, it was entirely fitting that this tedious, serious Etonian, on whose lips were the last dying echoes of the late nineteenth-century concept of progress without tears, should have had his moment in the middle of the turbulent and cruel twentieth century. He was a Disraeli hero who had moved into a service flat, or perhaps a deep shelter; a Bertie Wooster who had turned from the Drones Club to Toynbee Hall. As has been truly said in his days as an active politician, he was not only a bore; he bored for England.

Why, then, did he arouse, particularly among some of his

ostensible supporters, a frenzy of irritation, if not of positive dislike? After all, there are plenty of bores and nonentities among politicians of all parties. No one got furious with, say, Lord Woolton because he was not a dazzling conversationalist. Nor did a heavy hand in ladling out the spoken word prevent Lord Waverley or Lord Halifax from enjoying a reasonable measure of public esteem. Lord Alexander of Hillsborough was no Sidney Smith, and Mr. George Brown's oratory has always been more notable for sound and fury than sense. Yet these, and many like them, have patiently trodden the political mill, to receive in due course their due reward.

The simple fact is that nothing in Eden invited either admiration or abhorrence. He was just empty of content, like his television appearances in which a flow of banalities were presented in the persuasive manner of an ex-officer trying to sell one a fire extinguisher at the front door. His writings are the same. There is nothing wrong with them except that they are unreadable. One has to fight one's way through them; only dogged determination and a series of pauses to get one's breath for a fresh assault will carry one on to the end. When, as in the case of a joint Washington communiqué, President Eisenhower also took a hand, the result was a brew which makes Coca-Cola seem, by comparison, like Imperial Tokay.

Even so, quite a lot of Conservatives, particularly among his parliamentary and even ministerial colleagues, found it very hard to enthuse over Eden, and next to impossible to praise him. At best they put up with him. It was the same with Ramsay MacDonald during the second Labour Government. Labour Ministers and M.P.s for the most part just could not abide him, and at the same time they felt they had to endure him because he 'had a large following in the country,' because he 'spoke with authority in the counsels of the nations,' and so on—the self-same reasons, in fact, which induced Conservative M.P.s to endure Eden; to their subsequent deep regret at the time of the Suez fiasco. If there had been a Gallup poll when MacDonald was a Labour prime minister it would have shown, I am sure, as overwhelming a majority in favour of his leadership among the Labour Party rank-and-file as such a poll showed in favour of Eden's among rank-and-file Conservatives.

MacDonald and Eden, in fact, may be considered as having a great deal in common, down to the small but significant detail of frequently referring to us, the public, as 'my friends.' In the United States MacDonald was greatly esteemed; as also was Eden. Again, MacDonald had no more idea of how to deal with unemployment, the chief domestic problem confronting his government, than Eden had of how to deal with inflation, the chief domestic problem confronting his government. In his rather more shaggy, William Morris sort of way, MacDonald was as consciously elegant in appearance as Eden, and their diction bears many points of resemblance—a note of almost whimpering persuasiveness combined with a lack of precision which, in MacDonald's case, degenerated into total incomprehensibility.

In a sense, too, their roles were the same, though in reverse; MacDonald's being to convince the then much more powerful middle and upper classes that they had nothing to fear from a Labour prime minister, and Eden's to convince the now much more powerful lower classes that a Conservative prime minister is really on their side. Such a role cannot but give a touch of bizarrerie to those who undertake it, and though neither MacDonald nor Eden can be regarded as greatly dowered with humour, there is something inherently comical about both of them. In the eyes of posterity they are likely to appear as ribald figures whose earnest intentions and high aspirations bear no valid relation to the actual circumstances of their times, and therefore in retrospect seem funny.

None of this is Eden's fault. He is but a victim of history. The ship of state was already hopelessly waterlogged and incapable of responding to the tiller when he took over command. What was there, then, for him to do but to bend his efforts to soothing down the increasingly apprehensive passengers? Like the Republicans in the United States under President Eisenhower's leadership, the Conservatives under his were unable to find any *raison d'être* except to continue the policies of their opponents. They asked for a leader and were given a public relations officer; here is the news and this is Anthony Eden reading it.

How extraordinary then, that when, after the long years of waiting, Eden at last moved into Downing Street, he should have insisted on mounting the ludicrous Suez Operation, thereby infallibly encompassing his own ruin, and extinguishing for ever his country's Great Power pretensions. Future historians, if they are interested at all in so fatuous an episode, will offer their explanations. In propounding political and sociological ones, they should not overlook the personal, but perhaps decisive circumstance that Eden had long smarted under the lash of Churchill's barely disguised contempt. In nominating him as his heir-apparent, Churchill doubtless calculated that he would thereby protract to the maximum possible extent his own tenure of office. No one in their senses, as he saw it, could possibly prefer an Eden to him. Better a Churchill senile than an Eden in full possession of his faculties, such as they were! It is scarcely surprising, therefore, that when at last Eden did succeed Churchill, he should have had an obsessive determination to show that he, too, was mighty in action; that he, too, brooded over maps, sent for the Chiefs-of-Staff in the small hours of the morning, and could lead his countrymen through blood and sweat and tears to a glorious victory. Hitler had gone, but there was still Nasser. It must have seemed a prudent choice. In any manual for becoming a man of destiny, defeating the Egyptians would be exercise one. Alas, poor Eden stumbled even here. Full of Benzedrine, sick, a fugitive in Jamaica, his brief tenure of the centre of the stage was soon terminated, and he withdrew into the wings as the Earl of Avon to write his memoirs.

They have been appearing in successive bulky and weighty tomes. The style is reminiscent of every Foreign Office paper which has ever been written, minuted and stacked away in whatever cellar is reserved for these unillumined records of our time. Yet the work has, it cannot be denied, some weird fascination of its own. There is something almost majestic, if not sublime, in sentences like: 'The course taken by the German Government in unilaterally repudiating obligations into which they have freely entered, and in simultaneously acting as if they did not exist, both complicates and exaggerates the international situation.' One sees the young Anthony Eden starting off on what gives every promise of being a brilliant career. Socially, intellectually and personally he seemed destined for success. A distinguished record in the 1914-18 war, a first at Oxford in Oriental languages, impeccable family antecedents, an elegant appearance and an earnest disposition all equipped him for dazling advancement. In the lush pastures opened up in the age of Baldwin between upper-class Toryism and middle-class Socialism he must surely thrive.

Inevitably he gravitated to the Foreign Office. An astrakhan collar became him. What came to be known as an Anthony Eden hat grew on heads like this. By the Lake of Geneva, along the Quai Woodrow Wilson, wherever Benes beckoned and the Little Entente gathered, there was he to be found, first as a parliamentary private secretary, then as an under-secretary, then as a Minister of State and. finally as Foreign Secretary.

In politics, as in womanising, failure is decisive. It sheds its retrospective gloom on earlier endeavour which at the time seemed full of promise. Thus as one follows Eden's own voluminous and punctiliously pedantic account of the crises and conferences, the talks and diplomatic exchanges and orations of yesteryear—Abyssinia, Danzig, the Rhineland, non-intervention, sanctions, the Hoare-Laval pact—it is difficult to recapture the sense of urgency they once conveyed. They seem stations of the Cross which can only culminate in Gethsemane. Forgotten names crop up. M. Titulescu emerges briefly from oblivion; M. Politis rattles his fragile bones; Aloisi, Suvich, and a host of others whose names one once learnt to spell momentarily reappear on the public stage. The whole diplomatic circus of the thirties is assembled for one last commemorative performance.

Such an attitude is perhaps rather unfair. After all, those League of Nations committees (of Eighteen, of Five, of Six, of Thirteen, to name no others) were neither more nor less inept than the comparable United Nations ones to-day. Corfu or Cuba—what's the difference? Moreover, Eden's judgments and purposes, as he recollects them in tranquillity, were decidedly sounder than those of most of his ministerial colleagues. If he had been able to exercise full authority in the shaping of foreign policy he might well have made a better job of it. He could scarcely have made a worse.

From the beginning it was an uphill struggle. Baldwin appointed him Foreign Secretary with the grudging remark: 'It looks as if it will have to be you.' Baldwin's successor, Neville

Chamberlain, proved an even more woeful master. He was by no means content to be a sleeping partner, but grabbed up the cards himself and began playing them on his own account in a highly eccentric manner. Eden cites a letter Chamberlain addressed to Lord Halifax in which 'he wrote that the dictators were men of moods. If we caught them in the right mood they would give us anything we asked for. But if the mood changed they might "shut up like an oyster." ' In the same sort of way a newcomer to lion-taming might be advised to wait until the beast is in a good mood and then stroke its mane.

Finally it was too much even for Eden, and he resigned. One wonders why he did not do this earlier. He would seem to have been almost from the beginning at odds with the Government he served. He was always being asked to carry out policies in which he disbelieved and to undertake missions about whose outcome he was sceptical. Here, it seems to me, lies the fallacy of his whole career. He believed in diplomacy, a procedure as irrelevant to our present circumstances as embroidery in a factory which mass-produces bath mats. Believing in it, he could not but hope that somehow, some time, in confabulations with his opposite numbers, a solution would emerge.

In this expectation he hung on to office; went from capital to capital, sat ardently through interminable and tedious sessions at Geneva, drafted long telegrams and memoranda and wrestled assiduously with his colleagues, as with treacherous allies like Laval. It was like trying to dance a minuet with holy rollers. He knew the steps all right, but his partners just stamped on his toes and bruised his shins.

His memoirs tell us little about him as a man and all there is to know about the statesman he never became. The 700 pages contain only one joke—by King George V apropos Sir Samuel Hoare's resignation. 'No more coals to Newcastle; no more Hoares to Paris.' In any compendium of Royal humour it deserves a place.

An evening with bodgies and widgies in Melbourne

The faces of the bodgies and their female equivalents, widgies, were pinched and, for their years, sadly dilapidated—bad teeth, debauched eyes peering out uneasily from youthful features, sideburns (after their hero, Elvis Presley), and with it all an air of remote, unexpected innocence tinged with melancholy.

They described their police convictions and undetected misdemeanours with quiet pride—breaking and entering, larceny, carnal knowledge. They might have been going over cricket scores. It was difficult to remember that what they were talking about so vain-gloriously were serious crimes. They were showing off, and might well have been exaggerating, or even lying. It was not, however, what they had done, or pretended to have done, which was significant, but their attitude of mind.

Their clothing is lurid and basically American—long jackets almost to their knees, jeans or narrow trousers, brightly coloured socks. They work, earning between ten and fourteen pounds a week, of which they spend more than half on clothes and pleasures. As for school—they stayed the minimum permissible time.

'I expect I fell in with the wrong set,' one of them said. They, too, follow the prevailing fashion, and put forward environmental explanations of personal misbehaviour. There is quite a bit of whining mixed up with their boasting. Their parents scarcely seemed to play any part in their lives. They are prematurely adult—sleep with girls, drink, stay up late, come and go as they please.

We went on to a dance hall packed tight with rocking and rolling bodgies and widgies. A picture of Presley dominated the proceedings. I mentioned that I had read in the newspapers of how, when he reported for military service and his hair had to be cut, the suggestion was made that the precious snippets might be sold or distributed. This did not go down well. In bodgie ears it seemed a bit blasphemous, I felt.

The insistent Negro rhythm got going, and as the dancing worked up to its frenzied climax famous characters were pointed out—this one helped organise the pyjama party the other night, this one was just out after a stretch for robbery with violence, and so on. They were the big shots. There was no one present over nineteen, and most were fifteen or sixteen—a motley, runtish, spiritually under-nourished sort of gathering, lubricated by soft drinks and animated by an American-transmitted jungle beat. The tang of adolescent sex was in the air, or rather of carnal knowledge—perhaps of carnal ignorance, perhaps just hysteria. Who knows?

Waifs of a materialist society, I reflected, proletarian outsiders, surrealists of the gutter. They exist everywhere in more or less the same form. I have seen those long jackets and padded shoulders and ferret faces in Tottenham Court Road, Third Avenue, Montparnasse, the Kurfuerstandamn. It is a world-wide phenomenon, existing, if the Soviet Press is to be believed, equally on the other side of the Iron Curtain, where there are no pictures of Elvis Presley, no juke boxes, no erotic literature on easy sale.

These adolescents choose to stand apart, with their own fantasies, their own ways and language, preying upon the society from which they have deliberately excluded themselves. They cannot be accounted for by saying that they come from bad homes and have been neglected by their parents. Many of them have come from good homes and responsible parents. The social science copy-book maxims are not applicable. Nor are the psychiatrist's case-book maxims.

In a sense, the bodgies are over rather than under privileged. They are in full enjoyment of the material benefits which, it is constantly being contended, make for a full and serene life. Though Australian, they pursue happiness in the American style, and have the means so to do. If they are famished, it is spiritually; if they are deprived, the deprivation is within themselves rather than in their material circumstances.

It is no good asking them to become Boy Scouts. They will Be Prepared all right, but with a bicycle chain. Boys' clubs are unlikely to be of much use to them because they are not boys, but adolescents who have come to look old and wizened without growing up. The eroticism to which they, along with the rest of us, are continuously subjected, cannot be held accountable for them. This drenches one and all. They cannot be said to be products of horror comics. Rather, they *are* horror comics, written and produced with musical accompaniments and décor, by Mid-Twentieth Century Inc.

What, then, can be done about them? The police think physical chastisement is the answer, and resent not being allowed to administer it except with great discretion. Physical chastisement would no doubt serve to keep the bodgies off the streets, but it is improbable that it would eliminate them. Nor, for that matter, would moral homilies, and cheerful old sports, whether clerical collared or not, being hearty and cheerful over a pipe.

The bodgies and widgies, in all their different variants all over the world, must be considered as products of the fear and rootlessness and bewilderment which is noticeably present everywhere to-day. They are not criminals in the ordinary sense. Crime implies a motive and they have none. They are not just larrikins or hooligans, who, unlike the bodgies, hunted in exclusively male packs, and were addicted to violence rather than viciousness. These starvelings in their coloured clothes, with their drooping cigarettes, their furtive glances and quick movements, are emanations of an urban way of life which is probably more empty and aimless than any hitherto known.

Thomas Mann says in one of his books that, in a disintegrating civilisation, there are only two possible reactions—that of the saint and that of the gangster. The bodgies have chosen the latter.

Some future historian, I suppose, will one day survey this curious time of ours with the ironic detachment of a Gibbon. He is to be envied. What a rare harvest awaits him!— always, of course, assuming that we do not, in obedience to the death-wish which seems to possess us, destroy ourselves and all our records. Even if the records survive they will, in any case, be difficult to make out. Such a vast accumulation of lies and slanted information! Such contradictory conclusions and conflicting evidence! How will it all ever be disentangled? A resident newspaper correspondent in Moscow was asked by a wide-eyed visiting leftist, when Stalin's purges were in full swing, how far the court proceedings were to be believed. Everything was true, he replied, except the facts. It might be our epitaph. Never have so many facts been accumulated; never have such ingenious and efficacious means of propagating them far and wide been devised, but only to weave a great web of deception. The Dark Ages were noontide compared with our light.

My future historian will certainly want to devote a chapter, if not a volume, to the Christian churches in the mid-twentieth century. Their performance is bound to strike him as hilarious. They were funny enough when with crazy gallantry they tried to defend the Book of Genesis against Darwin's *panzers*; they are even funnier now that, belatedly, they have decided to join the army of progress just when it is in total disarray, if not in headlong retreat. They are like a citadel which resists wave after wave of attack; whose garrison, besieged, starving, decimated, holds desperately on, only, when the attackers themselves have lost heart and decided to abandon the struggle, to open the gates and sally forth bearing white flags. Contraceptives and copies of *Lady Chatterley's Lover* have been laid as propitiatory offerings on an expiring altar; the Red Sea opened, but the hosts of Israel, mistaking their direction, took the opportunity to return to Egypt and bondage.

Towards the end of the last century it would have seemed only too obvious that Christian institutions which bowed to the prevailing evolutionary current had the best chance of survival. Let them jettison their more ludicrous dogma and ceremonial. and take their place in the vanguard of progress; as it were, sell out their Heavens for what they would fetch and buy in Earths on a rising market. Then they could be sure of finding themselves on the winning side. Where are they now?—those ethical churches, those pearly gates opening on to the kingdom of heaven on earth, those hothouse blooms, nurtured by crossing the *Origin of Species* with *Hymns Ancient and Modern,* which made so fair a show in their day. All faltering or extinct. There is wind on the heath, brother, still, but it blows where it listeth, and is tainted with the stench of a charnel-house.

As things have turned out, it is 'enlightened' sects like the Unitarians which have withered on the vine, not 'obscurantist' Roman Catholicism. The Little Bethels are closing down, but the Scarlet Woman, drunk with the blood of the Saints, has unaccountably thriven in the age of science and enlightenment. Shaw is to-day more dated than St. Paul, and poor old Wells turned his face to the wall and cried his eyes out in *Mind at the End of its Tether* just because the atom had been split, when he of all people should have offered thanks. One does not expect a Salvation Army band to throw away their instruments and turn tail and run on Judgment Day. Walt Whitman, Edward Carpenter, William Morris—how far, far away their voices sound, whereas the crowning of a Pope attracts almost as many viewers as a royal occasion, and even rates a Dimbleby commentary.

My historian's astonishment would be all the greater that the Roman Catholic Church itself, having witnessed the ruinous consequences to its Protestant rivals of compounding with contemporary trends, should now seem set upon following a like course. Just when the Reformation appears to be finally fizzling out, another, it seems, is incubating in Rome. Luther escapes from John Osborne's hands into—of all places —the Vatican. The Church's profound pessimism about human life, miraculously preserved through the long false dawn of science, is about to be shed at the precise historical moment that it is most relevant and most urgently needed to save men's reason, if not their souls.

Pessimism has, indeed, been Christianity's great strength, and the reason for its survival. The concept of this world as a wilderness, and of human life as short and brutish, fits the circumstances of most people most of the time. The contrary proposition—that earthly life can be satisfying within its own dimensions and on its own terms, leads to such mental strain and confusion as to be scarcely tenable, other than briefly and artificially. The kingdom of heaven in heaven may be a dubious proposition, but through the centuries it has appealed both to sophisticates like St. Augustine and Pascal, and to all the simple-hearted who, legitimately disappointed with their lives here on earth, pin their hopes in a future beatitude beyond the grave. To proclaim a kingdom of heaven on earth, on the other hand, is both deceptive and intrinsically absurd. The maintenance of such a notion requires mental gymnastics so extreme and so strenuous that they usually produce dementia.

Thus if the kingdom of heaven on earth has dawned for us now, it is necessary to regard this age as exceptionally and increasingly humane, when in point of fact it has evidently been notable for slaughter, cruelty and destruction on a scale rarely, if ever, exceeded in history. We have to offset the Health Service against Hitler's gas-chambers, the Third Programme against the wanton destruction of many of the finest products of our civilisation like the city of Dresden, Parks of Culture and Rest against the monstrous annihilations of Stalin, Unesco against the millions of displaced persons (that blood-curdling term, itself an emanation of a lost mind reaching after a lost soul). We have to persuade ourselves that we are moving towards a condition of peace and enlightenment when, in fact, wealth and skills are being devoted on an inconceivable scale to making weapons capable of blowing us and our world to smithereens, such weapons being in the hands of tenth-rate demagogues like Lyndon Johnson and the hard-faced men, his opposite numbers, in the Kremlin who unaccountably succeed one another in power.

Above all, we have to persuade ourselves that we are

happy. This is the most difficult and sanity-destroying operation of all. The psychiatric wards are full of patients guiltily
conscious of having failed to be happy. The ever-increasing
numbers of the mentally sick (twenty million now, reportedly,
in America, the happiest land) have cracked under the
strain. Happiness in Scandinavia (another happy land, portrayed by Ingmar Bergman) often seems to fall out of the
window, Hemingway's happiness was a bullet he fired into his
brain. I gave my happiness an airing on the M 1, and it
collided with someone else's, spattering the tarmac with
blood. I swallowed my happiness in a little coloured pill,
I read it in the *Readers' Digest,* I saw it on a glossy page.
I even ejected it into my girl, but it gave her a pain. So
she had it cut out.

Deliverance from happiness would seem to be the greatest
need of mankind to-day, and the Christian churches are an
ideal instrument for bringing it about. The New and Old
Testaments are full of the hopelessness of looking for anything but tribulation in this world, and the senses stand
condemned as gross deceivers which enslave and ruin their
addicts. We are to die in the flesh to be re-born in the
spirit. One may carry so sublime a notion around with one
like the picture of a loved face, taking it out from time to
time to look at it with sick longing.

Yet, strangely enough, just at this moment when, of all
others, such a message is desperately needed, the trend in the
Christian churches is all the other way. One may, perhaps,
leave out of account the Anglican Church, which has long
been an object of derision. If it were to be disestablished it
would be seen to have practically ceased to exist. Its lovely
edifices are falling into decay; its superb *Book of Common
Prayer* scarcely redeems its shambling services; its clergy are,
for the most part, forlorn and negligible. Words cannot convey the doctrinal confusion, ineptitude and sheer chicanery
of the run-of-the-mill incumbent, with his Thirty-Nine Articles
in which he does not even purport to believe, with his listless exhortations, mumbled prayers and half-baked confusion
of the Christian faith with better housing, shorter hours of
work, the United Nations and opposition to *apartheid.*

One may sympathise with the difficulties of comprehend-

147

ing within one body St. Paul, the former Dean of Canterbury
and the present Bishop of Woolwich, as one looks in vain for
any guiding light of reason, or even sanity, in equating the
Pauline view of sex, with D. H. Lawrence's. The outcome,
in any case, is a shambles, amiable and well-meaning, perhaps,
but playing virtually no part in the lives even of the few who
continue to participate in Anglican worship.

That the Roman Catholic Church should now have embarked on the same road strikes a Protestant as more surprising. Through the years it has maintained its position, re-
fusing to be stampeded by the claims and pretensions of an
increasingly materialist world. The positions it has taken
up have always seemed to be, within its own terms of reference, sound and logical enough. Even on the highly contro-
versial subject of birth control I find its attitude more convincing than the breast-beating among its opponents over the
woes of excessive child-bearing. Far deeper and more ignomin-
ious suffering, in my experience, comes of sterility. Moreover,
my historian (returning to him for a moment) will surely
note as a highly bizarre circumstance the fact that the
strongest demand for birth control comes precisely when
the possibilities in the way of food production are seen to
be virtually illimitable, and when the whole universe is
about to be opened up, providing space to accommodate a
million, million times our present squalid little human family.

The Roman Catholic Church is the one remaining, and
far and away the strongest bastion of Christendom. If it is
now crumbling (as seems to be the case), and in process of
succumbing to the siren voices of material and fleshly well-
being wafted across the Atlantic, then the game is finally
up. The long tortuous path through history of this truly
remarkable institution will have ended at last, and the story
which began so strangely and momentously in Palestine 2000
years ago have finally lost its power to shape and animate
our human destiny. Affluence broadening down from hire-
purchase payment to hire-purchase payment will not salvage
it, nor the best of all possible birth-pills down the most
amenable of all possible gullets, nor more and better education, nor even votes for teenagers; none of the various
panaceas which have been or will be proffered. A light

will have gone out which has illuminated all our lives, shone through the art and literature of a long civilisation, and served to hold at bay, if only fitfully and inadequately, the wild appetites to gorge and dominate which afflict all our hearts.

England, whose England?

Each time I return to England from abroad the country seems a little more run down than when I went away; its streets a little shabbier; its railway carriages and restaurants a little dingier; the editorial pretensions of its newspapers a little emptier; and the vainglorious rhetoric of its politicians a little more fatuous. On one such occasion I happened to turn on the television and there on the screen was Harold Macmillan, then Prime Minister, blowing through his moustache to the effect that 'Britain has been great, is great, and will continue to be great.' A more ludicrous performance could scarcely be imagined. Macmillan seemed, in his very person, to embody the national decay he supposed himself to be confuting. He exuded a flavour of moth-balls. His decomposing visage and somehow seedy attire conveyed the impression of an ageing and eccentric clergyman who had been induced to play the part of a Prime Minister in the dramatised version of a Snow novel put on by a village amateur dramatic society.

We like to persuade ourselves that our leaders betray the trust imposed in them and distort the aspirations of those who elect them. Actually, they represent us all too exactly. The melancholy tale of our Prime Ministers, from Lloyd George and Baldwin, through Ramsay MacDonald and Neville Chamberlain, to Attlee, Anthony Eden and Harold Wilson, provides a perfect image of our fate. No one is miscast. Each left the country appreciably poorer and weaker, both spiritually and materially, than when he took over, giving an extra impetus to the Gadarene rush already under way. Churchill may be separated from the others in that he was confronted, in 1940, with an evidently desperate situation to meet which he invoked desperate remedies. Yet it may be doubted whether the overblown rhetoric he fed the English, in the written and the spoken word, was, in its ultimate consequences, appreciably different from MacDonald's exuberant incoherence or Eden's relentless banalities.

Macmillan, in any case, provided a symbolism which was perfectly appropriate. The crofter and the ducal connection; that antique rig with its faint flavour of burlesque; grouse-moor spats, and evenings wreathed in cigar smoke and rich with port; those meandering disquisitions, Trollopian, historical, floating loose, as it were, upon some aimless and inexhaustible tide—who could more fittingly direct our affairs in the mid-twentieth century? Never can I forget him in Kiev during his visit to the U.S.S.R. and Mr. Khrushchev. He was dressed in a tweed ensemble suitable for rural occasions, worn, I should suppose, at many a Conservative garden fête. His speech, delivered with old-style elegance, referred to how in the eleventh century a Ukrainian princess had married into the English royal house. Might not this union, he went on, be regarded as a happy augury for future relations between two countries whose history and traditions had so much in common? The crowd, as is usual on such occasions in the U.S.S.R., consisted largely of government officials, with a top dressing of plain-clothes police; solidly built, grey-faced men in issue suitings, containing ample room for a slung gun, and with wide trouser-ends. I studied their granite expressions as the Prime Minister's oratorical flow washed over them. In just one or two of their faces I thought I detected a faint trace of wonderment; a tiny flicker of an eyelid, a minute fold of incredulity round the mouth. The others remained inscrutable, their pleasure in their former princess's London nuptials, if any, well under control.

As Macmillan walked away with little Selwyn Lloyd, the Foreign Secretary, trotting along behind him, seemingly well pleased with himself, tall white fur hat perched on his head, and something crustacean in his gait, I realised that those two had gone about the troubled world before; in the parched plains of Spain, the one mounted on the lean mare, Rosinante, and the other on a donkey, looking for wrongs to redress and maidens in distress to champion.

Unmistakably, they were Don Quixote, Knight of the Woeful Countenance, and Sancho Panza, his squire.

As in Cervantes's masterpiece, one feels to-day that things are out of sync. The conductor is working from one score and the orchestra from another, with consequent total confusion in the resultant performance. The players have learnt their lines from another play than the one which is being performed; they make false entrances and exits, stumble over unfamiliar scenery, and turn in vain to the prompter for help and guidance. There is no correlation between word and deed, between the aspirations ostensibly entertained and what actually happens, between (to use Blake's dichotomy) what is seen with, and what is seen through, the eye.

Such is the prevailing impression when I look back at what has happened to and in England during the last five decades; since, that is, the outbreak of the 1914-18 war. I have a vivid recollection, at the age of thirteen, of going to Brixton after the first Zeppelin raid, and seeing crowds of people collecting, by way of mementoes, fragments of metal from the macadamised roadway. Most of these fragments were motor-treads, and had no connection with the raid, but were no less zealously collected for that. On Armistice Day my father astonished us all by producing a minute Union Jack when he returned from the City, and fastening it to the porch of our small suburban house, where it rather absurdly fluttered. In our socialist-pacifist household this action was as staggering as if he had announced that he was to be ordained into the Anglican Church. The Union Jack covered the chairman's table at Conservative gatherings; it was waved on patriotic occasions; it embellished pernicious leaflets. It was not for us.

I spent Armistice Day going on the top of a motor bus to its Woolwich terminal and then back to South Croydon. It was the first time I had seen human beings released from restraint; climbing on to the roofs of taxis, shouting, reeling, and clasping one another; dancing and, grimacing, and exchanging hats. In those days there was no radio to tell us about what we were doing and feeling; no television to mirror back to us ourselves and our hopes and desires. We had to make do with the *Daily Mail,* in which I read about the celebrations I had witnessed on the way to and from Woolwich. I think, therefore I am; it was in the *Daily Mail,* therefore it happened. The microphone and the television screen, and subsequent developments in popular journalism, were to make such propositions infinitely more actual in the years to come. I turned to the *Daily Mail* in preference to the *Daily News* with some trepidation. It was owned, I knew, by Lord Northcliffe, whose name my father used to pronounce with extreme displeasure, at the same time drawing a piece of string tightly round his finger like a noose.

My father's explanation of so astonishingly flying a Union Jack from our porch was that it signified on this occasion, not national pride, but national redemption; the ending of a war to end war, and the ushering in of the League of Nations, a land fit for heroes to live in and a world safe for democracy; the fulfilment of all the promises and prognostications dredged up out of Woodrow Wilson's Princetonian virtue, and Lloyd George's Welsh cunning, and the fathomless French duplicity of Clemenceau. It was, and to some extent still is, the fashion to complain that these promises were all broken and the prognostications all unrealised. My father soon, metaphorically speaking, lowered his flag to half-mast.

Yet the trouble really is that the promises have been all too well kept. How many housing estates have been built for heroes to live in! Hear old Beveridge's sheep's voice enumerating the benefits which Lloyd George aspired towards, and Attlee brought to pass! As for making the world safe for democracy, when has it ever been safer? Democracy in India, where millions go to the polls, choosing between Elephant and Lotus Flower in the maturest possible manner. In the U.S.S.R. and the People's Democracies, where polls of 95 per cent and more are regularly registered. In the U.S.A., where, thanks to television, rival candidates become personally known, a Real Presence, enabling the electorate to discriminate nicely between a Kennedy and a Nixon, a Johnson and a Goldwater. In the upper reaches of the Nile, where tall naked electors standing on one leg register their votes, and in our own boroughs and counties where votes are similarly registered by electors for the most part clothed and standing on two legs. Never, it is safe to say, has there been so much voting, on so broad a franchise, since the world began.

And the war to end war? After 1918, there was not, as it happened, another war, but only the same one, which is going on still. In that sense, the 1914-18 war might, admittedly, be better described as a war to begin war. As for the League of Nations, it duly came to pass. How well I remember it: that windy Quai Woodrow Wilson, and Ramsay MacDonald and his friends, and Anthony Eden idealistic behind his moustache, and Aristide Briand asleep behind his ampler one, and the Café Bavaria where journalists assembled to drink and dream up inside information. When complaints were heard that the League was somewhat ineffectual in actually terminating hostilities in Manchuria or Abyssinia, the reply always was that in other directions, like white slavery and narcotics, it was extremely effective. Thus, in August, 1939, the codification of level-crossing signs came up for consideration. The discussion was suspended when the Wehrmacht and the Red Army started marching into Poland from opposite directions, to meet in the middle. Whether it was ever taken up again at the United Nations, and if so with what result, I do not know.

The books about the war, Graves, Hemingway, Aldington; the poems about the war ('They have not died in vain'); the plays about the war, *Journey's End,* men in trenchcoats, tin hats, marching, singing; Edmund Blunden, Herbert Read (Sir); Lawrence of Arabia, alias Ross, and all his lies, which, if anything, only ministered, and minister, to the cult—grisly, shrinking, scruffily self-assertive prototype of all the scruffily assertive resistance fighters and fighting resisters to come, filling the deserts and the maquis and the mountains with authors in search of a hero; the other Lawrence (D. H.), Leavis his prophet, on the side of life, Saint Chatterley and all the Devils, in blissful sylvan union with her gamekeeper, though, according to perceptive Warden Sparrow of All Souls, by the back passage. The clergymen of the war, Woodbine Willie, Tubby Clayton, Dick Shepherd, mine hosts at the sign of the Lamb of God; poppies, graveyards with all the little identical gravestones stretching from here to eternity, the Prince of Wales fingering his tie; *All Quiet on the Western Front,* Old Contemptibles and Old Bill, cockney humour, to come in handy again in the underground shelters. "Arf a mo', Kaiser! 'Arf a mo', 'Itler!' with good old *Punch* throwing in its blessing all the way; minstrel boys, their wild harps slung behind them, who to the war did not go, Peace Pledge Unionists, Peace Balloters, never to fight again—never, never, never, never!

What a spectacular! What (as the reviewers say) a crowded canvas! What a yarn or slice of life, with *Good Companions* (Honest Jack Priestley) bringing up the rear, and, in the vanguard, the torch of culture borne aloft; Rare Tom Eliot with his Wasteland, squinting Jim Joyce with his vocabulary, Yawning Bill Yeats with his hive for the honey bee, and, coming along, Charlie Snow, Dilly Thomas, Johnny Osborne. Kit Logue, and Ken Tynan's Wolf Cub Troop, all wearing their badges as State Registered Satirists.

In such circumstances, a repeat performance of the 1914-18 war was inevitably called for, and was duly put on, under the direction of the Old Impresario himself, his stage cigar stuck in his mouth; siren-suited, jutting-chinned, a bulldog breed straight out of Cruft's if ever there was one. Some of his fellow-players in the original production had to be discarded for their creaking joints and stiff delivery, but there was plenty of new talent coming along; for instance, genial, ferret-faced Monty, with two badges in his hat and a heart overflowing with 'binge.' Soon the long, long trail was again a-winding; the home fires, thanks to the Luftwaffe, were kept burning, lighting such a candle by God's grace in England as (I trust) shall never be put out. Russian blood and American money sealed the glorious victory, and soon there was again a new and better world to be built.

See the three architects, met to de-limit its frontiers, shape its destiny, decree the punishment of the guilty and the reward of the virtuous; the Four Freedoms on their breath, the Atlantic Charter about their heads, enfolded in the luminosity of a common cause, a common dedication to life, liberty, and the pursuit of happiness for all mankind. Roosevelt with his large expanse of sirloin countenance, neon-lit; Churchill, British-warmed, fur hat rakishly awry, cigar rakishly jutting; and Stalin with his wary, slit eyes, staring, like some Mongolian shepherd, at a distant prospect, brooding on loot and murder and vast metal statues of himself to be erected in distant places. Imagine his heartfelt delight when Roosevelt, with the ingenuity of a Talleyrand, managed to slip out 'Uncle Joe'; when Churchill, shrewdly shaping up to Stalin's simple peasant shrewdness, demonstrated with match-sticks how his kingdom might be enlarged and his subjects increased, scribbling on a piece of paper the simple arithmetical division of their respective spheres of influence, and illuminating their discussion with primitive peasant imagery about not stuffing the Polish Goose too full of German food to the point of bursting. By way of preparation, he, too, had thoughtfully lighted such a candle by God's grace in Dresden as (I trust) shall never be put out.

Great was it in that time to be alive, but to be old was very heaven. The Four Freedoms reigned; in the rubble of Berlin and other demolished cities displaced persons picked their way, and constructed weird little caves to live in; cigarettes for currency, calories for food. In Nuremberg the fallen tyrants were brought to justice, Ribbentrop and the other accused hanging their heads and confessing to their judges, Soviet legal luminaries among them, that they had consented to the partition of Poland in accordance with the terms of the Nazi-Soviet pact as concluded between Stalin and Hitler. Thus was the majesty of international law upheld.

It fell to two newcomers to the stage of history, Harry S. Truman and Clement Attlee, to announce a momentous decision. The mice laboured and brought forth a mountain. Reading from a typescript, in a mechanical, expressionless voice, stumbling, childlike, after the words too eagerly to discover the sentences, President Truman announced the dropping of atomic bombs on Japan. Mr. Attlee likewise informed Honourable Members in the House of Commons, who rustled their Order Papers to indicate excitement, approval, and perhaps concern. Thenceforth the mushroom cloud adorned all deliberations. "Arf a mo', Krush!' But would there even be that much time? Millions now dying will never live. Ah! bearded, duffle-coated, twanging, chanting. Nuclear Disarmers; ah! Canon Collins in your belted cassock, and old philosopher Russell; ah! ten-gallon-hatted Jacquetta Hawkes, and all you resolute matrons and tousled girls, your souls go marching on.

Civilisation has already been saved twice, once by Lloyd

George and once by Churchill, and is now again in hazard. Who will save it this time, so that consenting adults may go on joyously consenting; *Cancer, Kama* and *Chatterley* continue to edify the young, delight the mature, and solace the old; no colour prejudice any more, no class prejudice either; an Empire now on which the sun never rises and a Commonwealth which never was; no poverty any more, bumper to bumper down to the sea in cars; our moral influence in the world mightier than ever before, though, let's be frank, old boy, our military might not quite what it was (God who made us feeble, make us feebler yet); we Greece to America's Rome, and, 'Your Royal Highness, Your Grace, Your Excellencies, My Lords, Ladies, and Gentlemen, as long as we, the two great English-speaking Democracies, stand together . . .' with cigar-smoke billowing upwards and brandy fumes billowing downwards; 'Hear! hear! Hear! hear!'

The New Towns rise, as do the television aerials, dreaming spires; the streams flow, pellucid, through the comprehensive schools; the B.B.C. lifts up our hearts in the morning, and bids us good night in the evening. We wait for Godot, we shall have strip-tease wherever we go. Give us this day our *Daily Express,* each week our Colour Supplement. God is mathematics, crieth our preacher. In the name of Algebra, the Father, Trigonometry, the Son, and Thermodynamics, the Holy Ghost, *Amen.*

Where the viaduct ends

Additional bits of Butleriana keep on appearing from time to time, the latest being Samuel Butler's Family Letters; more particularly his correspondence with his father, Canon Butler. None of this would seem to me to require any drastic revision of the essential picture which emerges from Festing Jones's monumental biography, reinforced by Butler's own private account of his relations with his friend Pauli, surely one of the most curious documents of its kind ever to be written.

During his lifetime, Butler's books, apart from *Erewhon,*

made practically no public impact. He toiled away at them, paid for their publication out of his own pocket, and wryly noted the meagre and mostly unsympathetic notices which they received. One has to admire the diligence and resolution which enabled him to persist on so unrewarding a course. Then, after his death, his long autobiographical novel, *The Way of All Flesh,* was published, and was an immediate success. When, some thirty years ago, I wrote a Life of Samuel Butler, I reached the conclusion that *The Way of All Flesh* was about the most *ignoble* novel ever written. Reading it in what purported to be a new text (it read uncommonly like the old one to me), edited by Professor Daniel F. Howard of Rutgers University, and taken from Butler's original manuscript, I found that my earlier opinion was largely confirmed. The publication of the Notebooks followed *The Way of All Flesh,* and Butler's posthumous reputation soared. Though it has diminished of late, it remains more soundly based than that of contemporaries like Gosse, who once, as he was never tired of complaining, so outshone him.

This enduring reputation can scarcely be accounted for on the basis of Butler's literary merits, such as they were. *The Way of All Flesh* is, on any showing, an unsatisfactory and decidedly tedious novel, *Erewhon,* too, though ingenious and, in its way, prophetic (for instance, the Musical Banks, which now actually exist in the United States), makes un-illumined reading. The dissertations on Darwinism, and on the role of habit in the evolutionary process are, I should suppose, little more than scientific curiosities, as the weird volumes on the *Iliad* and Shakespeare's Sonnets are literary ones. The Notebooks, too, have lost their bite, like the once daring witticisms of a Michael Arlen or a Noël Coward.

Butler's present reputation, then, derives rather from the sort of person he was, and what he stood for, than from his writings. Without meaning to, or even knowing he was doing it, he blazed a trail which many have subsequently followed. Like Columbus stumbling upon America when he thought he was finding a route to India, Butler stumbled upon the moral landscape which lay ahead when he thought he was carefully and prudently adjusting himself to the existing one. No one could have been, by temperament and inclination, mōre queasily conservative, more timid and conformist and respectable, than he was. Yet it so happened that he touched off a whole series of explosions whose reverberations are with us still. This is what makes him, unconsciously, so very funny. His jokes may have come to seem laboured and thin, but the colossal joke he *was* continues to be hilarious. Shaw, his devoted admirer, turned himself into a clown in order to be serious. With Butler it worked the other way round. He was so deeply and abysmally serious that he became a clown.

The point may be illustrated by three aspects of his character—his detestation of his father, his homosexuality, and his mania about money. Butler's correspondence with his father consists largely of financial wranglings. The Canon's greatest offence in his son's eyes was to go on living, thereby selfishly delaying the blessed moment when Butler would inherit. If the Canon had to remain alive, then, Butler considered, in common decency he should have disbursed far more readily and profusely than he did. Not only that. He was a plain, heavy-jowled, portentous old fellow whose inherited physical characteristics (not, like the financial ones, unfairly withheld, but all too readily passed on) Butler found little to his taste. It was, he felt, his father's fault that, instead of being self-assured and handsome like Towneley in *The Way of All Flesh,* he was diffident, gauche and unattractive.

Reading the letters which passed between them, one cannot but sympathise with the Canon. He was, of course, set in his parental attitudes. For instance, he wanted Butler to earn a living, which he resolutely refused ever to do. Yet as a result of the savage assault which Butler launched on him in *The Way of All Flesh,* the propositions on which the Canon had based his whole position were undermined and ultimately demolished. It became as fashionable to detest parents as formerly it had been to revere them. Butler, it is true, only lobbed an old-fashioned hand-grenade into the Victorian edifice of domestic harmony. Heavy Freudian artillery was being assembled to flatten it out. Historically, however, the first effective blow had been struck by Butler. Rebellious or Oedipus-stricken children yet unborn were beholden to him.

Butler's homosexuality was sentimental, furtive and timid. He and Jones, his biographer and inseparable companion in his later years, shared a passion for a Swiss youth named Hans Faesch, whom they saw off from Holborn Viaduct Station when he left for Singapore. Butler signalised the occasion by some verses which began:

Out, out, out into the night,
With the wind bitter north-east and the sea rough;
You have a racking cough and your lungs are weak,
But out, out into the night you go,
So guide you and guard you, Heaven, and fare you well.

This bizarre outpouring Butler considered to be 'the best thing I ever wrote.' He intended to get it published, with the title 'In Memoriam H.R.F.,' but changed his mind because, as he wrote to Hans, 'things have happened in England which make Jones and me decide not to publish it even anonymously.' On his copy of this letter there is a note to the effect that the event referred to was the trial of Wilde.

His longest, most troubled and most expensive affair was with Pauli, whom he met in New Zealand. Pauli, at that time, was working for a newspaper in Wellington, and Butler provided him with financial help to return to England, where he proposed to read for the Bar. They travelled back together, and thenceforth, however straitened his own circumstances, Butler continued to give money to Pauli, though they rarely met, and Butler did not even know where his protégé lived. Was it a case of blackmail? Mr. Silver, the competent editor of the Family Letters, dismisses any such possibility. I am not so sure.

In his study of the Sonnets Butler obviously finds a close parallel between Shakespeare's relations with Mr. W.H. and his own with Pauli. He suggests in all seriousness that the lines,

Why didst thou promise such a beauteous day
And make me travel forth without my cloak,

unmistakably indicate that Shakespeare had begun to make a pass at Mr. W.H., had then, as a result of a prearrangement with Mr. W.H., been surprised by some rowdies, and had to withdraw in disarray with some of his garments missing. 'So I, made lame by Fortune's dearest spite,' points to the fact that Shakespeare was quite seriously injured, but in the end,

Butler concludes, was able to live this deplorable affair down, while Mr. W.H.'s prank 'was generally regarded as blackguard sport rather than deliberate malice.' So far-fetched, not to say ludicrous, an interpretation, it seems to me, points to some equally ill-judged and ill-fated amorous episode between Butler and Pauli, perhaps on the steamer on the homeward journey as they sat side by side on deck-chairs under a tropical sky.

Be that as it may, Butler's attitude to Pauli continued to be humbly and wistfully adoring. He venerated his social ease, and the practical ability which enabled him, for instance, to arrange for the transfer of Cleopatra's Needle to London (Was there some phallic significance here?) Pauli himself remains a somewhat dim figure, but he obviously had an unusual talent for parasitism. When he died, it turned out that Butler was not his only patron. There were others. When they all met for the first (and last) time at his funeral, a slap-up affair with a special train, they were disconcerted to learn that the supposedly penurious Pauli had left an estate of some £8000, which, with a nice ironic sense, he had bequeathed to a mistress. One imagines those bearded and highly respectable mourners uneasily eyeing one another.

The character of Towneley in *The Way of All Flesh* is obviously based on Pauli, as Ernest Pontifex, the hero, is Butler himself. Towneley in Ernest's eyes, like Pauli in Butler's, represented everything he was not. He

'. . . belonged to one of the most exclusive sets in Cambridge . . . perhaps the most popular man among the whole number of undergraduates . . . big and very handsome . . . seemed to Ernest the handsomest man whom he ever had seen or ever could see . . . impossible to imagine a more lively and agreeable countenance . . . good at cricket and boating, very good-natured, singularly free from conceit, not clever but very sensible . . . father and mother drowned by the over-turning of a boat when he was only two years old . . . left him as their only child and heir to one of the finest estates in the South of England.'

Words cannot convey the total absurdity of Towneley's characterisation, exceeding even that of Lady Chatterley's father, the Royal Academician, and of the Snowmen. At one point, when Ernest is in a prostitute's room trying to induce her to mend her ways, he hears Towneley's step come 'bounding up the stairs as though of one over whom the force of gravity had little power.' When he bursts 'into the room saying, "I'm come before my time,"' Ernest slinks miserably off. Towneley, one feels, has already begun to unbutton even while Ernest's faltering step, over which the force of gravity has all too much power, is heard descending.

Butler disposed of the immediate exigencies of his own sexual appetites by weekly visits to a French lady in Handel Street, an arrangement which was later extended to include Jones, though not on the same day. Having thus dealt with their pressing necessities, the two of them were free to lavish their romantic ecstasies on Pauli, or Faesch, or, in a more generalised way, on Italian peasants and such like specimens of splendid manhood uninhibitedly piping down the valleys wild. Many a mute, inglorious don, and some not so mute, must surely have derived comfort and encouragement from their example. One has a faint sympathy for the Handel Street lady, who, when she had finished with Butler, had before her the prospect of Jones.

As for Butler's mania about money—it was lifelong and unremitting. No gold, no Holy Ghost, he noted down, and envisaged the further operation of natural selection to the point that babies would be born with five-pound notes wrapped round them for their early sustenance. After his first New Zealand venture, the only available source of supply was the Canon, who, as has been said, unbelted sparingly, and died belatedly. Butler's letters asking for news of his father's state of health were about as tenderly phrased as an income-tax demand note. At last, to his infinite relief, the Canon obliged, and all was well. It was the only happy ending Butler knew—being left a fortune, preferably by an aunt, but, failing that, by a parent. Thenceforth, Butler's life was untroubled, and he was able to establish himself as a one-man, or do-it-yourself, Affluent Society.

F

The economics of sunshine

So widespread and accepted is the contemporary passion for sun-bathing, and for getting tanned thereby, that it is difficult to remember how recent it is. Up till some four decades ago fashionable ladies would no more have thought of exposing themselves to sunshine than they would to-day to rain. The sunshade was an essential part of fashionable attire. Now, in all London, you cannot procure one except in theatrical costumiers. Peasants and labourers were liable to be suntanned, but this was just part of their inelegant way of life. The sign of social distinction was to be pale. How astonished, say, Lily Langtry would have been to know that her successors in the lush foothills of high society would go to almost any lengths, including crouching in front of ultra-violet rays and taking tan-producing pills, in order to give an impression of having been baked in the sun!

This cult of the sun, like all others, has been turned to commercial uses. Unguents, oils, special sun-bathing attire, bikinis and play-suits and darkened spectacles, have become big business. The largest trade in sunshine, however, is unquestionably done on the Riviera, now more commonly known as the Côte d'Azur—a name coined by a certain Stephen Liégard, a fervent Bonapartist who died in Nice in 1925, otherwise undistinguished, or at any rate unremembered. This narrow coastal strip, never more than twenty kilometres wide, stretching from Mentone to Saint Tropez, and, in the words of M. Raymond Cartier, *'entre une montagne sans humus et une mer sans poisson,'* has become the Mecca of sun-worshippers. Here they come in their millions, thigh-to-thigh on the beaches, bumper-to-bumper on the road, earnestly engaging in the most ardent of contemporary pursuits—leisure.

It began by being a fashionable winter resort. Russian grand dukes, English actual or would-be aristocrats, American millionaires, the rich from all over Europe, trekked to the Riviera in the winter months to enjoy the clement weather, gamble at the casinos provided for them, and generally demonstrate their superiority to the rest of their compatriots who had no alternative but to endure the fogs, frosts and other climatic hazards in their native habitats. There were also, inevitably, a number of adventurers, quacks and ponces—camp-followers of the affluent who subsisted upon their vices and gullabilities. Writers, especially those dealing with high society, found the Côte d'Azur congenial. Frank Harris found a sanctuary there, occasionally, according to his own account, getting his gardener to bring in a covey of young girls who obligingly took off their clothes and danced over the lawns of his villa, providing, as he put it, 'as pretty a sight as ever you saw.'

All of these scrupulously avoided the sun, and kept well away from the sea-shore, as did Queen Victoria, who, for four years in succession, took up her residence for six weeks at the massive Hôtel Regina. M. Cartier thus describes her retinue:

Elle arriva avec son âne Jacques, son maire du palais, le général Ponsonby, ses ladies-in-waiting, son médecin, ses six femmes de chambre, son valet de pied écossais, son chef français, ses gardes du corps hindous, ses douze valets d'écurie et quelques autres pièces de domesticité.

The *valet de pied écossais* was, presumably, the legendary John Brown, who doubtless brought along, on his own and his mistress's behalf, a good supply of his native Scotch to supplement the local wines. For her apartments the Queen paid 40,000 francs for the six weeks' visit—a very substantial sum at the then rate of exchange. And even this, M. Cartier says, was a *prix d'ami*.

The 1914-18 war and its aftermath put an end to this glorious period, during which the great hotels—Ruhl's, the Negresco, the Hôtel de Paris—were built and profitably conducted. The grand dukes disappeared to become taxi-drivers elsewhere; the very rich tended to look for other playgrounds, though there were a few old faithfuls like the Aga Khan. In their place there arrived desiccated colonels who had served in the East, and who found that their pensions went further, their drinks at sundown tasted sweeter and their wives were more tranquil on the Côte d'Azur than in

Cheltenham or Tunbridge Wells. Also, ladies of slender means and faded charms who brought tea-making apparatus which they set up in their pension rooms, and who were the chief patrons of English libraries which made their appearance in Mentone, Monte Carlo, Nice and other resorts.

The great change, however, was the summer season, which soon attracted many more visitors than the winter one. Hitherto, the Riviera had closed down from April to November. The local inhabitants, it is true, lived there throughout the year, but they were in the same category as Indian natives, who did not need, like sahibs, to take refuge in hill stations during the hot weather. How they managed to endure the oppressive heat, the mosquitoes and the sun's dangerous glare was their own business. From the point of view of the holiday-maker, the Côte d'Azur only existed for four to five winter months out of twelve. The hotels were barred and shut; only an occasional restaurant functioned, and the Promenade des Anglais was abandoned and deserted.

Now all this was changed. Hôteliers found the summer more profitable than the winter. The hot sun, which had been their enemy, became a lucrative friend. All along the coast, they edged nearer and nearer to the sea. In the casinos, instead of insisting on 'Smoking,' open-necked shirts and even shorts were permissible. Tourist parties made their appearance; north-country accents were heard and cut-price rather than luxury rates were the order of the day. Beaches, once deserted, began to take on the appearance of carpets of flesh, white shanks indicating new arrivals and bronzed limbs the eve of departure. The bourgeoisie had moved into the Riviera in a big way, driving the higher social echelons into secluded villas, yachts, and the relatively few hotels and restaurants, like the Réserve, which still found it worth while to charge inordinately so as to secure a select clientele.

England's departure from the gold standard in 1931 sent the tea-making ladies hurrying home, and brought destitution to the English libraries, but this represented a loss of respectability rather than of cash. The tide of tourists scarcely abated. At Juan-les-Pins the Prince of Wales played golf; the Spanish Civil War was fought out among American novelists while they smoked and sipped martinis after bathing at Cap d'Antibes; and film stars looked for press photographers along the *plage* at Cannes. The Côte d'Azur's luck had held. There was still a considerable winter migration, and a very much larger summer one, ranging from millionaires to bank clerks and typists on inclusive tours.

The 1939-45 war was a disaster of the first magnitude. If German officers on leave kept a few large hotels and a small but well-supplied black market going, the coast as a whole was desolate, with its local population—by this time nearly a million—left to starve on olives, wine and fruit, the only production of its barren soil. Even immediately after the war, it presented a sad spectacle. The futile American landing in southern France had caused quite an amount of unnecessary damage. Stucco had peeled; unpainted wood-work had blistered and swollen; villas and hotels bore all the sadly familiar marks of having housed military personnel and installations. An observer then might well have con-cluded that the Riviera's day was done, never to revive.

How wrong he would have been! A greater boom than ever was on the way. In addition to the old-style visitors—the moneyed Teddy-boys and girls, whose favourite haunt was to be Saint Tropez; the seasoned Rivierans like Aly Khan, Lord Beaverbrook, King Farouk, numerous displaced Guggenheims and sometime husbands of Barbara Hutton; the various categories of tourists—there were quiet new rivulets swelling the mighty stream. The better-off type of artisan, now for the first time accorded paid holidays, de-veloped a taste for moving southwards into the sun. Civil servants who had retired on minute pensions were attracted by house property on the Côte d'Azur which was bound to appreciate in value, could always be profitably let, and did not require central heating. Above all, there was *les campers*. In 1958, M. Cartier estimates, they amounted to 1,800,000, who stayed on an average for twelve days. Assuming they spent 1000 francs a day, they brought into the area some twenty milliard francs a year, which is about a sixth of the total expenditure of holiday-makers there.

Every indication suggests that the number in all categories will go on increasing. To-day one resort shades into another, with scarcely a gap between them. It is one huge Coney Island. Through the summer months plane after plane lands at Nice Airport, disgorging its passengers to disperse to their chosen resorts. From Aix-en-Provence, motorists grind their way to the coast in an unending procession. The trains are likewise crowded, and motor coaches from places as distant as Finland, as near as Marseilles, roar up and down the *corniche* roads. Real estate has appreciated by five times since the end of the war; Nice, Cannes, Mentone and Monte Carlo vie with one another in producing 'attractions,' all reported in the *Nice Matin* with dispassionate appreciation. Ironically enough, only the large luxury hotels are in the doldrums. Many of them have been converted into residential flats, and the ones which still function have a languid outmoded air. They belong to a past order of things. They are bespoke tailoring establishments in an era of mass-produced clothing; anachronistic survivals which cannot participate in what M. Cartier calls *'la grande réalité economique d'aujourdhui— les loisirs des masses.'* In this field, it is Sir Billy Butlin, rather than Messrs. Ruhl and Negresco, who holds the keys to the future.

The case of Kim Philby

It was in 1942 that I first made the acquaintance of Kim Philby, the so-called Third Man in the Burgess-Maclean affair who has now himself decamped to Moscow. We met at St. Albans, near London, where he was in charge of one of the departments of the counter-espionage sections of M.I.6, the war-time name for the Secret Service. He was an attractive, energetic man with a painful stutter. I remember how his hand used to clasp and unclasp convulsively with his frantic efforts to articulate.

His competence struck one at once, more particularly in view of the fact he had only just taken up Intelligence work after a moderately distinguished career as a journalist. Incidentally, it is characteristic of the naïveté which prevailed in M.I.6 circles, that Kim's journalistic achievements were grotesquely exaggerated. He might, to hear them speak, have been a combination of C. P. Scott, William Randolph Hearst and Northcliffe, instead of just a good average correspondent for *The Times* on the Franco side in the Spanish Civil War. The upper echelons of M.I.6 at that time consisted largely of service personnel most of whom had been thankfully unloaded, and miscellaneous eccentrics who could not have hoped to earn much of a living in competitive circumstances. They were liable to form an exaggerated view of worldly attainments, as, one imagines, are nuns and monks of the pleasure and excitements of a bordello.

My feelings about Kim were from the beginning, and remain, affectionate. We passed many pleasant hours together. He was able rather than intelligent; no intellectual, and always more interested in practice than theory. Thus I find it difficult to believe that he was at any time much of a Marxist theorist, or even particularly interested in politics as such. His attitude towards his work, was, I thought, unduly romantic; but then when one is, as I was, middle-aged, and involved in a war, a good many of those with whom one is associated strike one so.

Another aspect of Kim's character which struck me was a quality of violence. Inside him, one felt, there was something explosive, of which the stutter and that convulsively clenching and unclenching hand, were a manifestation. Alcohol, which he was liable to swallow in large quantities, intensified the explosiveness, to the point of making one apprehensive in his company, even though also drunk oneself.

He never spoke about his father, the Arabist, St. John Philby. At the time we met, Philby Senior was in confinement under the wartime Regulation 18 B (which also provided for the internment of Sir Oswald Mosley) for some alleged half-baked expression of Fascist sympathies. Yet one was somehow always conscious of this bearded, rather ridiculous paternal figure, with his Bedouin dress, and other Arab paraphernalia, made sickeningly familiar by his even more bogus counterpart, T. E. Lawrence. The effect of his father on Kim, I fancy, was to make him want to assert himself; to do something adventurous and spectacular which would draw the attention of people to him. If so, he has achieved his aim all too well.

I was sent abroad as an emissary of M.I.6, first to East Africa, and Kim became my boss. On visits to London it was always a pleasure to see him. In the office he wore an old officer's tunic, perhaps his father's from the 1914-18 war. I had the feeling that he would have much preferred being a combatant soldier, but was precluded, as he supposed, by his stutter. The same thing is true of most Intelligence officers, which is why they are so ferociously disposed towards one another. If the ferocity with which they conducted internecine strife, I often used to reflect, could only have been turned to military uses against the enemy, the Intelligence Corps would have been the most formidable of all.

I rarely discussed politics with Kim, and then only light-heartedly, but I remember a rather heated argument with him about taking advantage of the collapse of Italy to advance into the Balkans and get to Vienna, Budapest and Prague before the Red Army; a course I fanatically recommended as a counterpoise to Stalinist imperialism. Kim took a contrary view, but on military, not political grounds. There was nothing he said then, or at any time that I can now recall, which gave me the feeling that he was a militant Communist, or even, like so many liberals, a Soviet-addict. I thought of him as an adventurer who was always instinctively on the side of the adventurous.

He was, of course, a leftist, but then so, in my experience, were most of the wartime M.I.6 personnel. In the various Resistance Movements with which they were associated, they tended to favour the Communists, though more, I should suppose, out of stupidity and ignorance than deliberate fellow-travelling. Any planted agents among them somehow managed, like Kim, to escape detection. It is ironical to recall now that the French and Italian Communists got the money and arms which enabled them to establish themselves so strongly after the war, not from Stalin, but from Anglo-American secret intelligence sources.

Anyone like Mikhailovitch, conservative and pro-western in temper, got short shrift from Allied agencies; while Tito, who never disguised his loathing and contempt for most aspects of the way of life we were supposed to be defending, was greatly admired and beloved. After the war his enemies were obligingly sent back home to be shot, as were thousands of unfortunate Russian and Ukrainian defectors. Some at least of current Security and Secret Service troubles are a heritage from this time, when to deplore, as I did, the fatuous credulity of Churchill and Roosevelt at Yalta, and the supine obsequiousness of so many senior officers and civilian Top People towards Stalin was to seem a kind of traitor. It was the same attitude of mind which, in 1943, led some fifteen London publishers to turn down Orwell's *Animal Farm,* one of the very few unquestioned literary masterpieces of our time.

I spent the last year of the war in Paris as liaison officer with the French *Services Speciaux.* Belatedly and reluctantly, it had come to be realised that, with the forthcoming defeat of Germany, Intelligence activities should be given some sort of Eastward orientation. Officers on being posted were required to read an article which had appeared in the *Spectator* on Marxist dialectics and their application to Soviet foreign policy. The copy of the Spectator in which the article appeared grew dog-eared with use. Later, the article was cyclostyled, being marked, of course, Top Secret.

This documentation was subsequently augmented by a long paper prepared by an amiable don, Carew-Hunt, in due course published as a book. In accordance with the new policy, queries I received from Kim in London to pass on to the French increasingly related to Communist matters, though as Winston Churchill, the Prime Minister, was still proclaiming in the House of Commons, to thunderous applause, that the word of his old comrade-in-arms, Stalin, was as good as his bond, their impact was small.

Kim came over to Paris once or twice, and we spent several agreeable evenings together. I remember particularly one occasion when, after dining, he suggested that we should go and have a look at the Soviet Embassy, newly installed in the Rue de Grenelle. We both were a little tipsy, and walked excitedly and unsteadily up and down outside the Embassy (a most un-Bondish procedure, incidentally), wondering how this so forbidding and seemingly well-guarded building might be penetrated. Kim, as I recall, was unusually animated and eager; almost inclined to shake his fist at the citadel of our new enemy. If the last parliamentary statement about him is, unlike the previous ones, to be believed, he had already long since been recruited into the Soviet Intelligence Service, and was showing himself, and me, to them, rather than, as I supposed, ardently plotting their discomfiture. It was on the occasion of this meeting in Paris, too, that Kim, for the one and only time, spoke of his first wife. We were walking by the river, and he pointed up to an apartment where, he said, he had lived with her at the time of the Spanish Civil War. He vouchsafed no further information, and I asked for none. I was told afterwards that the lady was a German Jewess and a Communist.

I admired his continuing ardour after the wearisome years of combating German Intelligence, but could not share it. We had defeated the Abwehr (a victory whose bloom faded somewhat when one learned that its boss, Admiral Canaris, had been all the time on our side), and I had no intention, or inclination, to take on his Soviet opposite number. During the last months of the war in Paris I shamelessly addressed myself to my own interests and pleasures, devoting such energy as remained for official duties to trying to save a few of the more innocent French collaborators from their countrymen's ignoble wrath, the more furious because deriving from a sense of their own guilt. The peacetime Secret Service made no appeal, and I gladly returned to the relative innocence of journalism and Fleet Street.

Kim, on the other hand, remained in the Service, and there were those who predicted that he would in due course become its head. It is awesome to reflect, in the light of what we know now, that this might easily have happened; just as if Maclean had been able to stick it out he would almost certainly have become head of the Foreign Office. In terms of ability, enterprise, and seeming dedication to work, Kim easily outshone most of his colleagues. Asked about him once by one of his then seniors, I said that in my opinion he had most of the requisite qualities, but that I should not myself recommend his acceptance as a career officer in that particular Service because I considered that he was basically unstable and farouche.

Nonetheless, he was accepted and promoted. Some future Namier would find a rewarding study in a careful analysis of those who were thus taken on in the Secret Service and those who were rejected at the end of the war. My own impression at the time was that the foolish and the phonies, not to mention the occasional rogues, were almost invariably preferred to the more honest, straightforward and perceptive.

It is tempting to attribute this to treachery at the highest level. Actually, like so many of our current discontents, it arises out of the steady erosion of our social structure. A ruling class on the run, as ours is, is capable of every fatuity. It makes the wrong decisions, chooses the wrong people, and is unable to recognise its enemies—if it does not actually prefer them to its friends.

In the post-war years, I continued to see Kim occasionally, and to hear of his doings. He seemed to be thriving, and to be steadily advancing in his career. He was sent to Turkey, and then to Washington, where he had the important duty of acting as a link between British and American Secret Intelligence. As I vaguely heard from W., another wartime colleague who became a Conservative Member of Parliament (though without discontinuing his Secret Service activities), Kim had domestic troubles. His second wife, whom I always found particularly sympathetic and attractive, had suffered some kind of collapse, partly mental, W. told me. Looking back, it seems probable that this may have been brought on by awareness of Kim's equivocal position in the Secret Service. She is long since dead and beyond the reach of calumniators and the vengeful. Living with Kim must, in any case, have been a strain. He drank to excess, and was given to outbursts of unaccountable poignancy. Also he was extravagant over money. The family lived in some style, and I always assumed that Kim or his wife had private means. Subsequently, I learnt that this was not so, and would guess that Kim's involvement in espionage on behalf of the Soviet Government was more due to financial than ideological pressure. He liked to have money and to spend freely. Often in these security matters, the simple explanation is the true one. The odds are that Kim worked as a Russian spy because he was paid well (and tax-free, remember), and needed the money.

Then came the Burgess-Maclean row, and Kim's involvement in it through having accepted Burgess as a house guest in Washington. I had heard him speak admiringly of Burgess, whom I met only once in the company of a comically pernickety and gentlemanly homosexual lover, of great subsequent distinction. Burgess's combination of reckless untruthfulness, vanity and scruffy defiance, the whole dismal

171

package tied together with an Old Etonian tie, was not to my liking. Kim's contrary view I attributed to his romanticism and credulity; a trait, unfortunately, nurtured rather than corrected by Intelligence work. His own preference for womanising over sodomy was marked, so that no one could possibly suggest that his fancy for Burgess had any sexual significance.

As W. explained the situation to me, Kim had been guilty of an indiscretion, but nothing worse. He would have to leave the Secret Service, lose his pension rights and so on, but we, his friends, could help him to find employment in the sure knowledge that his conduct had been minutely examined, that he himself had been lengthily and expertly interrogated, without finding anything seriously amiss.

Such an assurance had to be accepted. In any case, I wanted to accept it. Low as was my opinion of M.I.6 and its home counterpart, M.I.5, I could not believe that they were incapable of effectively screening one of their own staff, with whom they had been dealing for years. If they could not screen Kim, who could they screen? Even then, before recommending Kim for a job, I asked W. to make absolutely sure, at the highest level, that he had not been consciously associated with Burgess and Maclean in their spying or in their escape. The assurance was forthcoming.

Now we are told that W. was deceived. Kim had been a Soviet agent for years, and had tipped off Maclean through Burgess that he was to be arrested. I find it difficult to believe that the deception practised on W., and at second hand on me, was accidental. In any case, I shall never be able to seek elucidation from W. Shortly after Kim's defection, like several others involved in this strange affair, he died.

As it happened, I failed to get Kim a job. Later, he found a sanctuary in *The Observer*, that Salvation Army shelter for the ideological drunks and bums of our time, where I have now found a refuge myself. Friends I tried to persuade to employ Kim proved recalcitrant. Had they perhaps been warned from some other quarter than the one approached by W.? That not all concerned shared W.'s confidence I learned by accident in Sydney, Australia. It was the day after Kim had held a press conference in London, and, on the strength of the assurances in Parliament of the then Foreign Secretary,

172

Harold Macmillan (presumably emanating from the same source as those furnished by W. and passed on to me), routed his accusers. At my hotel I happened to run into M., who also had been in M.I.6, and after the war served as an itinerant Foreign Office Security officer, in which capacity he had participated in Kim's investigation. We had a drink together, and spoke about Kim. How satisfactory, I said that he had now been completely exonerated.

M. shook his head, explaining that, in his view, Kim was far from having been exonerated. But surely, I said, if the Foreign Secretary and the head of the Secret Service give him a clean bill, if he receives (as he had) due financial compensation for dismissal, if he is recommended by M.I.6 for journalistic employment overseas, then he must be considered in the clear. I did not add, by way of final proof of his exoneration, that he was actually to work again for M.I.6 in the Middle East. This truly astonishing fact only came to light later. Even his dismissal, officially announced in Parliament, proved to be only a feint. It sounds incredible, but it is the case, that when he made off behind the Iron Curtain he was still one of our men in the Lebanon, and as such *persona grata* among diplomatic personnel there.

M. continued to shake his head, and to insist that, in his view, Kim remained under suspicion, if not, unquestionably a Soviet agent. I suppressed my indignation at such a suggestion, and we parted somewhat abruptly. It did not seem conceivable to me that M., a relative underling, could be better informed than his superiors, who, if he was to be believed, were either systematically lying, or so woefully ill-informed as to amount to dereliction of duty. Yet so it has proved.

Some belated effort was, presumably, made to unravel this strange affair, though if the same team was engaged as on the occasion of Burgess's and Maclean's disappearance they are unlikely to have met with much success. Our Intelligence and security services would seem to consist almost equally of fellow-travellers and Soviet agents, and disgruntled, indignant anti-Communists—a line up which reflects the Cold War, but does not make for efficiency. The only possible course now would seem to be to disband the whole show, fumigate its premises, and begin again.

As for Kim—I cannot see him settling down contentedly to a life of exile behind the Iron Curtain. Maclean is a born fonctionaire, and can be one in Moscow as readily as in Whitehall; Burgess, likewise, was able to live out his shabby, show-off life in the U.S.S.R. as well as anywhere else, especially as the British Treasury obligingly permitted the transmission of the requisite funds. But Kim is something different. Perhaps the vodka bottle will help him out. I sincerely hope so.

My life with the B.B.C.

Someone skilled in research, curious and ingenious, should undertake a history of the B.B.C. It is a capital subject. Professor Asa Briggs's massive work on the subject (*The History of Broadcasting in the United Kingdom*) which is in process of appearing, scarcely meets the bill. The professor is no Gibbon, nor even a Trevor-Roper. He writes like a man diligently plodding his way across a muddy plain; boots laden with slush, but resolved to reach the other side. Let us hope that some sprightlier pen will avail itself of the vast array of facts which Professor Briggs has so diligently assembled.

The Corporation is the most interesting and characteristic institution of our time. Its original pattern set by its Founding Father, John (now Lord) Reith, has been modified and elaborated, but not essentially changed. The basic rhythm remains intact. Even television has been digested, though with some anguish. All the rhetoric sycophancy, cowardice and fraud of a decomposing society has passed through its channels; like a gigantic prism, it has bent and coloured impinging rays in accordance with its own composition. By appearing to be free of governmental control, its subservience is the more effective. The Corporation may be relied on always, in the last resort, to operate on the side of conformism. The Party Line does not have to be formulated; it beats naturally in the hearts, speaks in the mouths, wanly illumines the eyes of those, like Lord Normanbrook, ultimately responsible for its direction.

The first Director-General, Lord Reith, was a kind of *exalté,* who made a mission out of fashioning the B.B.C. —the only truly remarkable man ever to have been eminently concerned with it. A curious and stormy blend of Scottish Calvinism, snobbishness and self-assertion rumbled furiously in his powerful but not very coherent mind; and this, combined with considerable acumen and ability, provided the first, and enduring, dynamic. The B.B.C. voice, so unlike his own, was to his specification. It speaks still, measured, articulate and genteel; somewhat hushed when death is the theme, otherwise presenting the weather and the woes which confront us in like accents, with only a very occasional emphasis in signifying a quotation.

From Lord Reith, too, is derived the note of piety which informs numerous B.B.C. offerings. That he took this aspect of the Corporation's role very seriously is indicated by one of the many legendary anecdotes associated with his name. It seems that a member of his staff was once discovered in amorous dalliance on a sofa in Broadcasting House. The man was at once fired; but subsequently the Director-General agreed to reconsider his case on the condition that he should in no circumstances be permitted to speak the Epilogue. It falls to few, like Lord Reith, to found and shape a decisive contemporary institution.

After him came the administrators—like the Indian Civil Service taking over the heritage of Clive and Warren Hastings. Sir William Haley transformed Lord Reith's creation into a mere machinery of acquiescence, and he was fittingly succeeded by a talented staff officer, Sir Ian Jacob, skilled in making appreciations, and in reducing even the wild strategic notions of Sir Winston Churchill to numbered paragraphs of flat, savourless prose. Sir William, with his Home Service mind and Third Programme aspirations, has found a suitable perch in Printing House Square, where he edits *The Times,* and, in the person of Oliver Edwards, faintly resurrects from their quiet graves writers who once deserved the praises of *The Times Literary Supplement.* Sir Ian has disappeared without trace in numerous City boardrooms, succeeded in Portland Place by Sir Hugh Greene, the first Director-General to be chosen from within the B.B.C. He reigns still.

My own relations with the Corporation have extended over some twenty years, with gaps when I was in disgrace. The first broadcast I gave, on the Third Programme, was about the Webbs. I caused some complaints—I never knew from whom or on what grounds. A letter from George Barnes (then holding the bizarre post of Director of the Spoken Word) informed me that the broadcast's announced repetition had been cancelled. The Corporation, of course, was in a position to take such action. It disposed of enormous patronage, in dispensing which it could be quite arbitrary. There was no obligation to justify, or even explain, its exclusions, preferences, and imperfect sympathies. The large number of dons, journalists, writers, politicians, and other miscellaneous publicists and intellectuals who appeared in B.B.C. programmes were easily induced to be compliant. They needed, or liked, the fees; the publicity which accompanied their appearances was professionally advantageous and personally gratifying. Thus it was not difficult to keep them well under control. Any who erred and strayed, failing to heed the sheepdog's admonitory bark, were just excluded from the flock.

After a decent interval, I was invited back on to the Critics' programme, then young and in the spring. This programme was recorded. Thus, if one of the critics, by accident, expressed himself, as the B.B.C. considered, over-emphatically or in a manner displeasing to the Corporation, the offending words could be, and usually were, deleted. How well I remember the scene!—arriving at Broadcasting House in time for a luncheon which, as I often reflected, tasted of the Home Service. One had, at any rate notionally, seen a film and a play, read a book, looked at an art exhibition and listened to a radio programme. After eating, the five critics, under the eye of one or more B.B.C. officials, launched upon their preliminary discussions before going to the studio. Unless something went wrong, by five o'clock it was all over. One was out in the street—a queer choking misery seizing one as one made one's way along Regent Street towards Piccadilly. George Orwell worked for a time in Broadcasting House. He told me once that it gave him the idea for the Ministry of Truth in *1984*.

There were other occasional programmes, like *Any Questions?* which had their own special oddities, notably the studio audience. I loved to see the man in charge expertly rousing these audiences (only too happy to have gained admission) to applaud; then banking them down, inducing them to laugh, and generally manipulating them in accordance with the exigencies of the programme—all by the wave of an arm, like an expert orchestral conductor. The studio audience, I should say, provides the perfect image of mid-twentieth-century democracy. At the time of Suez, I saw a photograph of troops by the Canal, all looking very glum except for one small party, which was being televised. They had their thumbs up and were smiling, as required.

The programmes I most enjoyed, however, were the Far Eastern department's panels. For these we would assemble in the evening, and the questions would be put—from Li Pang-yo of Kuala Lumpur, from J. Kichiwicki of Yokohama, from A. Ramakrishnan of Calcutta. Here the controls were relaxed. No one really cared what was said to Messrs. Li Pang-yo, J. Kichiwicki and A. Ramakrishnan. They were figures as mythical as we, the panel, were ourselves. Our encounter took place in the stratosphere, unheeded by the Corporation Brass, and, indeed, as far as I know, by everyone. I have travelled a good deal in the areas allegedly covered by these programmes without even encountering anyone, European or Asian, who had listened to them.

Then came television. I began by interviewing Billy Graham, and subsequently appeared fairly regularly in *Panorama,* again with gaps due to some misdemeanour at which I could only guess. It was very like sound broadcasting; indeed, was largely run by the same people, with the single outstanding exception of Cecil McGivern, who in some miraculous way managed to remain a whole man in the sunless land of the B.B.C. hierarchy—in the same sort of way that you will find among the closed faces in some prison or concentration camp one which still unaccountably smiles and reflects the glow of life. McGivern, in the end, was rather brutally sacked, and, after lingering on for a year or so in the wasteland of commercial television, with a kind of tragic aptness, literally set fire to himself and died.

In Lime Grove, as in Broadcasting House, I had the odd

illusion of hearing my own voice coming from far away, and speaking in alien accents on behalf of some being other than myself. Appearing on television cannot but be a form of exhibitionism. The actor at least has to play someone else; the television performer has to play himself. It is a part which, in my experience, soon palls.

It must, I think, be counted to the B.B.C. for virtue that it continued to employ me despite my strong advocacy of commercial television. Anything, it seemed to me, which broke the Corporation's monopoly would be to the good; and anyway its lesser employees (many of whom were extremely capable, enterprising and sympathetic) would at least have a possibility of alternative employment instead of being irretrievably subjected, as they were, to the parsimony and paternalism of Broadcasting House. The latter advantage has accrued: the monopoly remains. It is simply that two B.B.C.s have been made to grow where there was only one before. Matching men operate the ostensibly rival organisations—Sir Alexander Cadogan at the B.B.C. and Sir Ivone Kirkpatrick at the I.T.A., both sometime permanent Under-Secretaries at the Foreign Office; followed by Lord Normanbrook and Lord Hill. Is it any wonder that their functioning is undistinguishable?

My own *de facto* expulsion from the B.B.C. followed a row about some observations I had made in an American magazine on the subject of the monarchy. Whether it was the sentiments themselves (which, in any case, I had expressed rather more clearly and succinctly two years earlier), or some circumstance connected with their expression, I have no means of knowing. My agent just received a curt intimation that my contract would not be renewed. That was all.

I was glad that the last thing I had to do was to interview Augustus John. This admirable man, in the circumstances, provided a wonderful restorative, reminding one that the whole of mankind did not inhabit the airless, symmetrical upper floors of Broadcasting House, or consist of the Queen's more stridently loyal upper- or middle-class subjects. Only one thing worried me. I and others had put in a lot of work preparing a long television documentary, *The Thirties*. The programme had been scheduled, but to make sure that it really would appear, I asked

178

to see the Director-General. Sir Ian received me in his office—a short, buttoned-up figure, who looked at me uneasily across his desk. His suggestion was that *The Thirties* should be put off for three months. I said that a decision ought to be taken to show it as announced or to scrap it. He accepted this view—for which I am suitably grateful—and it duly appeared, to my great satisfaction.

Outside Sir Ian's office I found Sir Alexander Cadogan. He was bending over, I think to take off his galoshes, preparatory to going in to preside over a meeting of the B.B.C. governors, of whom he was then chairman. Going down in the lift, I thought how amusing it would have been if, at the moment of my encounter with Sir Alexander, an exile from behind the Iron Curtain, seeking freedom and anxious to signify his respect and gratitude to the B.B.C., had arrived on the scene.

'Here,' I should have said, pointing to Sir Alexander, and indicating the way to Sir Ian's office, 'is your new-found freedom. Pray, enjoy it to the full!'

Following the almost universally applauded departure of Sir Ian Jacob from Broadcasting House, I was reinstated in the B.B.C.'s favour, which I have continued to enjoy in the twilight of my days. This benign outcome of so much bickering and infidelity (committed, particularly, with Mr. Sidney Bernstein) does not muffle my awareness that the Corporation provides one of the great comic subjects of our time. It replaced the dear old Church of England (which in many respects it closely resembled, to the point, it has always seemed to me, that its Heads of Departments are Episcopal, and should sign themselves accordingly; as, George Light, Raymond Home, Archibald Third, etc.), as the focus of our own particular English brand of imbecility. Where outside Broadcasting House could there ever have been a Director of the Spoken Word? Who but its own precious Dimbleby could ever have referred to 'loyal Big Ben'? How impoverished one's own life would have been if one had never tuned in, for instance, to a chance encounter between a Chinese poet and a Cumberland shepherd! An ex-editor of *Punch*, of all people, has reason to be thankful for the B.B.C.'s existence. We had lost our curates, our charwomen, our strayed revellers; we were shortly going to lose our Poona colonels, our huntswomen, our irascible admirals. In such circumstances the Corporation was a godsend. It never failed us. I remember once, greatly daring, we decided to do a parody of the *Radio Times*. In the very week that our poor efforts at facetiousness appeared, the Third Programme announced a talk on 'The place of the potato in English folk-lore.' We knew we were licked, and decided thenceforth to accept heaven's blessings as they fell, without comment or embellishment.

Then there is Reith himself; one of the real oddities of our time, whose own Autobiography (appropriately named *Into the Wind*) gives some indication of the strange turbulences, the wild hopes and desires, which lie just under the surface of his portentous Scottish exterior. So furious a current driving so smooth a turbine. As a subject for a contemporary biography he would be, I should have thought, incomparable, combining in one first baron, as he does, the uplift, the earnestness, the drive and the solemnity, yes, and even, in a sort of way, the innocence, of an age dedicated to human progress, and at the same time, by some fatality, involved in bloodshed, destruction and confusion to a degree hitherto unparalleled in history.

In the thirties it was already clear, as Professor Briggs indicates, that the new medium, radio, and, potentially, still more television, were going to alter drastically the whole character of our twentieth-century societies. Here the Professor is an excellent guide. With great pertinacity and skill he traces the struggle, still going on, for control of a unique means of persuasion and of publicising political personalities. At an early stage the party machines saw their chance and grabbed it. Their chosen, anointed men were alone permitted to participate in political broadcasts, with the result, among many others all deplorable, that Churchill was largely kept off the air in the Chamberlain years. Some ground has subsequently been recovered, and the Corporation itself was able to live down the ludicrous Clause 4 of its original licence whereby it had to abstain from 'statements expressing the opinion of the Corporation on matters of public policy,' and from 'speeches or lectures containing statements on topics of political, religious or industrial controversy.' Even so, the party machines, alas, can still find ways of exerting themselves.

What, one wonders, would the framers of Clause 4 have thought of TW3? What, for that matter, does Reith think of *Juke Box Jury* or of Dr. Alex Comfort? His own religious specification was for a Christianity 'thorough-going, optimistic and manly'; equally displeasing, I should suppose, to Dr. Alex and St. Paul.

It is a far cry indeed from the days when a directive was circulated from the upper regions of Broadcasting House to the effect that all suggestions for competitions, outside the scope of the Children's Hour, were to be referred to the Director-General; when newscasters were liable to announce: 'There is no news to-night,' and when the Corporation's responsibility to give listeners what it thought good for them, rather than what they wanted or might like, was taken for granted. If I have seemed insufficiently grateful to Professor Briggs for his guidance through this fascinating territory, let it be remembered that a similar charge of ingratitude would lie against an early Christian who had been eaten, or at any rate nibbled, by lions, and then in paradise been presented with one of St. Thomas Aquinas's massive volumes on the Holy Trinity.

Frank Harris: his life and lies

It is a curious chance which has made Frank Harris's mendacious and lewd autobiography, *My Life and Loves,* a valuable literary property some three decades after it was written. As far as he was concerned, it represented a last desperate effort to raise the wind. Like many another, then as now, he turned to pornography as the readiest means of collecting quick profits. The first volume was printed in Germany, and some photographs of nude women were included by way of illustrations to drum up sales. To evade legal troubles publication was ostensibly for private circulation only. Harris's friends were expected to dispose of copies for him, just as they were expected when they visited him in Nice to bring out old Etonian ties and other upper-class regalia which he delighted to wear.

Actually, as Harris was always bitterly complaining, his profits from the autobiography were meagre and difficult to collect. His last years in Nice were increasingly penurious, and in the end he was literally on the run, pursued by irate creditors from furnished lodging to furnished lodging. I cannot imagine any single circumstance more calculated to enrage his ghost than the knowledge that his wife Nelly's heirs were benefiting financially from *My Life and Loves* on an infinitely greater scale than ever he did. 'Twenty-five thousand pounds for the paperback rights alone!' I hear him roaring in anguish out of Hades.

The book's enduring literary reputation, such as it is, would have struck him as well deserved and less than his due. Does he not characteristically describe it as 'the best autobiography ever written'? He could not, however, have been expected to foresee the golden harvest, in both fame and cash, which was to accrue to subsequent purveyors of eroticism, particularly in the field of his own speciality—young girls, on whom he was ever ready to lavish attention, though predominantly, it would appear, with finger and tongue. In any case, through the years *My Life and Loves* had a steady sale under the counter, and embellished the auto-erotic fancies of classroom and bedroom alike. Only now does it take its place, along with other money spinners in the game, as a Public Prosecutor's Special on open display.

A couple of years ago I went to have a look at Harris's residence at the time he was writing *My Life and Loves*. It was in Cimiez, high above Nice: a rented flat in the Rue Edouard VII, not, as he gave everyone to understand, a villa of his own. The concierge, an elderly lady in regulation black, remembered him well and affectionately. There was a hint of bottom pinching long ago in her reminiscent smile, I thought. Her memories of Nelly, on the other hand, were decidedly sour. Harris was accustomed, it appeared, to take a walk every evening. He perspired a lot, the concierge told me, and on his return would hang out his shirt on the balcony to dry. Somehow it gave me a vivid sense of him: the minute figure striding along and sweating profusely; stylishly dressed, with all the component parts of his attire— striped trousers, black jacket, winged collar—more or less correct, but the total effect definitely outlandish. Of all people, when I thought about him, he reminded me of Mussolini. Poor Frankie! Poor Duce! They both had a taste for white spats which persisted to the end. Harris was terribly conscious of his body's unappetisingness—so hairy and so small, with long arms hanging well below his knees. Ape's arms, he called them bitterly. With all his bounce and bluster there was something woe-begone about him: the dyed black moustache, pegged up by night and left pegged in the morning when he sat in bed writing his autobiography; the so resonant voice trumpeting forth, the vast meals consumed and then evacuated by means of his stomach-pump, the endless seductions.

In his delightful life of Harris published shortly after Harris's death Hugh Kingsmill demonstrates conclusively that there just is no reliable information as to where and when Harris was born, how he spent his childhood, and what happened to him before he appeared in London as the up-and-coming editor of the *Evening News*. Least of all in *My Life and Loves*. Harris was such an inveterate and extravagant liar that when by accident he tells the truth (as Max Beerbohm remarked, even Harris's inventiveness about himself sometimes ran dry) he can scarcely be believed. The truly extraordinary thing is that nonetheless, with the passage of time, a guarded credulity has come to be extended to his preposterous accounts of conversations with figures like Carlyle, Maupassant, Tennyson and (a particular favourite of my own) General Skobelef at Plevna. According to Harris they were together at Plevna in a desperate attack on one of the redoubts when their talk turned on women. At fourteen, Skobelef said, he had chased every pretty girl, with the result that at forty he was almost impotent. 'Good God, what a dreadful fate!' Harris exclaimed, and resolved to husband his own resources more prudently.

The ridiculous nature of such reminiscences (apart from difficulties over time and place) is well illustrated by what purports to be Jane Carlyle's description of the first night of her marriage, as allegedly retailed to Harris by Carlyle's physician, Sir Richard Quain, at a dinner in a private room at the Garrick Club. One imagines the scene: the port circulating, the cigar smoke rising. Then Quain embarks on his anecdote, telling it in Jane's own words to him:

'When we reached the house, we had supper and about eleven o'clock I said I would go to bed, being rather tired: he nodded and grunted something . . . A little later he came up, undressed and got into bed beside me. I expected him to take me in his arms and kiss and caress me. Nothing of the sort, he lay there jiggling like.' ('I guessed what she meant,' said Quain, 'the poor devil in a blue funk was frigging himself . . .') 'I thought for some time,' Mrs. Carlyle went on, 'one moment I wanted to kiss and caress him; the next moment I felt indignant. Suddenly it occurred to me that in all my hopes and imaginings I had never got near the reality; silent the man lay there jiggling, jiggling.'

In any collection of unconvincing club conversations this one must surely take its place with the hilarious exchange between Mellors and Lady Chatterley's father as recounted by D. H. Lawrence. It is not difficult to see that Harris has put his own inimitable gloss on Froude's suggestion that Carlyle was impotent, strengthening the authenticity by the use of direct speech. He would have made a great gossip-writer in our time. 'The truth of Harris's assertions about Carlyle cannot be resolved here,' Mr. John F. Gallagher, the editor of a recent edition of *My Life and Loves,* primly remarks in a footnote. 'It is a question of whose word one is inclined to accept.' I should say it was.

Another favourite episode of mine is Harris's account of a dinner given to the Lord Mayor of London, Sir Robert Fowler, by Sir William Marriott. Harris, naturally, was seated beside Lady Marriott. He was, he explains, an honoured guest at such gatherings, and 'for years never missed the Lord Mayor's Banquet,' being 'given a good seat at the Lord Mayor's table, nearly opposite him and the chief speakers.' At the Marriott dinner Harris

had just taken a spoonful of clear soup when my nostrils were assailed by a pungent, unmistakable odour . . . I looked at Lady Marriott and saw a shrinking in her face corresponding to the disgust I felt. I looked away again to spare her, when suddenly there came a loud unmistakable noise and then an overpowering odour . . . The atmosphere got worse and worse, the smells stronger and stronger, till

I rejoiced each time a servant opened the door, whether to go out or come in.

After 'another unmistakable explosion,' Harris could not but look again at my hostess. She was as pale as death, and this time her eyes met mine in despairing appeal. 'I'm not very well,' she said in a low tone, 'I don't think I can see it through!'

'Why should you?' Harris gallantly responded, and took the lady out on his arm, assuring her that, though the hostess, she would never be missed. Nor was she, he adds. Harris regarded himself as a specialist on polite behaviour, and was fond of boasting that his 'table manners were English of the best.' On one occasion he explained how, when put on to bowl in the Eton-Harrow match, he aimed the ball at a boy who deserved chastisement instead of at the stumps. Only those like himself brought up in the English upper classes, he went on, would fully understand the enormity of such an action.

These Harris fantasies, once their complete divorcement from reality is accepted, are not without their interest, and even charm. I like very much this exchange with Maupassant:

'I suppose I am a little out of the common sexually,' he resumed, 'for I can make my instrument stand whenever I please.'

'Really?' I exclaimed, too astonished to think.

'Look at my trousers,' he remarked, laughing, and there on the road he showed me that he was telling the truth.

Or, again, his suggestion that Ruskin was allowed, in Rose Latouche's last illness, to hold her for one whole night in his arms before she died. One imagines the negotiations with the Latouche parents to get their consent to such an arrangement, Ruskin being at the time in his late fifties and completely crazy, and Rose in her early twenties. Harris, obviously, for once had doubts about his plausibility, for he adds that 'notes of all this scene are so fragmentary . . . I can only translate, so to speak, my vague impressions into words.' Mr. Gallagher, however, manages to provide one of his reassuring footnotes: 'Nevertheless, what Harris says squares well with fact.'

Harris's own sexual exploits are described with gusto. They began (one cannot but feel authentically) with dropping his pencil in class when a child of ten with a view to staring up at the knickers of the little girls while searching for it: a spectacle which even then interested him more than the blackboard. Thenceforth, in the most literal sense, he never looked back. One notes an abiding concern not to squander his sexual resources, as, for instance, General Skobelef, that prodigious performer, had done. When retiring for the night Harris was accustomed to bind himself up to prevent nocturnal wastage. The only reliable indication I ever had of his own performance was from his amiable and gifted daughter, wife of an Anglican clergyman, who told me that a lady in a position to know (presumably her mother) had told her that there was nothing on earth which so scared the daylights out of poor old Frankie as a truly passionate woman. This judgment seems to me to be supported by Harris's own oddly inconclusive sexual disclosures.

Another side of him which remains inexhaustibly diverting is his valiant attempt to present himself to his readers as a kind of mystic: contemptuous of that which 'wanted wings to lift it into the blue,' dismissing whatever 'had nothing for the soul.' These high sentiments were propounded in his deep bass voice, and with a twirl of his moustache. Immediately after the stomach pump had done its work, he was inclined to reflect on the vanity of human wishes; when the girls the gardener had procured for him and his guests had finished their dance on the lawn, put on their clothes and gone home, his thoughts were liable to turn to Jesus and Gethsemane.

Kingsmill describes how when he was twenty-two he accompanied Harris to Paris, where they visited a brothel together. Some days later, walking along the Promenade des Anglais in Nice with him, Kingsmill became aware of an unfortunate consequence of his indulgence. Just at that moment he heard Harris observe: 'Christ went deeper than I, but I have had a wide range of experience.' I see the two of them: Kingsmill a good deal the larger, faltering a little in his step at the intimation of a disagreeable malady contracted; Harris bounding energetically along; the fading evening light. the white Mediterranean waves and the yellow beach, the lights coming out along the coast. If Harris belonged anywhere, it was surely there, and there his bones rest.

186

What price glory?

Asked who I thought were the three outstanding men of
action of our time, I answered without thinking: Gandhi,
Stalin and de Gaulle. On reflection I am inclined to stand by
my choice. Most Englishmen would have begun with Churchill,
but to me he has always been a slightly ridiculous figure,
mouthing the rhetoric of a past age to sustain the fantasies
of the present one. It was precisely this, admittedly, that
was required in 1940 to maintain the pretence, while waiting
for Russia and America to come into the war, that we
English were continuing to wage it. Once they were in
Churchill's role was exhausted. A good many Americans
would likewise, I suppose, have begun with Roosevelt,
manfully overlooking the appalling banality of his thoughts
and utterances in the light of his practical achievements in
counteracting the Depression and as a war leader. Sooner
they than I. Leftists of all categories, again, would doubtless
play it safe and opt for Lenin, whose writings—some ten
million words of them—I find unreadable, and whose brief
appearance on the stage of history ended in the New Economic
Policy, the negation of everything he had ever ostensibly
believed in or advocated.

Of my three men, Gandhi, without disposing of so much
as a popgun, got us out of India, where Churchill had said we
must remain for many a year to come. No one who saw, as I
did, the fabulous following he had among the poorest
of the poor in India could doubt the reality of his influence,
unsupported, as it was, by any sort of ceremonial trappings or
material resources. As for Stalin, he managed with unspeakable
brutality to get rid of the revolutionary riff-raff that Lenin
had bequeathed him, and in a matter of twenty-five years
or so transformed Russia from a shambles into a larger,
stabler, and more powerful empire than ever it had been
before. Those overturned monuments of him, we may be
sure, will be set up again when the very names of Khrushchev
and his successors are forgotten.

Then de Gaulle; in some ways the most extraordinary, certainly the most bizarre, of the three of them. Who would ever have believed in those far-off wartime days in Carlton Gardens, not only that he would take over in liberated France (that, after all, was always in the cards), but that he would become a dominant, if not *the* dominant influence in post-war Europe? The first glimpse I had of him was in the Connaught Hotel where he stayed in great modesty; a tall, lugubrious, but somehow splendid figure in blitzed London. I knew quite a number of his entourage and followers through doing a liaison job with the French Intelligence, then, as now no doubt, a battleground for every sort of internecine feud and faction.

It was interesting, in the light of this experience, to look over M. Pierre Viansson-Ponté's Gaullist *Annuaire*, added, by way of appendix, to his *The King and his Court*. In it he provides entries of varying lengths for all the leading figures, with the addition of an ingenious system of Michelin Guide-type symbols, ranging between a dog-kennel for a cabinet or staff job in London or Algiers, and an opened pair of scissors for any '*Specialité.*' The cruellest use of this last symbol is in the case of poor Captain Guy, a man almost as tall as de Gaulle himself, whom I remember as the General's A.D.C. and shadow from 1944 onwards, and particularly in the wilderness years in the Rue Solférino. His speciality?—'*Oublié.*' I had assumed he must be by now at least a general. Instead, it seems, he has just disappeared.

The two eminent Gaullists with whom I came into closest contact were Soustelle and the famous Colonel Passy. The latter, whose real name—Dewavrin—I was proud to know (name-dropping takes on an extra dimension when a *nom-de-guerre* is involved), with his pale blue eyes and gangster reputation, fascinated Allied intelligence officers; for the most part language teachers at schools and universities, carpet-sellers from the Middle East, and continental salesmen of everything from contraceptives to machine tools. We thought so dashing and attractive a figure was bound to do great things after the war. Imagine my astonishment, then, to read in M. Viansson-Ponté's *Annuaire* that Passy's present *specialité* is—Director of Bon-Marché. Truly God is not mocked.

Soustelle was something quite different. He was the one

I really liked; indeed, like, for I have seen him from time to time in the post-war years, always with pleasure. After the fiasco of the O.A.S. abortive revolt he has gone to ground, I don't know where, but hope most sincerely that his circumstances are not too disagreeable. M. Viansson-Ponté's piece on him is accurate enough. It recounts his fabulous academic success as a young man, his early Left Wing affiliations, his dogged devotion to de Gaulle through good and ill times, his *volte-face* on Algeria after being sent there as Governor-General by Mendès-France and ultimate break with de Gaulle over the General's abandonment of the *Algérie-Francaise* policy which, partly through Soustelle's manipulations, got de Gaulle power in 1958.

M. Viansson-Ponté considers that the change in Soustelle's attitude came as a result of seeing white French workers who had been massacred by Algerian terrorists; a sight which so appalled him that thenceforth he became a fanatical opponent of Algerian Nationalism. This, with all respect, seems to me mistaken, or at any rate an over-simplification. What happened, in my opinion, is that Soustelle, against his own deepest and best instincts, took to politics, and became an addict. He was like a Puritan who takes to sex, and who, precisely because his temperament is conditioned the other way—to asceticism—makes an idiot of himself: falls for the wrong woman, catches the pox, engages in excesses, and is finally run in for exposing himself (what the London police call 'flashing his Hampton') in St. James's Park. Soustelle is an intellectual, an instinctive anarchist; a poacher, not a gamekeeper. His devotion to de Gaulle, a power maniac to the marrow of his bones, made a gamekeeper of him, with catastrophic results. Inevitably, he found himself out on his ear. An American university should now seek Soustelle out, and offer him a chair of anthropology (he was, after all, assistant-director of the Musée de l'Homme at the age of twenty-five). If he accepted, some fortunate Faculty would gain a most brilliant and sympathetic addition.

De Gaulle is, of course, the exact antithesis of Soustelle, which is why sooner or later the break between them was bound to come. He is a born gamekeeper, who, even when he has been driven to snare a rabbit for the pot, has done it so majestically that rabbits scamper in begging to be caught, and other gamekeepers steal away on tip-toe for fear of disturbing him. The last time I saw Soustelle he told me of an exchange with the General which well illustrates the difference between them, as well as de Gaulle's weird, but, to me, quite irresistible, clowning. Soustelle, who had just returned from a visit to Algeria, remarked that all his friends there were bitterly opposed to the General's present policy. '*Alors, mon vieux,*' de Gaulle said, '*changez vos amis.*' It is as though, returning to my earlier image, the puritan-lecher should have complained that a girl he had acquired in a bordello only seemed to care for money. '*Alors, mon vieux,*' the tall, big-nosed madam replies, '*changez votre fille.*'

The account of de Gaulle himself in *The King and his Court* is admirably done and very amusing. M. Viansson-Ponté tells just the things one wants to know about the General: how he conducts himself at receptions and dinner parties, in his country house at Colombey-Les-Deux-Eglises, when watching television, etc., etc.; the little personal points of behaviour and etiquette which best convey his strange, elephantine drollery. It is interesting to note that his demagogic techniques are very contemporary, and American at that. For instance, he is a compulsive hand-shaker, and when he is on tour like Lyndon Johnson, often has to have his right mit tended, and sometimes bound up, after a day's campaigning. And this, surely, is quite in the mid-twentieth-century style of demagogy;

> To say that he mixes with the crowd is an understatement: he plunges into it, wallows in it. One can keep an eye on him not so much because of his height, but because he is the virtual centre of a whirlpool. Disappearing in one place, he pops up in another for a moment, then is lost to sight again for a long, underwater stretch, only to surface like a diver at the other side of the street . . . He has been seen to emerge with three buttons missing, uniform torn, hands scratched, military cap askew, but eyes sparkling with pleasure, looking delighted to be alive . . .

Moreover, de Gaulle has completely mastered the essential art of tell-politics. Coached by a good man from the Comédie Français, meticulously made up, and after hours of rehearsal in front of a mirror (what a sight that would be!), his performance on the little screen is decidedly impressive. He just loves it, and goes on and on and on. No one, naturally, can cut him short. His televised press-conferences, too, though, like the current White House ones, totally fraudulent, with questions and questioners arranged in advance, make first-rate television. Not since Napoleon (the Third I should add, to be truthful) has France had such a ruler.

In the French edition the section of M. Viansson-Ponté's book before the *Annuaire* ends with the General driving hell-for-leather to his house in Colombey, Mme de Gaulle beside him, hospitals along the way equipped with supplies of suitable plasma just in case, police on the alert. Through the glass partition the General urges the chauffeur on: '*Ne trainons pas, plus vite, je suis pressé.*' In the American edition there is an additional longish section which deals with some of the General's distinguished visitors, and with Gaullism in more general terms. I found this less interesting than the other part; a bit banal and pontifical, I thought, almost as though Mr. Lippmann had lent a hand. When M. Viansson-Ponté allows his native scepticism and sense of irony to take charge he is good; when pontificating, liable to be a bore. His attitude to de Gaulle is mixed, like that of most of his countrymen. He finds the General ridiculous but, in his inimitable way, sublime; a pain in the neck, but a historical necessity; alien to the whole tradition of republican France, but by now an integral part of the French political land-scape. If only he would go! If only he would stay for ever! Neither of these hopes can be realised. He will not go, he cannot stay for ever. '*Vive la République, vive la France,*' as he concludes his orations, and, notice, invariably in that order.

De Gaulle's essential character was formed before he came to London in 1940, as well as his basic ideas about history, leadership, and politics (see his early writings, '*Vers une Armée de métier,*' '*La France et son armée,*' etc.). All the same, his experiences as leader of the Free, later Fighting, French, and in dealing with Churchill and Roosevelt, helped to shape his resolute and extremely effective methods of exercising author-ity. I know of no more serviceable account of de Gaulle's relations with his western allies, particularly with Roosevelt, than Mr. Milton Viorst's *Hostile Allies: F.D.R. and Charles de Gaulle*. It is clear, readable, full of apposite quotations and references. Why Roosevelt should have had so insensate and relentless a detestation of de Gaulle is a question, I dare say, for psychiatrists, but that he had it is, as Mr. Viorst shows, beyond question. Churchill's instinct was, as usual, right, but he, too, found it difficult to get on with de Gaulle, tried to find a more complaisant replacement, and, in his usual feeble way, played up to Roosevelt.

The fact is that, without a trump card in his hand, de Gaulle took every trick, and made complete nonsense of Anglo-American stratagems and tricks; such as trying to put Giraud in charge in Algiers, or to prevent de Gaulle taking over in liberated France. Stalin likewise made rings around Roosevelt and Churchill at Yalta, but, after all, he had an enormous army, which was, as Churchill put it, tearing the guts out of the Wehrmacht. De Gaulle had nothing except a sense of history, his own stupendous rectitude, his towering moral superiority to the men he was dealing with. These assets proved, in their way, as decisive as did the feats of the Red Army to Stalin. Mr. Viorst's careful account of how it all happened makes fascinating reading.

What will be the final judgment on de Gaulle? It all depends on what happens. De Gaulle may well have espoused what turns out to be in the long run the losing side. All the same, nothing can alter his achievement. Amidst the rubble of a derelict civilisation, the spiritual darkness of a tottering religion, the vacuity, fantasy and vicious folly of a moribund culture, he has somehow managed to expound, if only in an illusory way, the bearing of a majestic past on a confused present and uncertain future.

The last time I saw him was in the Rue Solférino in the early fifties, when his political fortunes were at their lowest ebb. His following in the Assemblée had fallen to some seven or eight, led by the faithful Soustelle; all the pundits were convinced that he would never return to office. As they are always wrong, it seemed a good moment to seek an interview, which was accorded. Captain Guy showed me in. The General was sitting at a desk which seemed grotesquely too small to accommodate him. His pasty complexion gave an impression of ill-health; his head seemed tiny in relation to his huge bulk. He explained to me almost without taking breath how in due course, with an unworkable political system, a faltering economy and *pourriture* (one of his favourite words) at the top, there would infallibly be a breakdown, and a call for him to take over. I managed with great difficulty to put a question. Why, when he was in charge at the end of the war, did he not ensure that a more workable and equitable system was instituted? He had the power then; unlimited power. He looked at me with the sly ferocity he reserves for awkward questioners, then roared out: *'Ce n'était pas l'heure.'* The monologue was resumed. At the end I meekly asked what he proposed doing now. This time he looked benignly at me. *'J'attends,'* he said. It was, I decided, no bad posture, and so it has proved.

Public thoughts on a secret service

The Official Secrets Act, as is ever the way with such protective measures, is by no means an unmixed blessing for the various clandestine intelligence organisations whose clandestinity it aims at protecting. If it prevents embarrassing disclosures, it also sustains embarrassing misconceptions. Furthermore, it ensures that disclosures, when they are made, must take an ostensibly fictional form. When all has to seem to be invented every invention is liable to seem equally authentic—whether Mata Hari or Sir Compton Mackenzie's hilarious *Water on the Brain*; whether Ian Fleming's James Bond, or Graham Greene's *Our Man in Havana,* or Somerset Maugham's *Ashenden*. Incidentally, Mackenzie, Fleming, Greene and Maugham have all worked for M.I.6, the wartime version of the Secret Service. By means of careful exegesis it is possible to identify the common originals of some of their fictional characters.

Actually, despite the Official Secrets Act, practically everything there is to know about M.I.6's operations during the war years has, in one way or another, already been divulged. Its close wartime liaison with its American opposite number, the Office of Strategic Services, whatever other advantages may have accrued, was to prove ruinous to its security.

Deception and double-agent techniques, for instance, have been written up in great detail in American novels, memoirs and magazine articles. So have the methods and uses of cipher cracking. Every O.S.S. man has a best-seller in his knapsack, and the F.B.I.'s course is strewn with film rights.

The identity of the head of the Secret Service is supposed to be a closely guarded secret. Even in the internal telephone directory he appears as 'C.' No alteration was made in these elaborate security arrangements when the name of the then incumbent—Sir Stewart Menzies—was given out by Lord Haw-Haw on the German wireless at the time of the phoney war, following the capture of two British Secret Service men, Best and Stevens, stationed in Holland. One of them believed he was in communication with dissident Germans with whom he might arrange for the war to be brought to an end. He recklessly made (and kept) a rendezvous on the Dutch-German frontier, but, inevitably, his contacts turned out to be the Gestapo. A characteristic of all under-cover Intelligence agents is their almost inconceivable credulity. I suppose the unreal atmosphere in which they have, by the nature of their profession, to live and operate tends to loosen their own hold on reality. The real danger of trafficking in lies, which Intelligence work necessarily involves, is that it develops a propensity for believing them. In the same sort of way newspaper proprietors, unless they watch out, are liable to reach a point when they actually believe what is put in their newspapers at their own behest. A sceptical turn of mind like Dr. Johnson's is induced only by holding fast to truth.

The identity of 'C' was also disclosed, along with other information about the workings of M.I.6, in an article in the New York *Herald Tribune* by Stewart Alsop. I asked Alsop subsequently whether his disclosures had any repercussions. He said there had been some rumblings in Anglo-American Intelligence circles, but that Menzies himself had been appeased by the epithet 'legendary' which Alsop had, with sagacious forethought, applied to him. 'Legendary' is precisely what all Intelligence Brass, in my experience, wanted to be. They were all, in their own estimation, the central character in a Kiplingesque thriller, in which, when their agents were caught, tortured and finally executed, they always died with the words: 'Tell the colonel I kept the faith,' on their lips. This Intelligence folklore used to have a strong Indian flavour. M.I.5 (the home counter-intelligence organisation), and to a lesser extent M.I.6, were, before the war, largely recruited from retired Indian police and political Intelligence officers. They alone had the requisite experience. Nowadays, these cadres are no longer available, and anyway both organisations have grown vastly in size. Their more bizarre and endearing characteristics have, in consequence, as I have been given to understand. disappeared, leaving them uncommonly like the Board of Trade. I may add that, on one of the few occasions that I met Menzies, I formed the impression that he was amiable and shrewd in an indolent, easy-going sort of way. He certainly did not strike me as legendary.

Whether the identity of the present head of the Secret Service is as widely known as was that of some of his predecessors, is a subject for speculation. It will, in any case, certainly be known to any foreign Intelligence service which has bothered to find out. These zealously guarded secrets nearly always become common knowledge. Taxi-drivers in the war years were accustomed to refer to a well-known club as being 'opposite M.I.5.' Soon after the liberation of Paris, I myself overheard one person in a café ask another: *'Qu'est-ce que c'est, cette Baker Street?'* The reference was to an Intelligence hide-out where the most elaborate arrangements were made to ensure secrecy.

Clandestine Intelligence organisations are, generally speaking, as easy to penetrate as a co-operative store. They consist largely of personnel who either are, or become neurotics. and, therefore, are easily turned round or turn themselves round. Admiral Canaris, the head of the Abwehr, was, it appears, more or less working for us all through the war—a circumstance which was rather disconcerting for M.I.6 officers like myself, who fondly supposed that the Abwehr was fighting every inch of the way. It was like winning what seemed like a particularly stiff football match only to find that the opposite goalkeeper had been all the time deliberately letting the ball through his goal. No one seems to have suspected Canaris's untrustworthiness until late on in the war, if then. An enemy or turned-round agent inside the Secret Service is, for obvious reasons, the most difficult of all to detect—witness Blake.

Just for this reason, it is a favourite perch. It would be surprising if Blake were a solitary case. There are bound to be others, who may for the time being be lying low, but who can be activated as and when required.

Even in the case of the U.S.S.R. there have been more defections among senior Intelligence officers than in any other branch of the armed forces. It is a safe assumption that all Intelligence services know more about other Intelligence services than they do about anything else. In Istanbul, in the war, I have heard, when the German national anthem was played at a night club, a party from the German Embassy jumped to their feet and sang '*Zwölfte-land, über alles.*' For security reasons, in ciphering messages countries had to be referred to by allotted numerals, and Germany was twelveland. Secrets which are known to have leaked are guarded with particular ferocity. The most wonderfully complicated locks are put on the stable door after the horse has gone. When the Foreign Office clamped down on publication of George Blake's disclosures to the Russians, thus preventing them from finding out what had already been found out from Blake, a hallowed Intelligence precept was being followed. Information which has reached an actual or potential enemy is, like mercy, twice blessed. It blesses him that gives and him that takes, and is, therefore, doubly precious.

Double agents, in any case have a natural propensity to carry the game a stage further. They are feeding the enemy with a carefully concocted mixture of fact and deception, which is intended to deceive more than it informs. Why not, then, vary the mixture in such a way that it will inform more than it deceives? It is difficult to convey to anyone who has not been concerned in these weird transactions how great is the temptation to project and elaborate them endlessly, until their original purpose becomes quite lost to view. Similarly, an amorist begins with the idea of seducing women, and to this end engages in various stratagems and deceptions. These in time, come to seem an end in themselves, quite irrespective of their purpose. He finds himself so busily engaged in clandestine correspondence, keeping mysterious assignations, inventing cover stories and alibis, that he has neither time, energy or inclination to avail himself of the opportunities these activities are ostensibly intended to procure.

I remember passing through Lisbon in the war, having been engaged, on behalf of M.I.6, in transactions with some Germans elsewhere, and being almost irresistibly impelled to go and make myself known at the German Embassy. It was not out of a desire to be a traitor, or to take heroic risks. I just wanted to write another instalment in a whodunit of my own fabrication; to project the narrative a stage further. I should be surprised if some such consideration did not play its part, consciously or unconsciously, in Blake's transformation from a double-agent working for us into one working for the Russians. There may well have been a time when he did not know himself which side he was working for. This, at any rate, was a situation which quite often arose when, after the liberation of Paris, I had to try and unravel the basic loyalties of double agents who had been operating in occupied France. It is like—again using the parallel of the amorist—waking up in the night unsure whether the woman in bed beside one is one's wife or one's mistress—a dilemma which can very easily arise. Intelligence agents, like novelists, are under a constant inner inducement to over-elaborate their plots. One who worked for me always used to preface his verbal reports with: '*J'ai joué la comédie.*' It is the theme song of all Intelligence work.

In a war, Intelligence inevitably gathers to itself all the oddities, misfits and delinquents; all the dons, unfrocked clergymen and schoolmasters, who cannot be accommodated elsewhere. The basic qualification is linguistic, which, in England especially, is liable to produce almost anyone, from a Baghdad carpet-seller to a professor of Sanskrit. In M.I.6 these bizarre wartime reinforcements were interspersed with pre-war Secret Service professionals, now, alas, a vanishing race—men with monocles and sometimes spats, who used several aliases, and had exotic contacts all over the place. For them, the golden age of *l'Intelligence Service* was over. Just from talking to them, however, one could realise how delightful it must have been to live with all found in a foreign capital, with nothing much to do except arrange to collect the contents of ministerial wastepaper baskets, or cultivate ministerial mistresses, at the expense of H.M.G., of course. Nor should it ever be forgotten that under their ægis *l'Intelligence Service* acquired world-wide renown, and became a universal provider of harmless fiction.

There was also a stiffening of fairly senior officers from all three Services. I never did understand on what basis they had been seconded to M.I.6, and can only imagine that when, for instance, a Guards officers displayed an interest in, say, interior decoration, or a naval captain was seen reading *Great Expectations,* a convenient way out of the consequent dilemma was to wish him on to the Secret Service. Secretarial assistance was provided by upper-class girls who alleviated the ardours of war for all who were fortunate enough to come in contact with them. The security of their persons was by no means inviolate. But where their work was concerned they were impregnable. A bevy who arrived in Cairo could find no one to whom they felt entitled to disclose their duties, and so had to be sent home.

My first impression of this strange and diverse collection of human beings was that they must constitute a sort of false front or façade. When I had been fully vetted and tried out, I thought, I should be taken off to some other place, and there make contact with the real Secret Service. It took me quite a time to realise that this was not so at all, and that what I had assumed to be a false front was, in fact, the genuine article.

A characteristic of under-cover Intelligence, brought to my attention from the very beginning, is its love of mystification for mystification's own sake. Thus, having been a serving army officer, I had no civilian identity card or ration book. To procure these, I was instructed to explain that I had been away in America when the war broke out, and had only lately arrived in Liverpool. I produced this story with some trepidation, conscious that it could be shot down very easily. There was, for instance, no stamp in my passport indicating my alleged Liverpool disembarkation. No questions, however, were asked, and the official concerned handed me over an identity card and ration book without demur, having obviously been instructed so to do. Why, then, I could not but wonder, was there any necessity for me to collect my documents in person?

198

To have sent them over by messenger would have offended against one of Intelligence's basic canons, which is that nothing should ever be done overtly when covert means are available. It is interesting, and reassuring, to note, in the reports of the Guzenko Case in Canada and the Petrov Case in Australia, that this canon operates as strongly in Soviet Intelligence as in any other. Both cases contain many examples of similar unnecessary mystification. Indeed, Intelligence techniques would seem to be as standardised as air travel. Everyone's Man in Havana seems to be like everyone else's.

Training in the wartime days was understandably pretty desultory. Nowadays it is doubtless taken to degree standard —B.E.'s. Even so, I did receive a fascinating course of instruction in the use of invisible ink from a large, rather sombre man, who explained to me the relative merits of various solutions, as well as how to use a ball-pointed pen without marking the paper. In the last resort, he told me, bird shit (known in the trade as B.S.) would suffice. It had the advantage of being almost universally obtainable, though he personally had found town birds to be tantalisingly incalculable in providing supplies. For instance, one might put crumbs out on one's window-sill, and the birds would eat them without any B.S. being left behind. A more reliable method, he said, was to take a stroll through a park, and then, on seeing a good deposit of B.S., drop one's handkerchief as though by accident, and, in recovering it, scoop up the B.S. When I left for foreign parts I was given a good supply of tablets for curing headaches which, I was told, made first-rate invisible ink. As it happened, I never had any occasion to use them for this purpose, but they came in handy as a hangover specific.

In the station to which I was sent there was only one decent hotel, in which I lived, as did also my German and Italian opposite numbers. Though we never exchanged a word, there was a bond between us, if only because we were all bribing the same local police officers. The German, Leopold Wertz, gave every impression of being an ardent Nazi. I used to look over his private correspondence, which was brought to me by a friendly steward from the liner on which it was dispatched. It yielded nothing in the way of espionage material, but was humanly interesting. Somehow, having just read one of

Wertz's highly sentimental letters to his mother added a piquancy to the sight of him, obviously trying to be a credit to the Führer, across our hotel dining-room. He is now, I have heard, back in the West German Diplomatic Service, and prospering.

What has happened to the Italian, Campini, I have no idea. He was a large, luxuriant sort of a man, who made a big hit with the local ladies. I was rather hurt to learn how, after Italy's collapse, Campini, under interrogation, disclosed the fact that when he was driving his car by the sea and saw me walking along, he had a strong impulse to run me over. There should, I feel, be more solidarity among espionage practitioners than this.

Mystification for mystification's own sake is repugnant to adults, and is only acceptable to infantile and romantic minds. Hence the basic weakness of all Intelligence Services lies in their personnel, who tend to be immature. A *fantasiste* like Guy Burgess, for instance, is bound to drift into Intelligence work, and to thrive at it. But for his fortunate withdrawal to Moscow, he would almost certainly have thriven in M.I.6. His temperament was exactly right—flamboyant, untruthful, deceitful and energetic. Intelligence Services are unfortunate in that, the more suitable a person is for recruitment to them, the more disastrous he is like to prove. Blake was perfect. He had every requisite qualification and, by virtue of this, was the more apt to prove unreliable. Petrov, by Soviet standards, was an almost identical case.

By the same token, Maclean, if he had remained among us, would almost certainly have risen to be Permanent Under-Secretary at the Foreign Office. A ruling class on the run is capable of every folly, not the least of which is a propensity to advance unsuitable people in order to demonstrate its lack of stuffiness. From having in its heyday, excluded eccentrics and debauchees, in its decrepitude it goes to the other extreme, and actually prefers them to normal citizens.

The cost of the Secret Service has mounted even more astronomically than that of other government departments. It has the advantage of not having to account to Parliament for its expenditure, or to provide any public justification for its activities. Thus, there is no means, except by guesswork, of forming an opinion as to whether what is achieved is worth the money spent. I should myself doubt very much whether it was. Apart from high-grade defectors, radio interception and aerial reconnaissance, espionage is next to impossible in closed Communist Societies. Information collected by means of private agents is, for the most part deceptive. There are plenty of recent parallels in our own Intelligence reports, I am sure, to the C.I.A.'s fiasco over Cuba. The Intelligence agent, in the old-fashioned sense, has become as obsolete as the old-fashioned commercial traveller. He can only dredge up the same bogus statistics and misleading information as journalists and diplomatic attachés. He, too, has to draw his water from the poisoned wells which alone are available.

As for counter-intelligence—it must now be apparent to everyone that this is more or less inoperative. It is quite impracticable, as a whole series of recent cases have shown, to achieve even approximate security in an open society like ours. People can come and go freely, Commonwealth passports are easily attainable, and the transfer and provision of funds presents no difficulty. Illicit transmitting facilities, protected by diplomatic immunity, are available in most embassies, and there is a diplomatic bag to take more bulky material. Life is in every way made easy for the spy, and he need not worry unduly about M.I.5.

Indeed, the extraordinary thing is, not that spies can operate with relative impunity, but that any are ever caught. Just keeping someone under surveillance is extremely difficult, and costly in time and trouble. It needs about ten trained men on the job to keep one man under continuous observation. After all, Donald Maclean was already being watched by M.I.5 when he made off with Burgess. Screening, too, is just a word. Fuchs was screened; so was Blake, several times. In most cases it means no more than a very cursory investigation into friends and associates, political affiliations, and any other easily ascertainable biographical items. To screen a man thoroughly would be a whole-time job for a team of investigators for at least six months. They would have to find out everything about him and his past, as far back as his earliest childhood; examine mail, monitor his telephone, and peep through the keyhole at him in his most private moments.

Apart from the fact that such practices are distasteful, the manpower required would be prohibitive. Two-thirds of the population would be engaged in screening the other third. A Communist Society is geared to such purposes. No one can move without special permission, and everyone is classified, identified, and watched, at work and at home. Even then, people slip through the mesh, and the Political Police, though reduced in number and authority since the days of Yagoda and Beria, remain unwieldy by comparison with other State organs.

In our sort of society anything of the kind would be quite impossible. The choice, for us, is between security and freedom. And if ever we ceased to prefer the latter, we should soon find that we had nothing of any worth left to secure anyway.

Sons and Lovers *re-read*

It is difficult now to recall the first impact made by Lawrence's writing. There was a freshness about it, a kind of inward glow, which set him apart from his contemporaries. His reactions to life were so direct and so spontaneous that he gave one more the feel of a poet than of a novelist; his descriptive writing especially seemed uniquely alive. Coming across him after Lytton Strachey, Aldous Huxley, Virginia Woolf, and E. M. Forster was like walking over a springtime meadow with a pretty girl after lunching with Lady Ottoline Morel. He was exhilarating. Alas. the exhilaration has not lasted—though this, of course, may be more one's own fault than Lawrence's. The colours seem faded now and the subjects chosen foolish. Only the strength and verve of the line remain to recall the original enchantment.

Most discerning readers would agree that Lawrence's second novel, *Sons and Lovers,* is his best book, and that its earlier chapters are decidedly to be preferred to the later. This impression, as far as I am concerned, was confirmed on re-reading the novel after an interval of some twenty-five years. It seemed abundantly clear that Lawrence's great talent started deteriorating almost as soon as he began to write, and that it was bound to go on deteriorating to the end of his days. From the splendidly vivid description of life in a miner's household with which *Sons and Lovers* opens, to the incoherence and pretentious inanities of *Apocalypse* (so reminiscent of *Mein Kampf*) is a melancholy passage.

Lawrence, of course, was always writing about himself in different guises. At some point in the story a slim, forceful, withdrawn man, to women eerie but irresistible, is bound to make his appearance. Even the central character in *The Man Who Died* soon takes on the lineaments of a Nottingham boy who made good and grew a red beard. *Sons and Lovers* is Lawrence's own exclusive story; he spent the rest of his life producing variations on it.

I find no difficulty in deciding precisely at what point *Sons and Lovers* becomes irretrievably foolish. It is when Lawrence gets on to the sex life of his hero, Paul Morel. The efforts of Paul to seduce, first Miriam, and then Clara, are, as recounted by Lawrence, so laboured and unconvincing that they just cannot be taken seriously. As Johnson said of the plot of *Cymbeline*, they defy criticism because it is impossible to criticise unresisting imbecility. There would seem to be little doubt that Lawrence was impotent, or suffered under some physical disability which gave him a ludicrously excessive sense of the importance of a sexual fulfilment he was constitutionally incapable of ever experiencing. If, as I have often thought, sex is to the individual what politics are to the collectivity, then Lawrence's efforts in this direction are the equivalent of Ramsay MacDonald's oratory—long, meandering and largely meaningless.

This obsession with sex as the one source of enduring happiness, as a mainspring of action and an end in itself (for, throughout Lawrence's work, fornication is frequent but pregnancy rare) governed all his subsequent writing. The end was Mellors, in *Lady Chatterley's Lover*, sticking flowers in the hair on his chest and a single hyacinth bell in his navel —a scene which, in its combination of solemnity and absurdity is surely, as farce, unequalled. As Hugh Kingsmill has aptly remarked of it:

To be solemn about the organs of generation is only possible to someone who, like Lawrence, has deified the will and denied the spirit. If the sexual act is viewed apart from the other than physical emotions which accompany it, it is either comic or disgusting. Imaginative writers convey passion without using physical details, and are obscene only when they are being humorous about sex, like Rabelais, or are nauseated by it, like Shakespeare in *Troilus and Cressida* and *Timon of Athens* . . . After Lady Chatterley, Lawrence defended the book against the charge of being pornographical on the ground that pornography implies idealising of love, the man in the street being pornographical because he tells dirty stories, while insisting that a film-heroine must be a sexless thing of a washed-out purity. Owing to his inability to state anything correctly, Lawrence was a poor controversialist. Sexless film-heroines are unknown. All films end either with the disappearance of the last obstacle to the heroine getting into bed with the hero, or with the inexpressible anguish of both because destiny has decreed that they must continue to sleep apart. If a film ended with the heroine fixing a hyacinth bell in the hero's navel, the audience would either laugh like Rabelais, or leave the cinema in the mood of the later Shakespeare.

Sons and Lovers, in certain respects, is enormously like a Dostoievsky novel. It runs along in the same sort of vivid, confused, powerful way—like someone talking under the influence of a narcotic. Like Dostoievsky, too, it has a prophetic quality, which means, in practice, it popularises and projects contemporary charlatanry. Out of all its verbiage the sombrely significant countenances of popularisers, expounders and projectors of Freud and of Marx (a mighty if unedifying tribe) lift themselves up and bay the moon. I remember when I was living in Moscow there was a large glass apparatus, shaped like a venetian blind, which was exposed to public view. Looking at it from the left, you saw the bearded Marx; from the right, the genial Engels, and face to face, Little Father Lenin. Lawrence holds up a similar mirror to nature, only there is but one face—his.

Lawrence's obsession with class is at least as great as his obsession with sex. Everything he dislikes is labelled 'common'; as the Morel boys improve their circumstances they begin to call their mother 'mater' (was this ever really done outside the pages of the *Gem* or the *Magnet*?), and Paul, when he takes Clara to the Nottingham theatre, gets himself up in evening dress. At the same time, to offset this social climbing, the idea is developed that really the poor and simple are much 'nicer' than the comfortably off and sophisticated. The following conversation between Paul and his mother indicates the internal conflict which was taking place in Lawrence in this connection:

'You know,' he said to his mother, 'I don't want to belong to the well-to-do middle class. I like my common people best. I belong to the common people.'

'But if anyone else said so, my son, wouldn't you be in a tear. *You* know you consider yourself equal to any gentleman.'

'In myself,' he answered, 'not in my class or my education or my manners. But in myself I am.'

'Very well, then. Then why talk about the common people?'

'Because—the difference between people isn't in their class, but in themselves. Only from the middle classes one gets ideas, and from the common people—life itself, warmth. You feel their hates and loves.'

'It's all very well, my boy. But, then, why don't you go and talk to your father's pals?'

'But they're rather different.'

'Not at all. They're the common people. After all, whom do you mix with now—among the common people? Those that exchange ideas, like the middle classes. The rest don't interest you.'

'But—there's the life——'

'I don't believe there's a jot more life from Miriam than you could get from any educated girl—say Miss Moreton. It is *you* who are snobbish about class.'

She frankly *wanted* to climb into the middle class, a thing not very difficult, she knew. And she wanted him in the end to marry a lady.

Lawrence, of course, did marry a 'lady' (he used to use coroneted notepaper, and in particular cases would point an arrow to the coronet, accompanying this with a note to the effect that his wife was the daughter of Baron von Richthofen), and may be said to have fulfilled his mother's hopes that he would climb into the middle class. He remained socially restless, however, and continued to develop the point Paul made to Mrs. Morel about the common people emanating 'life itself, warmth.' Here again the *reductio ad absurdum of Sons and Lovers* is to be found in *Lady Chatterley's Lover*. Mellors, the gamekeeper, it is carefully explained, had been an officer in the war and, when he wanted to, could speak like a B.B.C. announcer even though, in his amorous transactions with Lady Chatterley, he used stage dialect.

With Lady Chatterley's father, Sir Malcolm Reid, described as 'the Royal Academician,' on the other hand, Mellors reverted to his officer-type speech. Witness the following exchange at Sir Malcolm's club, and surely the most fatuous piece of dialogue ever written; so fatuous that not even the Bishop of Woolwich, Mr. E. M. Forster, and the other distinguished witnesses for the defence at the Lady Chatterley trial were prepared to justify it as 'literature';

'Well, young man, and what about my daughter?'

The grin flickered on Mellors's face.

'Well, sir, and what about her?'

'You've got a baby in her all right.'

'I have that honour!' grinned Mellors.

'Honour, by God!' Sir Malcolm gave a little squinting laugh, and became Scotch and lewd. 'Honour! How was the going, eh? Good, my boy, what?'

'Good!'

'I'll bet it was! Ha-ha! My daughter, chip off the old block, what? . . . You warmed her up, oh, you warmed her up, I can see that . . . A gamekeeper, eh, my boy! Bloody good poacher, if you ask me. Ha-ha! . . . That sort of game is worth a man's while, eh, what? Ha-ha! I envy you, my boy . . . Oh, you're a bantam, I can see that. You're a fighter . . .'

Marxist critics doubtless contend that in *Sons and Lovers* Lawrence showed his awareness of the class struggle, and then turned his back on it. And, from their own point of view, they are perfectly right. He sensed the issue, but shirked it; he tried to establish a neutralist position which enabled him, on the one hand, to live, as it were, in the maquis of the upper classes, and, on the other, to continue to assert that all virtue and true vitality resided among the common people. In Taos, thanks to the hospitality of Mrs. Luhan and to her share in the profits of the Dodge enterprise in Detroit, he was able to extol dark unconsciousness as exemplified by local Indians. The class war cannot be evaded in such a manner. It is, for those who wage it, as real as any other war—indeed, more real, and its victories are not won on the playing fields of Eton, or even of Haileybury.

Part of the enduring interest of *Sons and Lovers,* that is to say, lies in the way, all unconsciously, it presents the pattern of the age. Paul Morel, like Lawrence himself, is a hero of our time, and the only begetter of a whole line of men from the north who come south to sleep with débutantes, write plays and novels about working-class life, and grow rich by looking back in anger. From his drab miner's home Paul looks nostalgically towards, as it seems to him, a brighter, more variegated world, where French is fluently read as well as spoken, and elegant, lovely women may be enjoyed without remorse, expense or the dread of disease. And how is this brighter, more variegated world to be entered? Only by strenuous effort; by eschewing what is 'common' and pursuing what is 'cultured'; ultimately, by breaking away from his own social origins. Like Paul, Lawrence set himself with a will to his French irregular verbs, and was in due course rewarded by acquiring a plump German baroness whom he could take over the hills and far away.

Matters, however, could not just be left there. Otherwise it would only be a Victorian moralistic success story of the type Dickens so delighted to write. In moving away from his proletarian origins, Paul, like Lawrence, had to persuade himself that, in fact, he was moving nearer to them. Like a rough diamond who has made a lot of money in the Midlands but still ostentatiously calls his wife 'Mother'; like a Labour M.P. (or Lord Snow) who anxiously explains that he has sent his son to Eton only because in society's present transitional state it is a better education; like a Conservative Cabinet Minister boastful of a grandfather who was an agricultural labourer, or his younger prototype seeking to be called 'Ted' or 'Jack'—so Lawrence's hero, Paul Morel, tries to compensate for social aspirations by a ceremonial social abasement. 'You're done for!' Lawrence snapped angrily to a lunch table full of Kenynesian literati assembled in Cambridge to make his acquaintance. Of course he was right. Done for they were, but so was he.

Sons and Lovers ends with Paul meditating departure. Like Coriolanus, he finds compensation for disappointments and frustrations in a world elsewhere. For Lawrence and for all his characters this is the only solution—to go somewhere else in the vague expectation that things will be different there. They are all ceaselessly on the move, only staying long enough in one place, first to praise it ecstatically, and then to hate it unutterably. (The single exception, oddly enough, is Australia, which to judge from *Kangaroo,* Lawrence rather liked, perhaps because it was so empty that he could almost imagine—his idea of bliss—that he existed alone in its vast expanse.) Lawrence was always toying with projects for getting a few friends together and 'making a life' somewhere or other. He was like the Nazis with their *alles muss anders sein.* The sense of a civilisation dropping to pieces dwelt with him, as with all of us, but he had nothing really to suggest except flight and imagined ecstasies of the flesh.

It is this that makes the latter part of *Sons and Lovers* such unsatisfactory reading to-day. The sentences are still alive; their phosphorescent glow has survived. But what hysteria! What sheer idiocy! It is like a wonderful dancer with no ballet to perform, a wonderful musician with no melodies in his head. Once he departs from the Morel household he is lost. From the real figure of Paul Morel's miner father he moves into the phantasy of Clara, who is herself solid and earthly compared with her prototypes to come, like Ursula or Gudrun in *Women in Love.* Incidentally, what a raw deal Paul's father had! He had to support a family all of whom treated him with undisguised contempt, or at best patronage. His drinking (a natural recourse in the circumstances) was held against him, and when genteel visitors came he was expected to keep out of the sitting-room. His circumstances provide an image of the usual attitude of well-wishers and improvers of the proletariat to actual proletarians.

It is perhaps a little unfair that in seeking the key to *Sons and Lovers* so vast a store of information about Lawrence should be available. Middleton Murry, Catherine Carswell,

Frieda Lawrence, Mrs. Luhan, Dorothy Brett—all these and numerous others have had their say. We know in nauseating detail all about Lawrence's quarrels, his fluctuating loves and hates, his ridiculous projects. We can fill in the picture of his life with sickening detail. This, however, should not blind us to the fact that bedded in it all was the most significant novelist of the first decades of this century. I cannot suggest a better means of recalling this fact than a re-reading of at any rate the first half of *Sons and Lovers*.

It is the least literary of novels; and its very naïveties add to this effect. Nothing could be more delightful than Paul Morel's early visits to Miriam's farm. They recall that wonderful expedition when Rousseau and two girls, riding the same horse, went looking for cherries. Nothing, again, could be more moving and tender than the scene in which Paul breaks the news of his brother's death to his father when he comes up from the pit. Such scenes are in a different category from anything written by any other contemporary novelist. It is only a pity that, like so much in our time, it should have ended in ranting, whining and sheer idiocy.

Twilight of greatness

The arrival of Sir Winston Churchill on the Riviera in the years before his death used to be as regular and invariable an occurrence as *Mardi Gras* or the Battle of Flowers. At Nice Airport the photographers would turn out yet once more, and M. le Préfect, or M. le Sous-Préfect, or just M. le Maire, await his arrival on the tarmac. It had all happened many times before, and everyone knew just what was expected of him. Local reporters from the *Agence France Presse* and the *Nice Matin* stood around in the vague expectation that there might be a story. Air travellers waiting for their planes, and spectators up on the airport roof, were glad enough to have something to look at. They clustered as near as possible to where the great man descended, and, when they saw him, raised a faint cheer, to which he responded by shakily lifting up his fingers in a V-sign.

The inevitable cigar, jutting out of his mouth, gave an impression of having been put there by someone else, as children stick an old pipe into a snowman. His face was glazed and vacant. It might have been immensely old or just born—the eyes faded and watery; the features muzzy, somehow out of focus, like a photograph when the camera has moved. One had a sense, under the surface varnish, of an inward melancholy. It is an illusion to suppose that those who cling tenaciously to life necessarily want to go on living. They often long to die; like Lear, hate those who would upon the rack of this tough world stretch them out longer. Their survival may be due to some reflex action. By lingering on, they may be expiating an undue rage to live. Bernard Shaw told his biographer, Hesketh Pearson, that each night, when he lay down to sleep, he hoped not to awaken the following morning. Sir Winston may well have been a like case, except that the chains which kept him earthbound ate mostly into the flesh, whereas Shaw's lacerated a mind which would not subside.

Churchill's prodigious constitution miraculously carried him through all strains and hazards, and left intact his capacity to eat and drink with enjoyment. The cautions and abstinences which normally accompany old age, and which his doctors prescribed, were not for him. He could still go through the motions of responding to applause when otherwise he seemed quite moribund. Cheers penetrated his deafness (which he resolutely refused to alleviate with a hearing-aid) even though words could not. The instinct, inculcated through years of practice, to brace himself for public appearances, still operated. As he went to his car, latterly with two nurses in his entourage, his footsteps were surprisingly steady, his bearing ostensibly alert. Old politicians, like old actors, revive in the limelight. The vacancy which afflicts them in private momentarily lifts when, once more, they feel the eyes of an audience upon them. Their old passion for holding the centre of the stage guides their uncertain footsteps to where the footlights shine, and summons up a wintry smile when the curtain rises.

Thus, from time to time, Churchill managed to find his way, alone and unaided, into the House of Commons. This was the scene he knew best; this the place where he had spent so many breathless hours of his long life. He returned to it by instinct—to the stale air, the untidy benches, the drone of unmeant and unheeded speeches, the pallid Front Bench faces, the occasional exclamations of approval or dissent, the laughter so easily and so fatuously aroused, all the drab panoply of mid-twentieth-century Parliament. When his bulky form appeared, whoever might be speaking, whatever was under discussion, the proceedings were, in effect, temporarily suspended. All eyes rested on him, in the galleries as on the floor of the House. With exaggerated obeisance, he would make his bow to Mr. Speaker, and advance upon his old seat below the gangway. Then, after some long drawn out by-play with his handkerchief, or a throat lozenge, he would lean across to ask a neighbouring M.P., in a sepulchral whisper, what was the business before the House, and who was that particular Member (pointing at him) on his feet. It might well be Macmillan or Harold Wilson whom he could not identify. His eyes seldom intimated recognition, and, when they did, it was from an old recollection. With the years, distant memories grow clearer. The present, and the recent past, are hidden from view under thick clouds of forgetfulness.

Attention would remain fixed on him. As he well knew, no speech would be heard, no question receive other than desultory consideration, while he was there. Honourable and Right Honourable Members, on both sides of the House, continued to be preoccupied with his strange, eerie presence among them. When he got up to go, their eyes followed him, as they did when he came in. After he had gone, and they had resumed their business, it took a little while for them to get back on to their own pedestrian wave-length. The atmosphere created by his incursion only gradually subsided. What was it about him which made him, even in his decrepitude, still tower above the others, and hold them in thrall? Not fineness of character—he was rather horrible. Not past services—in the House of Commons, of all places, it is true that (to use a phrase Shakespeare puts into the mouth of Timon of Athens) men bar their doors before the setting sun. Not famous orations—like all rhetoric, his wore badly. Even while he was still alive, few could listen without squirming even to the wartime speeches, so stirring at the time.

He had become a kind of totem. His continued existence provided a link with departed glory. Though his sun might have set, still, as long as he was there, some glow lingered about the western sky in which others might participate. He was produced, as totems are, to keep up tribal morale, which otherwise would sag under the weight of unfamiliar and disconcerting circumstances. Brittania no longer ruled the waves, but still did when Churchill was First Lord of the Admiralty. Narrower still and narrower might our bounds be set, not wider still and wider, as Conservative ladies fervently proclaim when they sing 'Land of Hope and Glory'; but it was Churchill who had said that he had not become His Majesty King George VI's Principal Secretary of State in order to preside over the dissolution of his Empire. Brave words, which had to be eaten during his post-war premiership under George VI's daughter, Queen Elizabeth II, when the dissolution of the British Empire went on apace! Even so, Conservative ladies continued to derive comfort and re-assurance from him.

On his last visits to the Riviera Sir Winston usually stayed at the Hôtel de Paris in Monte Carlo, as the guest of Mr. Aristotle Onassis, who owned the place. Or Mr. Onassis would take him for a cruise, along with Maria Callas, on his sleek yacht *Christina,* named, in the circumstances somewhat embarrassingly, after his former wife, Tina Onassis. When the party went ashore at some little holiday port, again there were cheers—'*Vive* Churchill!'—from groups of boatmen and fishermen and tourists who gathered in the Mediterranean sun to look at him, and at Miss Callas, and even at Mr. Onassis. Those who saw Churchill, as I did, walk down the Champs-Elysées with General de Gaulle, on his first visit to liberated Paris, when he seemed the embodiment of a resurrected Europe (at least, so we thought it then), might ruminate philosophically on the bizarreries of fame. How strange that applause, so tumultuous and heartfelt on the great stage of history, should only a few years later, find this faint, frivolous echo in so diminished a setting! Did he detect and note the difference? Who can tell? It was still applause. Mr. Onassis was no General de Gaulle, certainly, but an attentive, considerate and generous host; *Christina* no man-of-war, but a commodious and elegant yacht. V for

212

victory; and though that victory had been won, it seemed already an eternity ago, and had brought scant benefit and many woes, a V-sign made by its originator was still appreciated in Monte Carlo and along the Côte d'Azur.

The Hôtel de Paris, where Mr. Onassis accommodated Sir Winston, is one of the few remaining old-style expensive hotels on the Riviera. The others are steadily being eliminated by *le camping*, which, in accordance with the spirit of the age, thrives by taking a little money from a lot of people rather than a lot of money from a few. There is nothing of *le camping* about the Hôtel de Paris. The bars and dining-rooms and lounges are kept in restful and perpetual twilight. As far as is humanly possible, the outside world is excluded. Residents, if so inclined, may make their way to the neighbouring Casinos by an underground passage without submitting themselves to the elements even to the extent of crossing the road. The service is alert and efficient, and the cuisine justly famed throughout, and, indeed, beyond, the Alpes Maritimes; the suites are ample and luxurious, and the charges astronomical—though not, of course, for Mr. Onassis's guests, who pay nothing. Outside, Rolls-Royces and Cadillacs are neatly berthed side by side, awaiting their owners' pleasure. Sir Winston kept mostly to his suite, and appeared only rarely in the public parts of the hotel. On the occasions when he was respectfully wheeled, in his invalid chair, into the dining-room, the other diners would all look up, eager to catch a glimpse of him. For them, too, he was a totem, reinforcing their conviction that, whether or not there will always be an England, there will assuredly always be a Hôtel de Paris and a Côte d'Azur.

Before Sir Winston's friendship with Mr. Onassis ripened into intimacy, he used to stay in the Villa Pausa at Roque-brune, some two miles farther along the coast, with his literary agent, Mr. Emery Reves. This, too, is an ample residence, with a spacious stairway, and a large expanse of walls, which show off to advantage Mr. Reves's valuable collection of Impressionist paintings. It was formerly owned by Mlle Chanel, famous for *haute couture* and perfume, who tamed its Italianate luxuriance into the quiet shades of grey she preferred, preserving, in the large garden, a similar colour scheme by planting lavender under the old olive trees. Mlle

Chanel, incidentally, long ago when she was the intimate of the Duke of Westminster, knew Sir Winston well. She used, she told me once, to play cribbage with him, and found it expedient to let him always win. In those far-off days, Mr. Reves was still in his native Hungary, and Adolph Hitler, the unconscious instrument which brought him and Sir Winston together in Mlle Chanel's former villa, still in his native Austria. Such are the small, but still intriguing, byways of history's harsh course. Under the Reves régime, the Villa Pausa's décor has been preserved, though its Chatelaine, Wendy Russell, has superimposed a certain degree of Americanisation upon the household arrangements, daintily attiring the maids in Coffee Shoppe pink nylon—a shade to which she is addicted, and which predominates in her own elegant boudoir. As they say in Roquebrune, when conversation turns on the Reves ménage, made famous by Sir Winston's visits: *'C'est une vie en rose là-haut.'*

Mr. Reves, like Mr. Onassis, is a rich man. Sir Winston's hosts usually were. The difference was that, whereas Mr. Onassis's wealth was derived from shipping, Mr. Reves's had been derived from Sir Winston. He has the, I should suppose, almost unique distinction in our rough island story, of having benefited financially by associating with a Churchill. By astute and pertinacious syndication of Sir Winston's writings he enriched himself, and, of course, to a far greater degree, Sir Winston. Thus, when Mr. Reves entertained Sir Winston, he was, in a sense, looking after a valuable property. The property continued to be valuable even when Sir Winston could no longer produce. His works went marching lucratively on through the media of film, radio and television; his paintings continued to have a brisk sale as Christmas cards in the United States, and *Winston Churchill: The Valiant Years* provided both American and British televiewers with yet another version of his famous War Memoirs. The totem, like a guided-missile, proved effective at long range.

A ready means of being cherished by the English is to adopt the simple expedient of living a long time. I have little doubt that if, say, Oscar Wilde, had lived into his nineties, instead of dying in his forties, he would have been considered a benign, distinguished figure, suitable to preside at a school prize-giving, or to instruct and exhort scoutmasters at their jamborees. He might even have been knighted. A notable example of the operation of the same principle was Queen Victoria, who, in the earlier years of her reign, was so detested by her subjects that it was considered highly dubious whether the Monarchy would survive her death. Her gross and podgy figure repelled them, as did her morbid protraction of the normal period of mourning after the death of Albert, the Prince Consort. This unfavourable impression was intensified by her lack of consideration for her heir, later Edward VII, and by her curious associates like John Brown, the Scottish bailie at Balmoral, who, despite being usually drunk, was permitted gross familiarities, at any rate in speech. By the time of the Queen's Diamond Jubilee, however, all was changed. She had sat so long on the throne that her stupidities became endearing eccentricities, and her arrogance an old lady's whimsicality. Her turgid and heavily underlined Journals were lovingly edited, and to this day are liable to raise a snigger rather than a yawn. Dreadful statues of her, turned out by the score, were erected in prominent places throughout the country, and even shipped to far-off lands like India, where they still stand unsuitably in Calcutta, New Delhi and Lahore.

If this unpleasing old Germanic lady thus achieved fame and popular esteem just by becoming very old, how much more so was this the case with Sir Winston, who had notable achievements to his credit, and who had displayed, in the course of his turbulent political career, exceptional verve and resourcefulness. Yet, even Sir Winston, as few now care to remember, had periods of exclusion from office, and of intense unpopularity, particularly among his associates in the political party he happened to belong to at the time. I recall very well, in the middle thirties, when I was working on the London *Evening Standard,* how Churchill used to come occasionally to the office. Lord Beaverbrook, the owner of the *Evening Standard,* had engaged him to write regular articles on current affairs at what was then considered an exceptionally high fee. What a dispirited and disgruntled figure he was in those days! Any political journalist would have been happy to give long odds against his ever holding office again, let alone becoming Prime Minister. The Tories, whom he had re-joined when their political fortunes revived, could not abide him. He found a point of attack in their India policy, which, when it was put into effect in a far more extreme form some ten years later by a Labour Government, he let pass with scarcely a murmur. At the time of Edward VIII's abdication, he was howled down in the House of Commons when he attempted to make a plea on the King's behalf. Here, too, as the exiled Duke of Windsor found to his chagrin, Churchill in opposition was one thing, Churchill in office another. The nomadic Windsors received no more consideration from their former champion when he was in a position to do them favours than they did from Mr. Attlee, who owed them none.

By the time Churchill was very old any breath of criticism of his character or achievement was considered to be, not only in execrable taste, but almost blasphemous. This was a pity, if only because it detracted from his undoubted greatness. For a man as human and humorous and audacious as Churchill had been, to be turned into a totem, serving to protract illusions of grandeur, was a sad end to a splendid career. How fortunate were those Hindu rulers whose philosophy required them to retire to the forest for their last years, and thus disengage their minds from earthly preoccupations in order to prepare themselves for the death which could not be long delayed.

It is, of course, true that Churchill's totem role was particularly required in view of the visible decline of his country's fortunes. He was the last Prime Minister able to produce authentic Great Power credentials at international gatherings. Though, in fact, in his dealings with Stalin and Roosevelt, he was increasingly a junior partner, he appeared to be an equal. At the ill-omened Yalta meeting, he was mostly overborne, and sometimes treated with scant consideration, by his two associates, but in the final winding-up scenes they allowed him an equal status with themselves. He had the dubious distinction of being photographed, his Russian fur hat rakishly on one side, as one of the three pillars of the modern world, who, it was confidently believed, would draw the frontiers, and establish the conditions, for an era of enduring peace and prosperity. Things, as we know, took quite a different turn. Even so, the English are still inclined to look nostalgically into their old photograph album, which recalls grander circumstances than they now enjoy. Among the studio portraits it contains, Sir Winston's continues to be particularly prized.

Few men of action have been able to make a graceful exit at the appropriate time. Napoleon's retirement to St. Helena was enforced, restless and cantankerous; Lloyd George, for the last twenty-five years of his life excluded from office, continued till the end to hover round public affairs, managing to persuade himself that he was contributing to their course and direction. Even Sir Oswald Mosley, whose meteoric career in party politics ended ingloriously in the British Union of Fascists and incarceration during the war years, has been able to go on believing that the call would come for him to take over the government. Power-addiction, like any other, becomes in the end incurable. Its victims continue to crave for the drug even when it cannot be procured, or, if it could, when their systems are too enfeebled to react, other than fitfully and wanly, to its stimulus.

How much better for Churchill's reputation if he had brought himself, or been persuaded, to retire from active politics after his electoral defeat in 1945! Then his enormous services were a fresh memory instead of a too often told tale. The rhetoric which gloriously saved us from surrender to the Nazis had not staled with constant repetition; the great esteem in which he was rightly held had not degenerated into sycophancy, nor been used to sustain a legendary destiny which precludes effectively grappling with a real one.

It was not to be. He discarded the role of national leadership, which he had so richly earned, in favour of party leadership, for which he was ill-fitted, and which ill-became him. The red dispatch boxes, toys of office, held their old allure, and for them he threw away, or at any rate clouded, the memory of the time when he had been the spokesman, not of a class or a party, but of a nation and a cause. His post-war premiership was confused, meandering and self-willed—much more so than is even now recognised or admitted. He hung on as long as he dared, and as long as the poltroonery of his associates permitted. When, at last, he went, he bequeathed us Anthony Eden, who, in one ill-judged, ill-planned and fatuous venture at Suez, lost to, of all people, the Egyptians, what Churchill's heroic wartime leadership had saved from the Nazis. History, which is always ironical, has rarely produced a greater irony than this.

Surely, it will be contended, Sir Winston's place in history is sufficiently assured irrespective of how the twilight of his days was spent. Is it not the case that, as has so often been remarked, his deeds will live, and his writing be read, as long as England's fate interests mankind, and the English language continues to be spoken? As for his writing—I am not so sure. Participants in public events are seldom reliable chroniclers of them. Their egos are too involved, their views are too prejudiced, for them to achieve a historian's detachment. They find it difficult to recollect in tranquillity, and therefore to endow with enduring interest, what so excited them at the time. Effective men of action, by their very nature, have little sense of perspective. They are too obsessed with the present to trace its relation to the past and the future. Tactics obsess them to the exclusion of strategy. Like Napoleon, their only true principle is: *'On s'engage, et après on voit.'* History cannot be written in such a spirit. Gibbon, who, as an officer in the Militia, was a ludicrous figure, and at the Board of Trade a fiasco, could, with exquisite clarity, skill and elegance, unravel the story of Rome's decline and fall. Napoleon, on the other hand, when, on St. Helena, he looked back on the dramatic events in which he had played so dramatic and decisive a part, had nothing of any particular interest or significance to say about them.

In Sir Winston's case, the question is complicated by his rhetorical style, which, though it has been greatly admired by his contemporaries, posterity may well find distasteful. Already his *Memoirs of the First World War* have begun to pall. It would not be surprising if his *Memoirs of the Second World War* come, before very long, to create a like impression of being gaseous, over-written, and, in the light of subsequent events, too inappropriate to deserve attention. At his obsequies, the totem's positively last and most stupendous appearance, other lesser pens essayed the same grand manner, with not altogether happy results. 'The last frail petal of one of the great red roses of all England falls. And the sword sleeps in its scabbard,' wrote one. 'You can take tears to-day and catch them and call them the river that flows through

London's heart,' another began, and concluded: 'When I get to Heaven, he said, I mean to spend a considerable portion of my first million years in painting. To-morrow, perhaps, you will look up and there will be a rainbow in the sky. *Winston Spencer Churchill will be at work.*' Yet another: 'The river changed from lead to pewter, then to silver. The Tower glowed ash-tawny and alive beneath the inert grey blocks . . . a broad swathe of gold was flung down Tower Hill to the river as the road was sanded.' It was like one of those fantastic Asian sunsets, whose lurid, scarcely believable colours are followed by a deep, over-powering silence.

History, in any case, is the story of the victor. When I first went to India, in 1924, little Indian boys were taught at school that their country was torn with conflicts and prostrate until the English landed on its shores. Thenceforth, all was well. Now they are taught the exact opposite—that their country languished until the English were chased away. Which version is true? The answer probably is, neither. However unjustly or inaccurately, Sir Winston's place in history will depend on who, from the turmoil and discontent of our time, is seen to emerge as the victor.

The passion of St. Eatherly

In the profuse mythology of our time the Passion of Saint Eatherly is a choice item. Not even the martyrdom of Saints Sacco and Vanzetti quite equals the perfection of its symmetry, the architectural skill and elegance with which floor after floor has been added, until the whole majestic structure stands towering into the sky. How it all came about is revealed by Mr. William Bradford Huie in his book *The Hiroshima Pilot*. He provides an account—unique as far as I know—of just how a modern myth is created, elaborated and propagated, until its validity comes to be almost universally accepted.

The process has so great a bearing on the character of the contemporary world and the working of the contemporary mind that it is worth examining in some detail. Like all others,

219

the Eatherly myth exists in a variety of versions; synoptic, apocryphal, etc. Let us take as the standard one the version (quoted by Mr. Huie) by Robert Jungk, author of *Children of the Ashes* and *Brighter Than a Thousand Suns,* appended by way of introduction to *Burning Conscience,* a volume of letters exchanged between Eatherly and Dr. Gunther Anders, described as an Austrian philosopher.

In colourful terms, Jungk describes how Major Claude Eatherly of the United States Air Force, who 'commanded the Hiroshima raid,' had shortly after the war taken a look at the atomic desert which he had helped to create in the green and flourishing countryside of Japan.' He 'had gazed into the faces of his victims; he had seen their eyes fixed on him, had observed the expression of misery, of that lack of any desire to live after they had witnessed the end of the world.'

This experience, Jungk tells us, quite shattered Eatherly. He became taciturn and moody. As, however, he had done thirteen months of unbroken combat duty in the South Pacific, he was considered to be an ordinary case of battle fatigue and was sent to a New York clinic. There he was sorted out and discharged.

On hearing, when he landed at an airport near San Francisco on his way home, that his mother had died of cancer, he burst out 'to the waiting reporters . . . "It's a punishment. We shall all be further punished! We shall all have to make atonement."' As a 'much decorated hero,' Eatherly was to be fêted in his Texan home town, but in his contrite and shattered condition he felt unable to face the experience.

Subsequently, he joined the Israeli Air Force, and engaged in operations against the Arabs. Jungk does not tell us whether he looked into any of their faces. Presumably not, since he does not appear to have been unduly lacerated by the experience. When, however, back in America, he heard that President Truman had announced that America was to manufacture a hydrogen bomb, he 'tried in a hotel room in New Orleans to end his life with an overdose of sleeping pills.'

It was unavailing; he was still alive when discovered. Then, according to Jungk:

. . . a peculiar plan began to take shape in his mind. He

would, he decided, fight against this jingoistic tendency in America which had just elected a Second World War general to be its President. He would fight it by knocking that national paragon, that virtuous war hero, from his newly elected pedestal. He would compromise and expose him; and the victim of this act of unmasking would be himself, the Hero of Hiroshima . . .

In pursuit of this enterprise, Jungk goes on, Eatherly forged a cheque 'for quite an insignificant amount,' having, of course, 'paid the money into a fund for the assistance of the Children of Hiroshima.' He served a term of imprisonment, and then attempted a hold-up, whereupon the authorities decided that he 'was suffering from a mental disability attributable to war service' and he was discharged with a small pension, subsequently doubled.

The authorities 'would neither brand him as a criminal, as he had hoped, nor grant him that form of punishment through which he hoped to find relief from the great burden of guilt that oppressed him.' Thus, Jungk concludes:

The morally more healthy Eatherly could not come to terms with the sick society into which he was continually being let loose, because he had failed to develop that protective skin which enabled his normal contemporaries to accept complacently the crimes of Auschwitz and Hiroshima.

According to an earlier version (*Formula for Death,* by a French journalist, Fernand Gigon), Eatherly had a look at Nagasaki as well as Hiroshima, but 'remained poker-faced until after peace had been signed.' When he 'returned to Texas a much decorated hero,' he was 'greeted with processions, bands, flags, pretty girls, speeches by the Mayor.' Another refinement in this version was that Mrs. Eatherly, in seeking a divorce from her husband, said of him to the judge: 'He frightens me. He often jumps up in the middle of the night and screams out in an inhuman voice that makes me feel ill: "Release it! Release it!" Then after a moment or two, during which my husband seems to be in hell, he shouts: "Not now, not now! Think of the children! The children are burning!"'

Needless to say, the theme, whether in the Jungk or the Gigon version, met with a ready and sympathetic response in every enlightened breast. All the trumpets of the righteous sounded for Eatherly: old philosopher Russell threw in his blessing, and poet John Wain produced a long poem concluding:

> Say nothing of love, or thanks or penitence.
> Say only 'Eatherly, we have your message.'

Mr. Wain's poem in due course was broadcast by the B.B.C. Occasional sceptics and doubters were then confuted. With this imprimatur, the Eatherly legend had the same stamp of authenticity as the tablets setting forth the Ten Commandments with which Moses returned from his encounter with the deity. Eatherly was now firmly established as the man who dropped the bomb on Hiroshima and Nagasaki; who had gazed into the faces of the suffering Japanese victims, and, stirred by penitence, and wishing to expiate his sense of guilt, had turned to petty crime in order to suffer the punishment he felt to be his due, thereby inducing the authorities to regard him as mad, and getting himself incarcerated with his nightmares in a psychiatric ward.

It was at this point that Mr. Huie, like the German textual critics of the Gospels in the nineteenth century, embarked on his quest for the historical Eatherly. As they did, he went to the basic texts, in this case, the record of Eatherly's Air Force service, all along available for public inspection in Washington, though, apparently. no previous researcher or writer had bothered to take a look at it.

Mr. Huie easily established the fact that Eatherly had neither commanded, nor participated in, the Hiroshima raid. His role had been to fly at 30,000 feet over the target area before the raid to report on weather conditions. Far from having been engaged in intensive operations in the South Pacific, he went through the war (an unusual experience for a pilot) without hearing a shot fired in anger. No citation or record exists to indicate that he had been decorated or received a hero's welcome in his home town or elsewhere.

After the war Eatherly remained in the Air Force as long as he possibly could. He competed hard, but without success, for the honour of dropping the bomb at the first Bikini atomic test, and narrowly avoided being dismissed the service when he was caught out cheating at an examination. His honourable discharge, in the circumstances, could be considered fortunate.

From his Air Force associates, both officers and enlisted men, Mr. Huie was able to get a clear picture of Eatherly as they had known him—a tall, agreeable, smiling Texan, fond of gambling and chasing girls; a skilful pilot and a good skipper who seemed little interested in the war and its larger purposes, and gave no sign of worrying unduly about the slaughter and destruction involved. There could be no question of combat-strain because he was never in combat.

After the Hiroshima and Nagasaki raids, Eatherly for once showed some perturbation, arising, not from contrition, but from annoyance at being excluded from the subsequent publicity. With, for him, unusual prescience, he remarked to his crew: 'Books will be written about Hiroshima. Movies will be made,' adding: 'And nobody is ever going to know we were there.' Here, as it turned out, he was wrong.

In civilian life he was first involved in a curious and decidedly shady project to bomb Havana, using war-surplus stores for the purpose. Then he drifted into a life of petty crime and drunkenness, which led to a term of imprisonment followed by intermittent courses of treatment at a Veterans' Administration hospital for mental cases at Waco. At his divorce proceedings no mention was made of the nightmare cries referred to by M. Gigon. Mrs. Eatherly, questioned by Mr. Huie, denied she had ever heard them.

The intriguing question that arises is how this real Eatherly whom Mr. Huie met, and whose life and character he has unravelled, came to be supplanted by the legendary one, the subject of Mr. Wain's verses, the target of so much righteous indignation in so many parts of the world, bringing heartache wherever two or more nuclear disarmers were gathered together. It is tempting to imagine some supremely skilled Marxist propagandist or insensate anti-American at work. What a feat of propaganda would be the conscious transubstantiation of the failed airman on the make, the frustrated womaniser and drunk, into the broken-hearted humanitarian offering his own freedom and sanity as atonement for a monstrous collective crime!

Actually, as Mr. Huie shows, the transubstantiation resulted from an accident. Mr. Vachule, a reporter on the Fort Worth *Star-Telegram,* was covering local court cases. It happened that Eatherly, in the course of one of his federal prosecutions (this time for breaking into a post office), had to be transferred from the mental hospital at Waco to Fort Worth gaol. A deputy United States marshal named Robert Smith accompanied him. On the way they got talking. It turned out that Smith had also served in the Air Force, and they reminisced together. Vachule, another Air Force veteran, heard of their talk and went to see Eatherly in his cell. The result was a story headed 'World War II Hero in Trouble' which made the front page of the *Star-Telegram*. As Vachule put it to Mr. Huie (and his words could not be bettered): 'Let's say that I'm paid to find and write human interest stories that people want to read. . . . Some of what Eatherly told me I knew was incorrect. But other things he said proved to me that he had been a B-29 pilot. It was true that an Air Force major who had been at Hiroshima had now turned to a life of crime . . . well, I thought that was a good story . . . one worth working on.'

Compared with what was to follow, Vachule's first story was austere and factual. In it, Eatherly is quoted as saying that 'he wanted it understood that he is not blaming his mental condition or his troubles on his war experience.' 'I do feel,' he added, 'that I should be in a hospital rather than in gaol.'

Now the story really got going. As on a conveyor-belt, each hand that touched it added some new embellishment. *Newsweek* magazine, for instance, ran a story headed 'Hero in Handcuffs' which presented Eatherly as a picked pilot who had 'reconnoitred and selected and rendezvoused and led and witnessed and surveyed at both Hiroshima and Nagasaki,' and been awarded the Distinguished Flying Cross. It just took Mr. Vachule's story, and worked it up, without, as far as can be seen, checking a single fact. *Parade* magazine carried things further, with an even more fanciful story, which, it announced, was the result of a year's careful research by a team of reporters.

Vachule's story was given the N.B.C. 'Big Story' Award of 500 dollars, and was made the subject of a television show called 'Hiroshima Plus Twelve.' Asked by Mr. Huie how he liked the television drama, Vachule replied: 'Well, to put it mildly I was flabbergasted. I had been vaguely aware that some television shows use dramatic licence, but I wasn't prepared for what they did to my Eatherly story.'

Firmly embedded in it now was the notion of Eatherly's unconscious wish to atone. The psychiatrist in the TV show says to the reporter:

He (Eatherly) thought that he himself was responsible for all those deaths. So he yearned to atone for this act, he wanted to be punished for it. Instead, society treated him as a hero. This made his sense of guilt even more intense. There was only one outlet left for him. He had to commit anti-social acts . . . crimes . . . in order to be punished for what he believed to be unbearable personal guilt.

As one who has worked as a journalist for some forty years and who in retrospect takes a wry satisfaction in the trade, it is a pleasure to me to record that this final, imbecile twist to the Eatherly legend was entirely the contribution of psychiatrists. It was all their own work. Up to the appearance of Vachule's story, the ones who attended Eatherly at Waco had not even discovered the connection with the Hiroshima raid. They soon, however, made up for lost time, and managed even to persuade Eatherly (to his credit, quite a lengthy and difficult business) that he felt guilty.

Eatherly now began to receive large quantities of mail, and —what interested him more—money, with the prospect of making more. It slowly dawned on his not very quick-moving mind that he was a figure of international importance, and he reacted accordingly. He also learnt—and it is a cardinal point for our contemporary heroes and saints—that he must strive to have faith in what psychiatrists told him about himself, and approach his own portrayal in the printed word and on television screen in a believing and reverent mood. So conditioned, he came at last really to believe that he had dropped atomic bombs on Hiroshima, seen the faces of the victims and been accordingly seized with contrition and compassion to the point of sending them any money he could lay hands on and of going mad.

The gem of Mr. Huie's rare collection is undoubtedly the script of a film, so far, alas, unmade called *Medal in the Dust*. It is, the foreword announces, 'the story of Major Claude Eatherly, the Air Force pilot who led the Hiroshima and Nagasaki atomic bomb attack, then turned to a life of crime . . . a true story documented in military and police files.' We open with Eatherly engaged in a burglary. Then we

H

go back over his career; see him on his combat missions in the Pacific war, watch him being briefed ('You will select the target, Major'), and commanding the raid from the cockpit of his plane. Then follows his home-town welcome ('You're a hero, my boy. Didn't you know?') the death of his mother ('a thin, fragile woman, who has been beautiful in her day, but is now near her end'). An open Bible is before her. 'CLOSE UP OF THE BIBLE IN EATHERLY'S HANDS . . . CAMERA FOCUSES ON ONE LINE, the rest of the page being shadowed with grey. The line: 'Thou shalt not kill.'

CLOSE UP OF EATHERLY'S FACE as a strange expression comes over it . . . an inward look, as it were, with pain and guilt in it.

The rest of the screen-play maintains the same high standard, up to the final lines:

Your Honour . . . the thing that has broken Claude up is this . . . He wants desperately to tell people . . . more people . . . about the dreadful thing the Atom Bomb is . . . And nobody will even listen. Your Honour, if they would only listen . . . he might be one of the great voices in the world to-day.

It has long been my opinion that the most appropriate name for the times in which we live would be the Age of Credulity. Mr. Huie's exercise in research and common sense fortifies this opinion. Science (the very word has undergone a singular distortion; meaning originally a condition of knowing, it has come to signify particular branches of knowledge), which purports to inculcate scepticism, has surrendered the human mind to a degree of absurdity which would have astounded a medieval scholar, and made an African witch-doctor green with envy.

In the now little-read short stories of O. Henry there are two conmen—Jeff Peters and Andy Tucker—who regard it as unethical to sell gold bricks to farmers because it is too easy. Had these two worthies had the advantage and pleasure of reading Mr. Huie's *The Hiroshima Pilot,* they would have realised that compared with the fine flower of Western intelligentsia, farmers are a hard sell.

Julien Benda frightened us in the thirties with his analysis of the Treason of the Clerks. A further instalment of his great work is required on their credulity, which represents a greater danger to whatever remains of Western civilisation than the bomb Major Eatherly did not drop at Hiroshima. G. K. Chesterton remarked once that when men cease to believe in a deity they do not then believe in nothing, but in anything. Never has the truth of this proposition been more forcibly illustrated than by Mr. Huie.

India revisited

As the years pass, British rule in India comes to seem as remote as the battle of Agincourt. Shrinking obituary notices take care of its surviving dignitaries; the Indian orders and decorations, so avidly sought after in their day, expire with their recipients, relegated to glass cases or pawn shops, or just mislaid in attics along with uniforms, malacca canes, and other memorials of former Asian splendour. The very statues set up to commemorate viceroys and field-marshals in the scene of their glory begin to prove an embarrassment. They are unwanted where they stand, and it is difficult to find a home for them elsewhere. Our small island can scarcely accommodate its live population, let alone marble and bronze replicas of its once-famous dead.

Yet when I first went out to India as a very young man in 1924 few would have ventured to prophesy so speedy an end to British rule. It seemed well and firmly established. Some ten thousand English presided over the affairs of more than 300 million Indians. The Viceroy was one of the world's great potentates, and each individual drill-suited, topee-hatted Englishman, however humble his status in his own social hierarchy, was an aristocrat in the context of British India. The memsahib who might count for little in her native Wimbledon was a great lady by the banks of the Hooghly; private soldiers shouted 'Boy!' in their canteens when they wanted to attract the attention of an Indian servant with the same assurance as a Burra-Sahib in the Bengal Club. Even the Eurasians, however meagre their portion of European blood, liked to call themselves MacGregor, and somehow rustled up a pair of trousers in preference to a *dhoti*.

Filled, as I then was, with inflamed dreams of Byron at Missolonghi, not to mention Trotsky at Brest-Litovsk, my own attitude towards British power in India was one of the deepest disapproval. I wore Indian dress made of homespun, or *kadi*, in the Swarajist style, presenting, I should suppose, a peculiarly ludicrous appearance. I suffered agonies through trying to twist my stiff Anglo-Saxon limbs into a cross-legged stance, and developed eruptive Delhi boils through subsisting rigorously on a diet of rice. Above all I urged my students at the Travancore (now Kerala) college where I taught to rise up in rebellion against their English oppressors. Rather to my disappointment, the authorities did not hear of, or if they did ignored, my subversive activities. As for the students—while they agreed with me in principle, I found that they were more intent on their examinations, and subsequent government employment, than on becoming martyrs in the cause of India's freedom.

When I returned to India ten years later, it was to Calcutta. By that time wide cracks were appearing in the edifice of British rule. It was obvious enough that its days were numbered, and that Honourable and Right Honourable Swamis in the federal and provincial legislatures were shortly to take over. Many a humid Calcutta evening was spent discussing with a little circle of Bengali intimates what India would be like when that happened. Bengali intellectuals are notoriously given to melancholy and pessimism, and my friends were no exceptions. Yet none of them envisaged anything even approximating to what has actually come to pass since India achieved independence. They saw their subsequent rulers in a variety of unpleasing guises, but not as a projection of British rule, with an Indian Prime Minister for Viceroy. They could scarcely be expected to foresee that, when at last they got rid of the white sahibs, the brown ones who replaced them would go marching on more or less in the same direction.

A visit to Delhi and Simla, after an interval of thirty years, confirmed the impression that the White Man's Burden has merely been shifted to Brown Men's shoulders. It is true that in what was to have been the Chamber of Princes there sat only tribunes of the people, members of the Lok Sabha or

Parliament, with but one royal personage among them—the delectable Maharanee of Jaipur. Also that in what used to be the Viceroy's House resided President Radhakrishnan, some-time Spalding Professor of Eastern Religions and Ethics at Oxford University; and in the Commander-in-Chief's house, Mr. Nehru. When I was last in India, these dis-tinguished edifices were being constructed, still with a view to an indefinite succession of English, or anglicised Indian, occupants. Their style is decidedly Occidental; such Oriental flourishes as they embody are rather in the manner of a Taj Mahal restaurant than of the Taj Mahal.

Mr. Nehru was kind enough to receive me for the purpose of recording a television interview. While the camera-crew were setting up in a room in his house, I strolled about the extensive garden. There were rose-beds, herbaceous borders, lawns and flowering shrubs, reminiscent of Kew Gardens and the Home Counties, which in Delhi's drastic weather needed much coaxing and care. This, I fancied, might now be dwind-ling. The garden seemed imperfectly kept. Its decay was can-celled by a fantastic sunset, which hung over and submerged it, and all New Delhi; Lok Sabha, Government offices, the whole English custom-built capital, along with the six other ruined ones in the vicinity, all likewise constructed by conquering invaders. It was the moment of pause between the scorching Indian day and the velvet night, full of stillness and poignant fragrance, for ever unforgettable.

Mr. Nehru suddenly appeared among the television cameras by himself, without any prior announcement or train of underlings. He seemed, I thought, somewhat shrunken in stature, and older than his seventy-three years. His white Gandhi cap, flowing white coat and tight white trousers, which have come to be almost the uniform of the Congress party's upper echelons, conveyed, despite their simplicity, an impres-sion of elegance, added to by the invariable flower pushed into his coat. He had, I decided, a patrician air, unlike Gandhi, who, outwardly, was a little gargoyle of a man, with big ears and a wide mouth. His distinction came from within.

When young, Mr. Nehru was exceptionally good-looking. He continued to the end to have a decided style about him. No one could embody more exactly than he the dilemmas and perplexities of his country. His manner of thinking, the whole temper of his mind was not only 'Western,' but specifically English of the late twenties and early thirties. After conversing with Mr. Nehru one felt that, by some weird irony of history, the last old-style progressive voice of our time had made itself heard where once the Moguls reigned, not to mention Lord Curzon. One might, indeed, have closed one's eyes and imagined that the Peace Ballot, the Left Book Club, the Popular Front and all the other sombre insignia of the inter-war years were still being tumultuously paraded. The saddest consequence of British rule is all the ideological debris left behind when it ended. The streets are littered with White Papers and Royal Commission Reports, quietly munched by cows still piously permitted to wander among the Secretariat Buildings.

Mr. Attlee, one of his then intimates told me, went off alone to the cinema on the afternoon after he had taken the decision to partition and then withdraw from India. While he was puffing at his pipe in the three-and-sixpennies and Lord Mountbatten was dusting down his uniforms, the scene was being set for the bizarre drama in which Mr. Nehru was to play the leading part. It struck me, talking to him, that he was aware that some dénouement was approaching, if not already upon him. Gone were the halcyon days when he could pronounce *Guardian* editorials to a seemingly attentive and appreciative audience of all mankind. That phase was over. The Chinese, when they invaded India, shattered for ever the assumptions on which it was based. After all those years of wearing his heart on his Left sleeve, Mr. Nehru had to attempt a kind of Indian impersonation of Winston Churchill, with offerings of blood, sweat and tears, enriched by finest hours.

The transition did not come easily to him, and I entirely sympathised. As he explained, the sheer brutality, bad manners and general coarseness of the Chinese Government's communications was a rude shock. His previous exchanges with Mao-Tse-tung and Chou En-lai had been couched in elegant, cultivated terms. The deterioration in style, he suggested, might have been due to reading Karl Marx in Chinese, an arduous and stylistically debilitating experience. There is,

230

I must admit, something pretty forbidding in the thought of going up and down those assemblies of little pictures and spelling out *Das Kapital*. Then again Mr. Nehru found himself at odds with figures like Bertrand Russell who for long had been his guides and heroes. He might have argued, not perhaps with the fullest conviction, that Gandhi, if he had been still alive, would have recommended resistance to Chinese aggression rather than submission through fear. Russell, however, had specifically stated that he considered India to be the aggressor in the Chinese dispute.

This was too much to take even from a *Guru,* especially in view of the fact that all the fighting took place on Indian territory, and the great bulk of prisoners held when the fighting stopped were Indians in the hands of the Chinese. Yet Mr. Nehru continued to call himself a neutralist and nuclear disarmer. He still venerated Russell. The everlasting gap remained between what should happen, and what actually had happened, with Mr. Nehru posed precariously across it.

His acceptance of his straddled position was endearing. Most of those in authority lean one way or the other, becoming, in consequence, either odious tyrants or tedious demagogues. We who survey with (speaking for myself) growing distaste the spectacle of the pursuit of power, may be compared to a pianist in a brothel. When a client, driven by necessity, comes into the establishment, and looks round at the girls provided with a distaste almost equal to our own, we are naturally drawn to him. Such a client was Mr. Nehru.

The Lok Sabha was debating the continued usage of English for official purposes. It was a theme which brought out the mental ingenuity and verbal agility of Indian parliamentarians. For the most part, they spoke in English even when they were pleading for its obliteration or railing against its use, in that characteristic lilting tone, due, it has been suggested, to the fact that the first language teachers in British India were underpaid Welsh missionaries. Procedure and modes of address continue to follow fairly closely the Westminster model. Only sartorially was there any wide divergence. The single pair of Western trousers present was worn by a nominated member, Mr. Anthony, representing the Eurasian community. Otherwise the prevailing mode was Indian, with Gandhi caps the equivalent of the toppers that used to adorn the House of Commons front benches.

It is surely a strange historical chance which has fostered English-style parliamentary government in Indian, as well as a lot of other equivalent social, academic and forensic ritual. As the years of separation extend the divergencies from the home produce cannot but increase. One wonders at what point they will cease to be recognisably akin; when Indian English will be so different from English English as to constitute another language needing to be learnt. Or whether, as is perhaps more likely, in India there may be conserved, with museum exactness, the form and nomenclature of an English way of life which, in its place of origin, has been submerged by an American one, or in any case disappeared. Already leading articles in Indian newspapers, lectures in Indian universities, the oratory of Indian parliamentarians, the raillery in Indian Army messes, have a decidedly old-fashioned flavour. Perhaps sociologists will one day explore these for the light they shed on their extinct originals.

This, of course, assumes that the momentum left behind by British rule, and the institutions and practices transplanted in India with it, will continue to carry along the present régime. As of now, while the English book-reading public feasts upon the *Kama Sutra,* their Indian equivalents remain faithful to *Lady Chatterley,* 'The Waste Land,' *Milk Wood,* and the *Oxford Book of English Verse.* It might not always be so. Even the bonds of Eng. Lit. might one day break asunder.

I drove to Simla from New Delhi, taking in Chandigarh along the way; the new capital of the Indian part of the divided Punjab, designed by Corbusier and about as appropriate to its setting as would be the temple at Madura on the South Downs or the Monte Carlo Casino by the Ganges.

Simla is a truly English production. It was part of the audacity and insolence of British rule to suppose that, in the hot weather, the whole vast, teeming Indian sub-continent could be governed from this mountain eyrie in the extreme north. Government departments and wives used to trek up to Simla in enormous caravans; debs looked avidly for husbands there, and the Viceroy transferred his court to Vice-regal Lodge. Now a statue of Gandhi overlooks the Ridge where the Viceroy used to take the salute at ceremonial parades. People sleep in the bandstand where regimental bands used to play. Viceregal Lodge is unoccupied, with all the gilt furniture still arranged as though for a reception; three small thrones set side by side for the Viceroy, the Vicereine and the Governor of the Punjab, and a large portrait of the King-Emperor on the wall.

In the event of a nuclear war, I was told, President Radhakrishnan would take up his quarters there. Or it might be turned into a very select school. Or, alternatively, it might be left as it is, with all the other empty palaces which litter India; the least impressive architecturally, but certainly the oddest.

Hugh Kingsmill

Those of us who knew Hugh Kingsmill Lunn (he dropped the surname for writing purposes) have continued to keep his memory alive among ourselves. It is rare, when we are together, for us not to find some occasion to recall some observation of his, or refer to one or other of his books. Outside his intimates he has, I fear, been largely forgotten. His books are all out of print, and though most of his brilliant intuitions—for instance about Matthew Arnold and Dickens—have been sustained by subsequent research, credit is rarely accorded him by name. More often than not, those who draw on his conclusions, if they mention him at all, do so disparagingly. How delightful, then, for us who love and revere Kingsmill still, that the first full-length study of him and his works should be undertaken, not by one of the diminishing and ageing band of his intimates, but by a young man, Michael Holroyd, born into the world Kingsmill was leaving! It was, for me, an intensely moving experience to read Holroyd's book; the more so because it was mature and perceptive to a degree one would scarcely have expected in so youthful an author.

When, later, I made Holroyd's acquaintance, this favourable impression was only heightened. He seemed to have got the hang of Kingsmill in an almost miraculous way. Indeed, there is something miraculous about the whole venture—in Holroyd's having stumbled upon a writer so remote from his generation, and immediate awareness of his unique qualities; in his patient and resolute pursuit of information about Kingsmill and his writings; in the diligence and courage which enabled him to complete his task.

Kingsmill is the only human being I have ever known in whose company I never suffered one moment of boredom; whose solid figure I never saw looming up, and whose voice I never once heard, except with unalloyed happiness. I first met him in Manchester in 1929, when I was working there on the *Guardian*. His brother Brian, whom I knew through my wife's family, had often spoken to me about him. So had Louis Wilkinson, the first authentic man-of-letters with whom I was acquainted. Wilkinson had, at that time, a red spade beard, and wore a black hat with a large brim, and seemed to my adolescent eye every inch a writer. He described how once he had come upon Kingsmill unexpectedly, and had seen him gazing somewhat disconsolately at his face in a mirror. The description stuck in my mind. Intimacies cast their shadows before them; they begin in advance of acquaintanceship. This is why the first sight of someone who will be dear to one is never as a stranger. Love originates in a past too remote to be measured, and is projected into a future likewise immeasurable. You take someone's hand, look into their eyes, even in certain cases enfold them in an embrace, before you know, or even think to ask, their name.

Thus, when I saw Kingsmill coming to the barrier at Manchester Central Station I at once knew him, and began talking to him as to an intimate. Thenceforth we went on so talking, on and off, until he died, twenty years later almost to the day. He was a substantial man with a rolling gait, rather like a sailor's. His head was exceptionally large; his hair, already grey, sparse and dishevelled. He never wore a hat. His complexion was ruddy, and he conveyed an impression, even when he was full of troubles, of immense cheerfulness. Happiness glowed in the innermost core of his being—a happiness based, not on his circumstances (which were often atrocious), but on an inward serenity, a close and unbreakable relationship with the sublime realities of human life. Kingsmill's complaints were always addressed to the phenomenal world, which he saw as a shadow hiding the real one, like the moon momentarily obscuring the light of the sun in an eclipse. 'Poor old mankind,' he would sometimes mutter, as he might affectionately about some friend who had run into a lamp-post, or fallen down a man-hole.

His cheerfulness was, I dare say, a certain handicap to him professionally. I have noticed a strong predisposition to believe that writers should, like Don Quixote, wear woeful countenances. There was little trace of woe in Kingsmill's countenance. A hostile reaction to our laughter was not uncommon when we were together; for instance, on the top of a bus, or walking along the Strand. People did not like it. There is something about laughter which calls in question the whole edifice of established authority, and, equally, established opposition to it. As Kingsmill would put it, laughter, on behalf of the imagination, challenges the will, and those who laugh are, therefore, inimical to order and propriety.

Kingsmill's laughter was highly characteristic. It came from within and spread outwards. Some notion would start him off, and, as he developed and expanded its absurdity, so his laughter would wax correspondingly. I remember once, when he and Hesketh Pearson and I were lunching together at the Horseshoe in Tottenham Court Road, we started speculating about the weekly visits which Samuel Butler and his friend Jesting Jones used to pay severally to a French lady residing in Handel Street nearby. As Kingsmill explored the theme —Which of them went first? What was Madame's verdict on their relative performances? Did Butler take with him a sponge bag containing his kit? And so on—our laughter rose. Finally, we decided to go to Handel Street, and identified the house. Standing in front of it, Kingsmill produced such a hilarious picture of these two bearded sentimental homosexuals on their curious errand that we were reduced to hanging helplessly on to lamp-posts to contain our mirth, to the astonishment, and I dare say irritation, of occasional passers-by. Even now, if ever I pass Handel Street, the memory of the scene returns, and makes me want to laugh again.

The idea of getting Kingsmill to Manchester was to try and arrange some reviewing for him on the *Guardian*. To this end I took him along to the office. We leader-writers worked in what was known as the Corridor; a place of shadows doubtless haunted, among others, by the tortured ghost of C. E. Montague. I introduced Kingsmill to the literary editor, Alan Monkhouse, but could see from the beginning that the interview was not going well. The sensitive, talented, but somehow forlorn Monkhouse shrunk from him, as, to my amazement, people often did. He was too strong for them. It was sometimes suggested that his manner was not of the best. In the sense that he never could feign interest in anyone or anything which he did not feel, there may have been an element of plausibility in this. His own thoughts and speculations were so absorbing that he was often oblivious to his surroundings, and might finish off a plate of cakes, or monopolise the fireside, without knowing what he was doing. This was liable to annoy a certain type of person, as was Kingsmill's relentless honesty of mind, called by those who feared and shunned it, tactlessness.

In any case, the *Guardian*, and the already creaking, groaning, derelict Liberalism it represented, had no place for him, or he for it. On our way home in the evening, we looked over the next day's leaders, noticing, with much hilarity, one which began: 'One is sometimes tempted to believe that the Greeks do not want a stable government,' and went on to express the hope that 'moderate men of all shades of opinion' would rally round someone or other. Thenceforth, we often spoke of 'moderate men of all shades of opinion.'

It is difficult to convey the delight, the variety, the sparkle and the immense verve of Kingsmill's talk. Merely quoting observations he made will not serve. They have to be fitted into the theme out of which they emerged, into the wealth of illustration used to embellish them, into the flow of quotations and references of which he had so seemingly inexhaustible a store. For his numerous anthologies he practically never needed to look anything up. It was all in his head, and he could prepare one (as I have known him do) in a matter of ten days, and without reference to any library other than his own few shelves of books.

To me, his talk was, and remains, one of the greatest pleasures I have ever experienced. It was not only that he talked himself; he stimulated talk in others. No one was ever less oracular than he, or more ready to listen and be amused. He made one feel mentally alive as no one else I have ever met has. He raised one up to his own level. To this day there is not one book I spoke with Kingsmill about whose pages do not still glow with his memory. Once, when we were in the British Museum (a place we both loathed, and which I have never entered since his death), we overheard one of the uniformed attendants ask another where so-and-so was. 'He's in the Illuminated,' was the reply. Kingsmill took one into the Illuminated. In a sane world he would have been a don; but then, in a world as sane as that, there would be no need for universities as we know them. The teachers I had at school and Cambridge were derisory, and made no impact whatsoever. I forgot them at once and everything they taught. It was from Kingsmill I learnt that the pursuit of understanding is so enthralling that all others seem, by comparison, lustreless; that, as he so often quoted, all the world's in a grain of sand, and ecstasy lies in holding it up to catch the light.

Kingsmill's visit to Manchester was entirely dedicated to talk. He had lately come out of hospital, where he underwent some minor operation, and dilated upon how happy he had been, looked after by amiable nurses, and secure against any demands, personal or monetary, from the outside world. He liked whatever shut him off from the business and noise of life, and provided a lull for him to meditate and take his ease. Thus, nothing pleased him more than to settle into a first-class railway carriage with a long journey before him. This indulgence was permissible as long as he could procure a free pass from the travel agency founded by his father, Sir Henry Lunn. When that got into difficulties his railway travelling was correspondingly curtailed. Even his time in captivity in the 1914-18 war had in retrospect a pleasant glow. He used to say that it would have been perfect if he could have drawn on it from time to time as required, instead of having to take it in a lump sum.

While he was with me in Manchester, Kingsmill had some notion that Hesketh Pearson, then a professional actor, would pass through Salford on his way back to London from Glasgow, where he had been appearing. We spent an agreeable Sunday morning walking up and down the platform of Salford Station; not among the world's beauty spots, but to me, then, in the new enchantment of Kingsmill's company, delectable enough. Pearson, I need scarcely say, did not appear. Nor, as I subsequently learnt from him, was there any particular reason to suppose that he would. Kingsmill's congenital impracticability derived from an engrained habit of entertaining the, in his eyes, eminently reasonable assumption that whatever he thought desirable was bound to happen. Nor did he ever cease to be surprised and hurt when this assumption proved unfounded. Even so, in retrospect I see our fruitless vigil on Salford Station as holding a promise of the many happy hours that the three of us were to pass together.

The next time I saw Kingsmill was in Hastings, where he was living in a wooden house called The Old Mill, on a hill overlooking the town and the sea. He had returned to England from a sojourn in Thonon-les-Bain to, as he said, face his creditors. Having taken this honourable and courageous action, he went on, it was preposterous to expect him to carry matters further and pay them. He had a deep love of Hastings which lasted to the end of his life and which I came to share. His father, in the mysterious operation of his enterprises, had acquired control of the Albany Hotel there. When he was young, Kingsmill lived in it, relatively free from financial and other cares. It was, perhaps, the memory of these youthful times which endeared the place to him. The Albany was an old-fashioned establishment, patronised by an elderly, and often decrepit, clientele. Kingsmill described them once, with some acerbity, as excrement living on increment. In the 1939-45 war it was first evacuated, and then received a direct hit which has totally obliterated it.

It was in the five years before 1939 that I saw most of Kingsmill. He was still living in Hastings, but in a larger, more solid house in Laton Road, and I was living in the village of Whatlington, some seven miles away. We met frequently; Pearson came often to stay with one or other of us, or in the

George at Battle. Brian Lunn was also residing in Hastings with his two children, in a house built, and formerly occupied, by a monumental mason. Half-finished tombstones lay about the garden, and the interior arrangements had a vaguely funereal aspect. The lady who conducted the household was named Mrs. Pitcher; the widow of a petty officer in the navy, sharp-tongued and somewhat bizarre in appearance, in the style of a pantomime dame, but kind-hearted and capable. Brian, with his wide expanse of rubicund face, and of equally rubicund bald pate, was a familiar figure in Hastings, as, wearing the late Petty Officer Pitcher's white shorts, he made his way to the sea in all weathers for a morning bathe. He provided the subject for Kingsmill's novel, *The Fall*, by, on one occasion, falling from the top of a London bus. The subsequent temporary derangements of his wits suggested to Kingsmill another Fall; this time out of the fantasy of the will and into the reality of the imagination, instead of the other way round as in the Garden of Eden. This finer shade of significance in Brian's accident was momentarily eclipsed when we visited him together in hospital. Two male attendants, who were standing by in case of violence, took the opportunity to withdraw, and Kingsmill and I looked at one another with an anxious eye across Brian's—as we hoped—recumbent body.

It seems to me now, looking back, that those summers, before the hideous chain of events from August, 1939, were full of sunshine. I saw Kingsmill most days, or had long telephone conversations with him. Either I would bicycle into Hastings, or he came out to me, taking the bus to Battle, and walking the last mile or so to Whatlington. Usually I would meet him along the way, delighted when his solid figure came into view, and he began to wave, and shout his cheerful greeting—'Hullo, old man! Hullo!' His cheerfulness, which made some shudder like an east wind, arose out of his basic attitude to life. He saw the imagination and the will locked in interminable conflict. The imagination generated love, serenity, literature, faith, laughter, understanding; the will, their opposites—in the individual, appetite for sensual satisfaction, and in the collectivity, for power. Kingsmill came to live so exclusively in the imagination that the pursuit of power, and all its ancillary imbecilities—on a broad front, ranging from Hitler to D. H. Lawrence, and taking in the various contemporary Utopians, or dawnists, as he used to call them—filled him with a kind of derisory wonder. This was one of the reasons his company was so pleasurable. He had no part in the age's grisly buffooneries. I asked him once what he did when, in the First World War, he found himself among the enemy. 'I tried to convince them that my intentions were pacific,' he replied. In an age of collectivism, all collective remedies and hopes seemed to him intrisically fallacious. As he put it in his introduction to *The Poisoned Crown*:

> What is divine in man is elusive and impalpable, and he is easily tempted to embody it in a collective form—a church, a country, a social system, a leader—so that he may realise it with less effort and serve it with more profit. Yet, as even Lincoln proved, the attempt to externalise the kingdom of heaven in a temporal shape must end in disaster. It cannot be created by charters or constitutions, nor established by arms. Those who set out for it alone will reach it together and those who seek it in company will perish by themselves.

The clarity of Kingsmill's vision, and the opposition he so amusingly and good-naturedly, but confidently, offered to prevailing trends, may have cost him the moderate popular success he humanly craved, but it also brought an inward happiness and serenity which few of his contemporaries were capable of even understanding, still less experiencing. However sour or apocalyptic one's mood, with him laughter was always lurking round the corner; above the dark clouds there was the azure sky—that sense which never can quite desert us, and which abode with Kingsmill more than with most, of the sheer blessedness of being alive. Once we stood looking down on old Hastings on a still autumn evening. From each separate chimney there came a wreath of smoke; like souls, he said, climbing up into the sky.

In the worst days of the London blitz, Kingsmill was staying in Pearson's house in St. John's Wood, and spent a lot of time listening to gramophone records of Beethoven's slow movements, to which he was greatly addicted. Pearson and his wife had moved to be near us at Whatlington, and Kingsmill's only companion was a certain Aunty Bea. She had also, by marriage, a Rumanian name which nobody seemed to know, and was a lady of somewhat unequal temper and no great physical beauty, who nonetheless got along famously with Kingsmill. This oddly assorted couple took little account of the mighty deluge of bombs, which, in Kingsmill's eyes, were just another example of the will's insanity. They made endless cups of tea, and Kingsmill addressed the running commentary on life which so delighted his friends, in their absence, to Aunty Bea. What she made of it, if anything, has never been discovered, but subsequently she always spoke appreciatively of the time she spent with Kingsmill. As she was normally of a decidedly critical temper, this was an outstanding tribute to the charm of his company.

In the first years of the war Kingsmill had various teaching jobs, which he greatly enjoyed for the work itself, and, above all, for the relative easing of his financial troubles that they provided. Money worries were his torment and certainly hastened his end. Though he was very abstemious himself, and lived modestly enough with his wife and three children, he never could seem to earn enough money to meet his expenses. There was a constant delivery of unpaid bills, solicitors' letters and other intimations of penury at his house, to the point that he hated and dreaded the post, and delighted in public holidays when none came. How often he would set off to London from Hastings under the urgent necessity to lay hands on some money and with no clear idea how to do it! On one of these occasions, seeing no alternative, he decided to approach Shaw. He found him in his sitting-room at Whitehall Court, sitting bolt upright in a chair, and looking, as Kingsmill put it, as though made of cotton-wool. On such occasions, out of shyness and distaste, Kingsmill was liable to be brutally blunt, and confine himself simply to saying in an angry tone of voice that he was in need of money. Shaw heard him out, and, without a word, reached for his cheque-book, and wrote a cheque for ten pounds. Kingsmill afterwards considered that he should have stood out for fifteen pounds. It was, in any case, a final settlement for whatever unease Shaw felt at Kingsmill's straitened circumstances compared with his own affluence. I should add that, as far as his friends were concerned, if money passed from them to him, it was invariably on their initiative, and involved no initial embarrassment or subsequent pain.

Kingsmill's inability to cope with his money requirements was part of an innate unworldliness which was not, as is so often the case, in any way affected. He never could quite reconcile himself to being a resident on earth, but rather felt himself to be a visitor, who continually marvelled at the strange sights it offered and the truly extraordinary behaviour of the natives. He would lurch against things and against people, physically and metaphorically, because his eyes and heart were set on another scene, of which his actual circumstances were but a poor image. This clumsiness, of behaviour and of disposition, was an integral part of his whole character and attitude of mind, and as such, to his intimates, most touching and lovable.

As far as his finances were concerned, matters were made worse because, up to the age of forty, he had been accustomed to a condition of relatively effortless affluence. His father took him, along with his two brothers, into the family tourist business, and as long as that throve, Kingsmill was assured of an adequate income without undue inroads upon his time and inclinations. He never could quite see why or how this agreeable arrangement should have come to an end, and was inclined, in moments of irritation with his money worries, to suppose that he had been deliberately excluded from the Lunn business. Actually the business itself, for a variety of reasons, had ceased to thrive, and there was no superflux (a word Kingsmill particularly liked, as used by King Lear when he belatedly discovered the existence of the poor:

> Take physic, pomp,
> Explore thyself to feel what wretches feel,
> That thou mayst shake the superflux to them,
> And show the heavens more just)

to be shaken in his direction. It is true that the break-up of Kingsmill's first marriage coincided with his ejection from the business. Even so, his matrimonial troubles only, at worst, hastened what would sooner or later have become inevitable anyway.

I had a faint acquaintance with Kingsmill's father, Sir

Henry Lunn, largely as a result of occasionally travelling to London in the same railway carriage. He was a tall, large man, with certain similarities to Kingsmill in his face and voice, though, physically, Kingsmill more closely resembled his mother, whom I scarcely knew at all. Sir Henry had begun his life as a Methodist missionary in India; then, as a result of organising a religious conference at Mürren, drifted into the travel business, at which for a number of years he throve. There can be no question but that he became, in the most literal sense of the world, a humbug, whose public sanctimoniousness and private eye for the main chance went ill together. Kingsmill was, of course, particularly aware of this dichotomy in his father's disposition, and reacted accordingly. Someone not connected with Sir Henry could see the funny side; as when he described to me how, having persuaded certain bishops to attend the Mürren Conference, W. T. Stead told him never to go back to curates. It was not as though, as I pointed out to him, someone had told Christ, after the conversion of St. Luke, not to go back to fishermen. Sir Henry, in the English way, sought refuge from his guilty pleasure in material prosperity by dedicating himself with increasing abandon to snobbishness. This, as Kingsmill agreed, was the only theme of true disinterestedness in his life. In the end, aptly enough, it brought about his material ruin. By providing too many peers and dons with free holidays he came near to bankrupting his business. Only the Hellenic Travellers, the Albany Hotel and his free railway pass remained from the wreck of his fortunes. He entrenched himself in these scattered positions, and held out to the end, dying at sea on a cruise, in a company which contained a sprinkling of non-paying nobility who served as bait to attract the more numerous commoners who paid.

Sir Henry, it seemed to me, had more affection and regard for Kingsmill than might have been supposed; certainly than Kingsmill himself supposed. He was constantly puzzled, however, as to why the undoubted talents, and even reputation, of this one of his three sons should bring him so little material reward. His efforts to mend Kingsmill's fortunes were unavailing, and sometimes decidedly bizarre. On one occasion, for instance, he involved Kingsmill in a project for introducing into England an operation for prostate trouble, to which he had submitted himself in Switzerland, and which had the advantage of leaving intact such sexual capacity as the patient might have. Sir Henry set about promoting the enterprise in his own inimitable way. He found a retired colonel in Budleigh Salterton who was prepared to testify to the operation's efficacy, and had leaflets printed to this effect, which were to be addressed to everyone over the age of fifty who appeared in *Who's Who* and other such works of reference. It was obviously essential that the colonel's communication, delicately hinting that his sexual prowess remained unimpaired, should have a Budleigh Salterton postmark. This Kingsmill undertook to procure. Pearson and I saw him off, but, to our subsequent regret, were not able to accompany him on his strange mission. He had a large sack of the colonel's testimonials which, when he arrived at Budleigh Salterton, he hoisted on to his back, and, staggering under the weight, made his way to the local post office. There, he announced with some understandable diffidence that he 'had a letter or two to post' and the colonel's testimonials were duly dispatched. On his return to Hastings he found one of the letters on his own doormat. It unnerved him a little, he told me subsequently, to find that, being over fifty and in *Who's Who*, he qualified as a recipient. I should perhaps add that the colonel's appeal was in vain. Some legal or professional objection to the recommended operation arose, though whether because it was considered unsound, or because it offended against Anglo-Saxon prejudice in favour of eliminating sexual pleasure whenever possible, I have no idea.

In the latter years of the war Kingsmill worked on *Punch*, and I visited him occasionally in the Bouverie Street office. The first time, as I recall, a sort of chill struck me; no doubt a premonition that I was going to be entombed there myself for five years. How often, during that five years, I regretted his absence as I struggled unavailingly with the hopeless task of making the English laugh! A more cheerful meeting-place was the office of the *New English Review*, where the amiable Miss Cast (also now, alas, dead) ministered valiantly and lovingly to Kingsmill's vagrant clerical needs during the time he was literary editor, and whence he took review copies of books to sell at an establishment nearby; a transaction for which he ever had the greatest possible respect and esteem.

His appearance was always so robust that it was difficult to believe that his health was failing. Yet there were signs. He grew tired easily, and once, when some lucrative but tedious writing assignment was proposed to him, he burst out that little time remained, and he could ill spare any of it for such work. I noticed that, as he said this, his eyes filled with tears. After his first spell in hospital, he stayed with me in Regent's Park, where I was then living. He seemed to recover, and we spent many happy hours in the park, which Kingsmill always loved because, he said, it was a gentle and restrained image of nature, which could be so turbulent and so cruel. The second time he went to hospital in Brighton was the end. Pearson and I visited him. We went separately to tire him less and make the visits more. The last time I saw him he was very weak and held my hand—an unusual thing for him, who was, by temperament, undemonstrative. He had, he said, some good news to impart; something wonderful which had come to him about our human situation. He never did manage to get it out, but nonetheless, unspoken, it has often comforted me. As I get older and approach my own end, it even seems to me that I know what he had in mind to tell me. His sense of humour remained unimpaired. One of the nurses, he told me, had remarked to the doctor that he was holding on to life like grim death. He was in a public ward, and as usual had delighted and fascinated his fellow patients. I used to ring up the hospital in anguish every morning for news of him. The last time, owing to some telephonic accident, I intruded upon two strange voices. Though I could not distinguish what they were saying, they seemed to be full of a malice and foreboding which chilled my blood. When I got through to the hospital I heard that Kingsmill was dead.

I am constantly reminded of him still—at the Kardomah Café in Fleet Street where we so often had tea at a ridiculously early hour; down Bouverie Street where the office of *Punch* is; in the Inner Temple where we so often strolled; in Whitehall Court (which Kingsmill said looked like a little Kremlin in the sunshine) which was a constant meeting-place; in

Harley Street where we once went in the very early morning
and stood outside Hallam's house, remembering Tennyson's
lines about the noise of life beginning again:

> And ghastly through the drizzling rain
> The noise of life begins again,
> On the bald street breaks the blank day;

in Charing Cross Station where we often took the train
to Hastings together; above all, in the Silence Room at the
Authors' Club where his voice would boom a delighted
welcome. 'Balmy breezes are blowing in from the sea outside,'
he wrote from hospital in a letter just before he died, 'and
all past springs revive, but I hope that this decaying old husk
will release me at not too long a date to recover all the
beauty of those old days in some other form.' His hope,
I am sure, was not in vain.

The Fabians

There has long been a need to supplement and bring up to
date Edward Pease's somewhat dry and guarded *History of
the Fabian Society*, first published in 1916. Mrs. Margaret
Cole was an obvious person to undertake the task. Her *Story
of Fabian Socialism* is a notable achievement—vivacious,
packed with information, and leading one painlessly through
the various ideological disputes which the Society inevitably
encountered. She writes as a participant rather than an on-
looker, and has known personally, often intimately, most of
the leading figures concerned. She and her husband, the late
G. D. H. Cole, bridged the two phases of Fabianism—from the
original audacious take-over bid to participation in the management of the resultant Welfare State.

Her difficulty has obviously been an excess of material.
Her own memories and her own and her husband's writings,
a multitude of relevant memoirs, biographies and autobiographies. Mrs. Webb's superb Diaries covering almost the
whole period, the Society's records and enormous output,
and the contribution of individual Fabians like Shaw and
the Webbs whose pens were never still—the documentation

is overwhelming, and to contain as much as she has in a single volume was a remarkable feat of compression.

Then there are the Fabians themselves, a bizarre and fascinating company, who set themselves certain defined aims, and to a quite extraordinary degree achieved them. Mrs. Cole would be less than human if she had not at times allowed herself to be deflected from the Society and its works into a consideration of the curious assortment of characters who founded and directed it. All the elements for an excellent musical comedy are present in this earnest tale of righteous endeavour. Perhaps one day we shall have it, with Shaw in the title role, and with Hubert Bland and Wells as the two wicked seducer-uncles, Mrs. Besant as the *femme fatale,* and the Webbs riding on to the stage on a bicycle made for two.

I was brought up to regard the Fabians with awe. This was in the days of their obscurity, before they all became peers and professors and Privy Counsellors. When one or other of them came to lecture in Croydon, a visit to our little suburban house would usually be included. These were golden days for my father. To him the Fabians were the fine flower of mankind, and he treasured every remark they made, every little idiosyncrasy of behaviour, as Sir Walter Scott did the wine-glass out of which George IV had drunk. Even though they might be inclined to condescend (when I married her niece, Mrs. Webb wrote of my father, in a letter to her sister, my mother-in-law, that he was 'a very worthy person, though of modest means'), in his eyes they could do no wrong. This was not just because he agreed with them, and was wholly in favour of what they were trying to bring about. He venerated them for their learning and intelligence, for their mental self-assurance, and even, with an oblique kind of snobbishness, for their seeming aloofness from the plodding self-education and tedious wage-earning in which he was perforce engaged. His hope for me, alas disappointed, was that I might one day be like them.

This adulatory attitude, inculcated in childhood, did not survive a closer acquaintance with the Fabians and their activities. I thought I detected in them faults of arrogance and complacency, and even a certain inherent absurdity in their whole attitude of mind and behaviour. They did not conform at all to my romantic notions of what revolutionaries were like. Those talks at Passfield Corner, with Mrs. Webb standing and warming herself in front of the fire, and Sidney perched on a chair with his little legs not quite touching the ground, and the dog Sandy cavorting on the hearthrug! They were so sure about everything; so confident that they knew exactly what was required to set everything and everyone to rights. When the Webbs went to visit Trotsky, exiled on the Island of Prinkipo, Mrs. Webb was fond of relating, Trotsky had remarked that a bloody revolution might well be necessary even in England. 'We told him, "No!",' she had retorted. They had a way of thus pronouncing yea or nay with oracular finality.

The Coles, of course, as Mrs. Cole relates with gusto, started off very much in opposition to the Webbs and the Fabian Old Gang. Her first encounter with Mrs. Webb was far from being mutually satisfactory. Mrs. Webb, as a matter of fact, had an instinctive antipathy to other females who achieved intellectual or political distinction. This was for males, and females (apart from herself) should confine themselves to participating in the reflected glory of masculine brilliance. 'If you could have been the beloved of the dozen ablest men you have known,' she wrote in her Diary, significantly after finishing one of Wells's novels, 'it would have greatly extended your knowledge of human nature and of human affairs.' Other women have had the same idea, but expressed it rather differently. Mrs. Webb, in any case, felt that the 'perturbation caused by such intimacies' would have deprived her of the possibility of benefiting from them in terms of increased knowledge. She may well have been right.

Even so, looking back, Mrs. Cole is rightly disposed to dwell upon the great gifts and achievements of the Fabians. As she said to me once, long ago, of Mrs. Webb: 'We shall never look upon her like again.' Nor shall we. I really liked her very much, particularly the malicious, gossipy side of her. She would tell one the most outrageous things, with great glee, about Ramsay MacDonald and other eminent associates. The unpublished portions of her Diary are, I am sure, full of such treasures, one day to be enjoyed.

On the occasion of the interment of the Webbs in Westminster Abbey, the then Prime Minister, Mr. Attlee, remarked that everything the Fabians had striven and worked for had come to pass. It was, if one came to think about it, a curious observation. The world was in a condition of confusion and prostration unknown for centuries—infested with displaced persons, heaped with rubble, and, as a result of the discovery of atomic fission, confronted, for the first time in its history, with the possibility of its own extinction. Clearly, it was not these sombre circumstances that Mr. Attlee had in mind as having been worked and striven for by the Fabians. He meant himself and the social legislation his Government had introduced. Yet the one could scarcely be admired without reference to the other. It is the disparity between the Fabian achievement and the world setting in which it came to pass that has tended to detract from its impressiveness in contemporary eyes. Admiration for a tasteful window-box display is diminished if the building incorporating it happens to be on fire.

The Fabians were necessarily creatures of their time, and took for granted the existing power systems, particularly the British Empire. This was why some of them, as Mrs. Cole recalls, warmly supported the Boer War. 'The world,' Shaw insisted, 'is to the big and powerful by necessity; and the little ones must come within their borders or be crushed out of existence.' It was a decidedly totalitarian view, but he at least was perfectly consistent in holding it. He warmly approved of Mussolini and Hitler, and particularly Stalin, whom he considered to be one of nature's Fabians, and a perfect exponent of the inevitability of gradualness. The Webbs, too, when they were in the Far East, found the efficient Japanese greatly to their taste, and despised the disorderly Chinese. Again, having abominated the Soviet régime in its early revolutionary phases, they, as they put it, fell in love with its Stalinist version because it was strong, narrowly dogmatic and bureaucratic. Even the terrorism was not wholly displeasing. How the Webbs stand in the U.S.S.R. now, in the light of the present attitude to Stalin's rule, it is difficult to say. The new bosses can scarcely expect us to follow their example, and have the Webbs removed from the Abbey as their hero, Stalin, has been removed from his mausoleum in the Red Square.

This unquestioned acceptance of the validity of power was, it seems to me, the Founding Fabians' basic fallacy.

On the one hand, they supposed that Britannia would obligingly continue to rule the waves while they quietly and methodically set about adjusting arrangements at home to their satisfaction. On the other, they were ready to accept the pretensions of any power-maniac who purported to share their aims. As Anne Freemantle writes in *This Little Band of Prophets*, for the Fabians power 'was as beneficial as electricity.' The only thing that mattered was to get a hand on the switch, and to this end they bent all their efforts. The possibility of a power cut or short-circuit never seemed to occur to them; still less that the current, instead of bathing mankind in a glow of carefully adjusted benevolence, might burn the very earth to a cinder.

Miss Freemantle's volume, an American paperback, provides a useful addition to Mrs. Cole's. It is inclined to be meandering and naïve, but nonetheless can be dredged for valuable material conscientiously assembled. In the case of the famous Wells row, for instance, Miss Freemantle provides details about its amorous aspects which are lacking in *The Story of Fabian Socialism*. Wells described what happened, from his own point of view, in *Ann Veronica*, and took his revenge on the Webbs by his portrayal of them, as the Baileys, in *The New Machiavelli*. His irregular conduct, in word and deed, led, as I have heard, to a motion being proposed and carried at a Fabian meeting that 'Mr. Wells is a cad.' Again, the character of Bland, the Frank Harris of the outfit, emerges with greater clarity at Miss Freemantle's hands than at Mrs. Cole's. To me, he has always seemed an inexhaustibly fascinating figure who really deserves a whole biography on his own—as he put it himself, 'a student, an expert in illicit love,' and as Sir Robert Ensor somewhat priggishly put it, 'a scamp clothed in a frock-coat, striped trousers and monocle who preyed on his wife while having relations with other women.' Through it all he remained a sedate pillar of the Society.

It is sometimes assumed that the Fabians ended with Shaw and the Webbs, as they began with them. This, as Mrs. Cole shows, is far from being the case. Largely due to the efforts of the Coles, the Society was reactivated, and remains a going concern, with useful Colonial and International Bureaux, as well as its normal activities of organising summer schools, bringing out pamphlets, and permeating whatever and whoever, friend or foe, seems worthy of permeation. A volume of New Fabian Essays, edited by R. H. S. Crossman, if it could not be expected to have the impact of the original one, still aroused much interest and discussion.

How history will judge the Fabians is difficult now to decide. Will they seem to posterity to represent a spirited but forlorn effort to repair a way of life which was anyway doomed to extinction? Of pioneers who truly found an answer to the problem of resolving and humanising twentieth-century social and economic conflicts? Was it a blueprint they devised or a petition in bankruptcy? Were they the first élite in a new series or the last in an old one? In any case, they will surely never be forgotten, both because of what they were and of what they achieved.

The Queen and I

Some years ago I wrote an article in the *Saturday Evening Post* on the English Monarchy. It aroused, at the time, a good deal of controversy and abuse, and even now I am occasionally asked whether I think Princess Margaret ought to have married Group-Captain Townsend, or whether the Duke of Edinburgh is a good husband, as though I were some kind of expert on such questions. This is far from being the case. My knowledge of the Royal Family is confined to what appears about them in newspapers and magazines. Since I read little of this vast, and, to me, nauseating outpouring of printed matter, and am, in any case, sceptical about the authenticity of a great deal of it, I may be said to be more meagrely informed on the subject than are most of my fellow-citizens, who tend to read it all avidly and credulously. Even so, having, at a journalistic chance, been pitch-forked into the subject, with consequences quite unforeseen at the time, I find myself continuing to brood intermittently on it.

The deadly solemnity with which my article was received, and the furious indignation it generated, made me feel that the Monarchy, at any rate as a social phenomenon, deserved to be taken more seriously than I had previously supposed. Nothing is more illustrative of the true nature of society than a brush, such as I perforce had, with its manipulators. One sees then, in terms of a personal experience, how Lenin's famous axiom—who whom?—really works. The actual flywheels and pistons are discerned beneath the machine's quiet, reassuring hum. It is like the difference between being a prison visitor and doing a stretch oneself.

At one point, I went to see an eminent lawyer to consult him as to whether an action for libel lay in the distorted newspaper accounts of what I had actually written about the Monarchy, and in the offensive and professionally damaging comment based thereon. Of course there had been libel, he said, pacing up and down his office, but I must never forget that, in view of the circumstances, and the particular matter at issue, I could not count upon a jury or a judge taking an unprejudiced view. It was eerie, and a little alarming, to have the theory of 'People's' justice, as administered in Communist countries, thus expounded by this Dickensian figure— winged collar, dark suit, liability to press his fingertips together—in the antique quiet and tranquillity of one of London's Inns of Court.

Before I became a delinquent, my natural impulse was to regard the Monarchy as essentially comical. With all the appurtenances of supreme authority, as crown, throne, regal address, the Monarch has come to exercise none. Any rural district counsellor, in practice, has more say in the conduct of public affairs. On those frail shoulders rests the burden of an empire, one of the more ponderous and high-minded commentators like Mr. Dimbleby was liable to remark at the time of the present Queen's coronation. One might as well say of Miss Barbara Hutton that on her frail, or not so frail, shoulders rests the burden of Woolworth's. There is no Empire, but only a holding company—the Commonwealth —set up to dispose of its dwindling residual assets, on whose managerial board the Queen does not sit, though she has inherited a sizeable block of non-voting shares. This is an essentially humorous situation, which a Jonathan Swift or a Mark Twain would have known how to handle. It is a traditional music-hall joke, in which pretension and actuality are grotesquely at variance. Courtiers back respectfully away from a Royal presence which can neither harm nor, appreciably, benefit them; ladies drop creaking curtsies to an image of authority which history has rendered ineffectual and irrelevant.

Even obsequiousness and sycophancy, to have reality, must be directed towards some end. The captain who officiously helps his brigadier on with his overcoat hopes to become a major. The salaried underling who hurries forward to settle a millionaire into his Rolls-Royce hopes to steer some of the other's wealth in his direction. The gigolo who declares passionate love to a wizened heiress hopes to participate in her affluence. If the brigadier disposes of no patronage, the millionaire of no surplus cash, and the heiress cannot be led to the altar, these acts become merely derisory. Nonetheless, it is an indubitable fact that the Monarchy, in its contemporary version, has attracted more adulation, not less, with the extinction of its power and authority. Ostensibly at any rate, it is most beloved when it is most futile. Kings who claimed to rule by Divine Right were indifferent as to whether or not they were popular with their subjects. Divine approbation sufficed. Henry VIII would have seen no point in consulting Dr. Gallup had that worthy been functioning in Tudor times. Subsequent Hanoverian monarchs were too bestial in their ways, and exorbitant in their financial requirements, even to envisage the possibility of attracting the people's love. It was the people's cash they wanted. Now that the Royal family's sole responsibility is to present an image of domestic felicity, to flap a hand and flash a gleaming smile at the adoring multitude, they have become as sought after, crowded round, gazed upon, and generally adulated as any film star.

It might plausibly have been supposed that, as the English social structure became more theoretically equalitarian, the status of hereditary authority would decline. This has happened in, for instance, the case of the House of Lords, which, precisely because it has been deprived of all effective legislative power, no longer commands any respect, or even interest. Its proceedings are seldom reported in the popular press, and then only when a peer chances to make some eccentric pronouncement on matters like adultery or sodomy, which are inherently newsworthy. Other hereditary offices, such as Lord-Lieutenancies of Counties, have become almost totally forgotten. Incumbents are appointed to them as they fall vacant, but their names make little impact outside the columns of *The Times,* that Forest Lawn of expiring authority, where defunct offices and officers are interred, to the notes of sonorous background music, and encased in asbestos platitudes to ensure everlasting preservation. All the more curious is it, therefore, that the Monarchy should have undergone a quite contrary development, becoming, as it shed its power, ever more popular, and the subject of an ever more rapacious curiosity.

A constitutional monarchy, as such, has much to recommend it. The case for one is presented cogently and impressively by Walter Bagehot in his classic essay on the subject. As he points out, a State requires a Head, who can communicate with, and receive, other Heads of State, and generally provide a focus for the mystique, as distinct from the exercise, of government. There are decided advantages in making this Headship of State hereditary and Royal rather than elective, and so liable to be hitched on to the unedifying gravy-train of universal suffrage politics. The essential feature of a constitutional monarchy, however, is that it should be completely subservient to the legislature. If, as Bagehot graphically puts it, the legislature were to pass a bill for the Monarch's execution, he or she would be bound to sign it or abdicate. Incidentally, I was imprudent enough to quote from Bagehot in this sense, thereby calling down on my head particularly vehement accusations of being scandalous and seditious. There can be little doubt that a popular English newspaper which serialised Bagehot's Essay (still, very properly, used as a text-book for history students at state schools and universities) would thereby bring itself into public odium.

In the light of the undoubted advantages of a constitutional monarchy, its adoption in the United States deserves consideration. President Eisenhower, for instance, would have made an impeccable constitutional monarch. It is interesting, in this connection, that, on first taking office, he publicly stated that he saw the functions of the Presidency in such a light. His lack of interest in government, which laid him open to criticism as a President, would have been a virtue in a constitutional monarch. As for his addiction to golf—when I think of the relaxations of some of our past English sovereigns, this one seems innocuous, if not positively praiseworthy. The chance for an Eisenhower Dynasty would seem to have passed. We shall never now, alas, see on the stage of history King Ike I, or better, in view of America's greatly increased power and extended responsibilities throughout the world, the Emperor Ike. Perhaps the Kennedy line, richly endowed as it is with heirs and successors, may yet find its way into the *Almanach de Gotha* and the Book of Common Prayer.

The abusive letters and telephone calls, and other public and private insults evoked by my, as I fondly supposed, sensible and amiable observations on the Monarchy, reflected a state of mind which I could not but regard as morbid and potentially dangerous. What, I asked myself, was the explanation? How did it come about that English people, who, in the ordinary way, are sane, humorous and easy-going, should, on so trivial a pretext, behave like a Jew-baiting Nazi mob? It is, of course, possible, and even probable, that the actual numbers involved were much fewer than might have appeared. The abusive letters, though largely illiterate, suggested, by their notepaper and manner of address, rather genteel than proletarian origins. The voices which screamed insults down my telephone had about them likewise a faint flavour of gentility. An anonymous correspondent who wrote to my wife rejoicing that our youngest child had been killed in a ski-ing accident was able to type, and even, approximately, to spell. It was in clubs, expensive restaurants and first-class railway carriages that I was made to feel uncomfortable rather than in omnibuses and pubs.

In these days of mass communications, it is next to impossible to tell how far what purport to be manifestations of popular emotion are authentic or contrived. The Press may be unanimous, but it is controlled, to a great extent, by a handful of not particularly edifying individuals. Similarly, radio and television. The so-called Press Council, which in England is supposed to uphold high standards of journalism, is a stuffed shirt affair. Its members, to adapt a famous line of Dryden's, for knighthoods will cry whore to their own

mother. When, from time to time, they administer ponderous
and self-righteous rebukes to individual journalists and newspapers, I am always reminded of how Mr. Winkle, having
got involved in a fracas along with the rest of the Pickwick
Club, was seen to take off his coat and begin belabouring
a small boy. It did not surprise me, therefore, that, far from
providing any redress when I found myself in the stocks, they
joined the caterwaulers. We shall never be able to differen-
tiate, nor will posterity, between our true hopes and desires,
and those implanted in us or attributed to us. My own conclusion, drawn from this experience of momentarily interfering with the propagation of the legend of popular monarchy,
is that only a specialised few invest authentic passion in such
legends. The rest are swept along on a tidal wave of sub-
liminal, stereoscopic emotion. Skilled and numerically insignificant cheer-leaders know how to produce and manipulate
the Voice of the People, while still righteously insisting that
it is the Voice of God. Government by hysteria, unhappily,
can easily be identified with government by popular acclaim.
In the Country of the Blind he who can see is King, and
in the Country of the Dumb, he who can make himself heard.

However few or many, with conscious purpose, participate
in the legend of popular monarchy, there can be no question
about the efficiency and efficacy with which the legend is promoted and sustained. It goes from strength to strength. No
fatuity is too oleaginous to serve its purpose. The spotlight
which shines upon the Royal family grows ever brighter.
Their doings, their comings and goings, are ever more minutely
examined and displayed. A legend which can incoroprate
Mr. Anthony Armstrong-Jones, not to mention his former
friends and associates, as this one has with notable success,
is strong indeed. It is true that, in the interminable expound-
ing of the legend, there is noticeable, from time to time, a
decided undertow of irritation and malice. The most practised hands, constantly spelling out the same story, filling the
same frames with the same pictures for the same strip, grow
weary and sullen. Even so, the Monarchy's popularity rating
has never been higher, Gossip-writers cannot have enough
of it. Pulp magazines thirst for it as the hart after the water-
brook. For photographers it is Midas-treasure. Leader-writers
and sonorous B.B.C. voices intone its rubric on all possible

occasions. The characters may be few and ordinary, and in themselves of limited interest; the script may be repetitive, undergoing only occasional and minor variations; but the show remains triumphantly at the top of the Top Ten. Even in Mr. Ned Sherrin's successive versions of a late night satirical show the Monarchy proved a favourite theme. The obsession is operative even in reverse.

Part of the explanation of this is to be found in the intensification of snobbishness which, surprisingly, has accompanied the transformation of England into a Welfare State. Never have class divisions been so acute and anguished as since they were, theoretically, abolished. The nerves of class consciousness have been made raw and inflamed by the administration of what purported to be a sedative. Instead of a cure for this collective asthmatic condition being affected, new and virulent allergies have been set up. The rich man in his castle, the poor man at his gate, were, at one time, according to the well-known hymn, expected to take for granted one another's due estate. This was, admittedly, easier for the former than the latter, but such was the accepted arrangement. Now, death duties and supertax have forced the rich man to turn over his castle to the National Trust. The castle gate is open, on payment of a small fee, to all poor men who care to enter it, as many do, examining with eager curiosity the furnishings, the sanitation, the pictures and the *objets d'art*, if any. Class infiltration has taken place on a vast scale, but has only served to exacerbate class-consciousnes. Equalitarianism, preached by the Labour Party, and put into effect through legislative and fiscal measures, has produced an unprecedented sense of social inequality. The sheep have leapt out of their pens in search of better pasture, leaving the unhappy shepherds, who first opened these vistas to them, with a dwindling flock, and looking decidedly silly.

Public schools which once counted their waiting lists in scores now count them in hundreds. The fees go merrily up, and so do the numbers of those seeking entry. Peers may be, as legislators, at a heavy discount, but, socially they are booming. Their marriages and divorces, their travels and real estate deals, their feasting and their fasting, are eagerly reported. In the days when Dukes of Bedford appeared in history books, they never had anything like the showing

I

the present Duke gets on television when he opens a nudist camp in his ancestral seat, or joins Mr. Perry Como on a merry-go-round. Everyone wants to speak like a B.B.C. announcer, to dress like the Windsors; to experience, if only through the lush prose of women's magazine fiction, the sense of being socially superior. How ironical, and yet how like life, that that universal yearning should have come to pass, not as a result of insistence on the sanctity of class divisions, but as a result of an alleged passion to abolish them!

The social mountaineers, setting forth with their nailed boots and climbing equipment, doggedly essaying now this peak, now that, see in the distant mists an ultimate summit—the Monarchy. This is the pinnacle, not, indeed, ever to be climbed by them, majestically unattainable, but endowing their puny endeavours with validity. If there were no Everest, who would bother with Box Hill? Keeping up with the Joneses is glorified because of Armstrong-Jones. I remember, years ago, seeing in some Soviet museum a picture from Czarist times, showing God in his Heaven beaming down radiance on the Czar and his family, who in turn beamed down radiance on an ecclesiastical dignitary, who in turn beamed down radiance on a mujik and his family. A contemporary English version would show arc-lamps as the source of the original radiance, with this being passed on from crown to coronet to bowler hat to homburg to cloth cap. The Bolsheviks attacked the Czarist social mystique from the top downwards. They abolished God, and butchered the Imperial family in a cellar, thereby disposing of the legend of the Little Father for ever. The Labour Party made a feeble and confused assault on our English social mystique from the bottom upwards. It has proved a ludicrous failure, leaving what they sought to destroy to flourish and proliferate as never before.

The Monarchy, then, in that Snobcracy into which the Welfare State, contrary to the ostensible wishes and expectations of its founders and promoters, has transformed itself, provides a distant and alluring horizon. It has, also, at least in some minds, a more practical function. When the social fabric rattles from the deep reverberations of our time, and the winds of change howl and shriek in the outside darkness, it is comforting to feel that in our old English homestead we have one truly stable element, the Throne; one truly beloved figure, the Monarch. In Victorian times industrialists managed to persuade themselves that they were held in high regard by their employees, landowners that they were venerated by their tenants. Such fantasies have long ago been laid aside. Profitable, and possibly socially beneficial speculative enterprises like take-over bids, it is recognised, find little popular favour; landlords, of whatever variety, are not the recipients of affectionate glances and hearty greetings as they look over their building-lots or latest block of flats; a banker or stockbroker or director may be a prince of good fellows in his club, but well knows that his public appearances are unlikely to be spontaneously applauded.

How reassuring, then, for such persons, that the Throne should be authentically popular! The public esteem and affection in which it is held provides collateral against which they can increase their own already heavy overdrafts on their popularity accounts. Small wonder that the Stock Exchange roof is shaken when the brokers, stiff as ramrods, sing the National Anthem. Company directors, over their third expense-account brandy, are liable to shed a loyal tear; real estate, oil and insurance men drink the loyal toast with full-hearted and full-throated ease; Generals and General Electric, Their Graces, Their Excellencies, Their Worships, Honourables and Right Honourables, all likewise lift up their glasses, and their hearts with them, to the Queen. God bless her! In green rooms and board rooms alike, in episcopal palaces, palace grills and palais de dances, wherever two or three are gathered together for whom the Garter, the Thistle, and even the humble O.B.E., are crocks of gold at the rainbow's end, there shall loyalty be found.

In the poker game of politics the Monarchy is regarded as an ace, to be held in reserve, and only played if there are dangerous depredations on the bank. This doubtless accounts for the esteem in which it has lately come to be held in what *Pravda* and *Izvestia* call 'ruling circles' in the United States. There was a time when the Hearst and Luce publications, not to mention the *Chicago Tribune*, were little disposed to venerate the Court of St. James. Now it is very different. The subjects King George III lost crowd eagerly around Queen Elizabeth II. Crawfie goes down as well in Birmingham,

Alabama, as in Birmingham, England, and a coronation is as unctuously presented by American television networks as by the B.B.C. itself.

Shortly after the appearance of my article on the Monarchy, Mr. Mike Wallace invited me over to New York to be interviewed by him on the subject. He kindly accommodated me in his house. While we were sitting chatting together, there was a long-distance telephone call from California. As Mr. Wallace found himself, when he picked up the receiver, getting involved in a long and obviously acrimonious conversation, he thoughtfully motioned me to listen in on an available telephone extension, which I cheerfully did. The voice I heard (belonging, as I subsequently learned, to one of the chief executives of the TV network for which Mr. Wallace then worked) was raucous and deeply perturbed as it rebuked Mr. Wallace for interviewing me at all, and appealed to him, if the interview must take place, not to be 'soft' with me.

'Don't you realise,' it said, in a final effort at persuasion, 'that this Queen is the only bulwark against Communism?'

I should add that Mr. Wallace persisted sturdily with our interview, though, presumably out of deference to the anxieties of his employers, it was not transmitted to Washington, where the Queen and Duke of Edinburgh were then staying.

The Founding Fathers of the American Republic would surely have been surprised, and perhaps amazed by the perturbation of Mr. Wallace's caller from California. They would scarcely have expected one of their Republic's more substantial citizens to regard an English sovereign as the mainstay of freedom and the American way of life. In the Kremlin, too, I can imagine a hilarious reaction. Among the Soviet Bosses' preoccupations, as they labour to make the world safe for Communism, it is difficult to believe that the English Monarchy looms very large. If this ace were ever to be played, they must legitimately have calculated, it would assuredly turn out to be a two of clubs.

Such considerations, however, are far from the minds of the crowds who throng the streets when a Royal car is going by, of the readers of *Women's Own* or *Woman's Realm* avid for details of Princess Margaret's home life or the Duke of Edinburgh's latest quips; of the loiterers outside Bucking-

ham Palace staring through the railings at all times and in
all weathers irrespective of whether or not the Queen is in
residence, in the vague expectation that something will
happen, someone will appear. What impels them? What are
they after? To see a vision of themselves transfigured? To
commune with majesty in their own lineaments? To participate, however remotely, in the glitter of a palace and the
splendour of a throne? Their faces wear the anonymous rapture of televiewers. Like a strip-tease audience, their ecstasy
lies in seeming to possess what is inexorably beyond their
reach. They see through a glass coach darkly. They are kings
and queens, not even for a day; just for a passing moment.

Monarchy, for them, is part of the mystique of our time,
which is itself a kind of Caliban's dream, full of sound and
sweet airs, so that, like this strangest and last of Shakespeare's
creations, when we wake we cry to sleep again. The dream
passes across television screens, is recounted in print and
spoken through microphones and written in neon lights, shines
forth in chromium fittings, speeds along majestic highways,
climbs into the sky in gleaming, mountainous buildings, is jet-
propelled through space and rocketed into the very stratosphere, where it twinkles and orbits among the stars.

What a dream it is! And yet, how perilous! Suetonius
describes how the last Roman Emperors insisted on being worshipped as gods. As their earthly pretensions became more
unconvincing, they were the more insistent on their divine ones.
Their kingdom was shrinking to almost nothing, the barbarians
were closing in, but a debauched and sycophantic Roman
population was still induced, and required, to accord them
divine honours, and mouth empty praises of their virtue and
valour. Let us beware that a like fate does not overwhelm us.
We, too, are well endowed with bread, along with much other
affluence. We, too, have circuses, piped into our homes, astutely
and persistently whispered into our ears, to reach the deepest
recesses of our unconscious minds. We even have a Britannic
Majesty, presiding over a non-existent Empire, and so ingeniously spotlighted and produced as to reduce the wide
world's dangerous and thronging stage to this small dimension.

I first met C. P. Snow (later, Sir Charles Snow, and now Lord Snow of Leicester) some thirty-five years ago in Manchester. As I recall him in those days, he was a large, red-haired, rather wistful-looking but still resolute man of about my own age. I was then twenty-seven. It emerged in the course of our conversation over tea that he was poised between being a writer and a scientist; had already written a thriller or so, but, I had the impression, leaned then in the direction of science. How good a scientist he was, I had, of course, no means of knowing. Nor, for that matter, have I now.

An impression that stayed with me was of a worldly man. Worldliness is, by its nature, a highly romantic attitude; only mystics know how to be sceptical. Snow, I felt, was romantically worldly. Though, politically, he belonged to the Left (at that time, I should suppose, the fairly extreme Left), things like money and social eminence and success held great allure for him. My own romanticism (a late-Victorian throwback) was the converse of his. Success, I had convinced myself, was the hallmark of failure; the rich could only be contemptible, and what was worse, bores. Thus, the idea of an ostensible intellectual like Snow wanting to be rich and successful struck me as bizarre, if not reprehensible.

Actually, as I see now, romantic worldliness like his is a great promoter of success in the field of action, though inimical to any other than the most mediocre achievement in the field of the imagination. The mists of desire obscure life's landscape, whether to portray, describe or understand it; they facilitate its conquest. Thus, Napoleon had so romantic a notion of the glories and delights of power that he was able to grab it, in the same way that a greedy child grabs the best cakes. He took so glamorised a view of the thrones of Europe that he was able to overturn them, and then stand them up again to accommodate his repulsive Corsican relatives.

262

Similarly with a certain type of literature. For instance, Stendhal's novels derive much of their driving force from his abject and ridiculous romanticism about being distinguished and important. One can trace the same thing, in a rather different way, in Proust. Snow is no Stendhal certainly. Still less is he a Proust. One has, in fact, to accept Dr. Leavis's preposterous and portentous tirade against him to the extent of agreeing that Snow is a negligible writer. All the same, his great popularity in England and America, and still more in Western Europe and the U.S.S.R., may be attributed to his romantic worldliness. He is the man rubbing his nose against the plate-glass window of Vanity Fair, and telling the others who can't even get near the window what it is like inside. Pascal, a non-worldly man, said that judges and sovereigns had to be attired in elaborate regalia because otherwise the threadbare nature of their authority would be exposed. Snow, contrariwise, finds the regalia marvellous in itself, and deduces from it the reality of the authority beneath. His only authentic grouse was that he had no regalia to wear himself. Well, now, as a peer and sometime member of Harold Wilson's Labour Government, he has.

Whatever may have been his inclination all those years ago when we met in Manchester, as things have turned out he has pursued neither science nor literature, but grazed in the no-man's-land between them. It is as an academic fonctionaire that he has made his mark, his novels being a by-product. They are narrated by Lewis Eliot, who is obviously himself; a fellow of Christ's College, Cambridge; an occasional civil servant and a knight (Will he be raised to the peerage in subsequent volumes?); a scholar of sorts, and a lawyer—but he might just as well be a novelist.

The latest offering, *Corridors of Power,* is about a Tory politician, Roger Quaife, who undertakes a rather indeterminate political operation directed towards extricating the Government from its nuclear commitments. Considered as an exercise in political strategy the whole thing is quite exceptionally silly and difficult to follow. There is no particular need to try. After a series of ups and downs, Quaife is worsted, and has to resign. His downfall is assisted by an affair he has with the wife of a fellow-Conservative M.P.; described by

Snow with all the sensitivity and subtlety of an elephant pounding through a cornfield.

The dynamic of the novel, as of the series of which it is a part (there are, I gather, four more to come), lies in the lush descriptions of the alleged workings of power in England through the House of Commons and the Government, through the civil service and high-born families who use money, patronage and influence as lubricants. There are the country house week-end gatherings at Barset, Diana Skidmore's house in Hampshire; the dinner parties at the Quaifes' house in Lord North Street, Westminster, presided over by Quaife's energetic wife, Lady Caroline, or Caro as she is known to her friends, and, of course, to Lewis Eliot; encounters with Lord Lufkin, an industrialist, and Lord Houghton, or Sammikins, who 'had published a short book on Anglo-Indian relations . . . it seemed anti-Churchill, pro-Nehru and passionately pro-Gandhi.'

Poor old Sammikins! He never should have come out in the open as an admirer of the Mahatma. It got him into trouble with his family and political associates. Words cannot convey the imbecility of this vision of power as conceived in Snow's ponderous, totally humourless and endearingly innocent, or at any rate naïve, mind. To transubstantiate, as the dear old fellow has done, those moustached Westminster hostesses into divinities; to take Barset back to Trollope and Lord North Street back to Disraeli; to fabricate out of universal suffrage democracy in its, and England's, decrepitude a high drama of derring-do, a Salvation Army Agincourt—this is something that only Snow could, or would, have attempted.

Let me take, by way of illustration, a single sentence which caught my fancy. Snow mentions that 'during the winter the gossip began to swirl out from the clubs and the Whitehall corridors.' One imagines that so substantial figure; that huge moon face, unsmiling, portentous, looking across St. James's Park. Then, wetting a finger, holding it up to the wind, with an expression of great gravity: yes (head on one side), yes, sure enough he can detect a decided current of gossip swirling past him from the clubs and Whitehall corridors.

From the Athenæum, perhaps, where seedy clerics and

atrocious dons desperately wash down bad food with bad wine. Or the Carlton, home of out-moded Conservative politicians in black coats and striped trousers hoping against hope for a telephone call that never comes to summon them to be under-under parliamentary secretary at the Ministry of Nothing. Or White's whose red-faced members suck down their tenth Bloody Mary, still keeping a weather-eye open for Lord Boothby, or even Randolph Churchill. Or the Garrick, frequented by noisy lawyers, moronic actors, and American newspaper and television correspondents who manage to persuade themselves that they are consorting with the mighty in their seats. Oh, Joe, oh, Drew, come out from behind that decanter of port! I know you. As for Pratts—dear, gallant old Snow is on record as having reflected, while taking a drink in its dismal premises, how remarkable it was that he, a poor boy from a poor home, should ever have found himself in this haunt of the smart and the great. As it happens, it is the only club mentioned by name in *Corridors of Power*. So perhaps it is from Pratts that the rumours swirled.

As for the Corridors—we journalists who have paced them often and long enough in search of a story; who have visited those sad, sad knights in their ministries, looked at them across their desks; grey, listless men with black brief-cases stamped with the Royal Arms (ministerial equivalent of the air-line bag), which they take with them, to and fro, between Whitehall and their homes in Putney or Wimbledon—we just can't accept the swirling rumours. What wouldn't we have given for just one tiny swirl to take back to the office and knock out on a typewriter. The truth is that journalism unfits one for reading Snow. One's state of mind is all wrong. I give up. Those last four volumes, as far as I'm concerned, shall remain unread.

A decidedly amusing situation was created when Snow was teamed up with Frank Cousins, boss of the Transport and General Workers' Union, to look after our technology, thereby stepping out of his novels into politics. I have long held the view that power is to the collectivity what sex is to the individual. On this basis, writers like Snow obsessed with power may be compared, within their own terms of reference, with writers like D.H. Lawrence obsessed with sex. They display the same sort of seriousness; no more laughs in the corridors than in the woods when Lady Chatterley and Mellors were on the job there. They are, as it were, power-pornographers. For Snow to join a government was rather as though Lawrence had taken a job as a gamekeeper. I am personally extremely grateful to Mr. Harold Wilson for having created this diverting situation, and only wish that he would cap it by taking Dr. Leavis into his government now that Lord Snow has left it. What could Leavis be? The promised Ombudsman, perhaps. Or our first Minister of Culture.

Fanny over the counter

A very minor poet of my acquaintance, now dead and totally forgotten, used to make periodical appearances in London from the remote West Country where he lived. He was very poor, and his style of living, commoner then than now, comprised a minute cottage with a neglected garden, some shelves of books a good proportion of which were still in their dust-jackets, membership of the Wine and Food Society, a typewriter (though he cultivated an ornate hand-writing for his verses and private correspondence) and a wife. His visits to the metropolis were rare enough to be an occasion. He would arrive by the night train, a short, stumpy, rubicund man with a wide expanse of bald pate, and at once get, as he put it, lit-up, having brought with him a couple of bottles of Algerian wine in his bag for the purpose.

We used to meet, if at all, in an obscure and somewhat seedy little club to which we both belonged. One would hear with a vague disquiet his lit-up voice booming away as one entered the club and hung up one's overcoat. It was not that one wanted to shun him. On the contrary, he was rather a dear fellow. Only one knew that, in his festive mood, he would insist on telling one about the woman he was going to have that afternoon before taking the night train back to his country retreat. She would be terrific, old man—some stupendous Nordic blonde with mountainous breasts; or a black girl with sinewy thighs who would eat him up, or a Jewess from Cadiz into whose cavernous black eyes he would dive,

266

gasping for breath. He even, to show the catholicity of his tastes, spoke darkly about a clergyman's lady from his locality with whom he had assignations in a room near Paddington Station. She was, it seemed, no oil painting, but prepared to do anything, but anything, old man.

Later, when his circumstances grew increasingly penurious, and the bottles of Algerian wine required to light him up multiplied to four, or even five, his account of his projected amorous adventures became ever more strident and unconvincing. He also took to railing against his contemporaries and times. They lacked gusto and true sensuality, he claimed. The spirit of Rabelais (one of his great heroes) had disappeared from the earth, yielding place to prigs and pansies (he was very against the latter); and he cited the case of his Autobiography, which he was then ostensibly engaged in writing, and which, he said, with its eighteenth-century flavour, was bound not to please.

Actually, to the best of my knowledge, it was never put to the test. No autobiographical manuscript has come to light. He appears to have spent his last years in almost total indolence, consumed, I fear, with ill thoughts and remorse: that particular melancholia of the failed writer which is fed by contemptuous envy of successful contemporaries, who sell their tens of thousands where he has sold only his hundreds, receiving honours and rewards which he and they when young, as scruffy undergraduates and pinchbeck bohemians about town, had scornfully derided. Even on his rarer and rarer visits to London, and lit-up, the melancholia tended to persist. I caught a glimpse of him once at the club, mouth open and fast asleep, with an expression of utter lostness. When I sat down nearby he awakened with a start, at once shouted for tea, and launched off on one of his tirades about namby-pamby writers and timid publishers, only pausing to get his breath and remark with a leer that he must be off to keep an assignation. 'She's terrific, old man, terrific,' I heard him muttering as he made his way out of the club.

It was the next time I saw him, or the next but one, that he confided in me that the women he waited upon were now imaginary figures. Even the clergyman's lady had stopped coming to London and had joined the Buchmanites. 'I've no money, and I'm old,' he said with an unusual air of desperation, implying that not even his zest could compensate for deficiencies so basic: eighteenth or twentieth century, it was all one to those without money and without youth. The course he had been forced to adopt, he went on, for lit-up occasions, was to fix in his mind some bizarre erotic image, say of an Indian squaw, or of an Eskimo woman tucked sedately into a fur-lined, brocaded sleeping-bag, or of some amazing alabaster harlot in Alexandria, doe-eyed and slumberous. Then, on arriving back at his cottage late at night, tiptoeing upstairs, he would pounce upon his sleeping wife, endow her with one or other of these roles, and ravish her.

The scene, as I envisaged it, was touchingly comical: the faltering, tipsy footsteps, the fumbling hand on door-latch, and clumsy undressing; the impenetrable darkness mercifully hiding paunchy, squat figure and gargoyle face uncertainly approaching the sanctuary of bedclothes, in whose small compass all fantasies could be snugly contained, like a tiny, snug ship at anchor on a wide troubled ocean. As it happened, I had once seen his wife when visiting their part of the country. She was a grey, wispy sort of woman, indomitably cheerful, interminably embroidering with coloured wool, turning books into braille for blind readers (working on H. G. Wells's *God, the Invisible King* for some reason on the occasion that I met her—surely a case of the blind leading the blind, if ever there was one) and ever ready to type the manuscripts her husband never wrote. How she made out in her unconscious squaw, Eskimo or Alexandrian impersonation I have, of course, no idea.

This man had, or claimed to have, an extensive and varied collection of pornography on which he no doubt relied to keep the erotic fires burning. It was from him that I first heard of *Fanny Hill*, a classic in the genre, which has been a clandestine best-seller in numerous languages for some two centuries, and is now at last on free sale and setting up records on both sides of the Atlantic.

Pornography and erotic literature have always been easy to sell. To-day they are booming as perhaps never before. My deprived generation had to search for smut in the Bible, and to wade through the tedious, and often fatuous, pages of Kraft-Ebbing and Havelock Ellis in public libraries. Trembling and fearful, we looked at lewd films in some squalid Marseilles brothel, or hid a copy of Frank Harris's *My Life and Loves* in our luggage when we returned from Paris.

To-day the young, in this as in so many other respects, are pampered. The garnered erotica of the centuries is readily and cheaply available to them, including our own not inconsiderable vintage, our Bond, our Durrell, our Henry Miller and our Burroughs, all on open display, and with perfectly respectable imprints. No necessity any more for plain wrappers, for watching one's chance to make a purchase when unobserved. The young lady comes forward and packs up *The Chapman Report* or *Sex and the Single Girl* without a blush or a frown, as though one were buying Thomas à Kempis or *Sonnets from the Portuguese.*

In this plethora of riches I perhaps exaggerate the elegance and vivacity of *Fanny Hill,* described by Boswell (who, needless to say, was an avid reader of it) as 'that most licentious and enflaming book.' Maybe it is just that it has for me some evocative quality of randy adolescence as it used to be—pre-Freud, pre-Kinsey and pre-Chatterley; before the Forbidden Tree had been liberated, or the Serpent been made Regius Professor of Theology, or Eve equipped with the latest oral contraceptives. The author, John Cleland, was a needy man-of-letters of sorts, who knocked the work off at great speed under dire financial stress. He was paid twenty guineas for it, and its first publishers netted £10,000, a tidy fortune. Subsequent publishers all did well out of the book. This is very much in Fanny's vein. She liked to have money herself, and to be surrounded by people also with money, but displayed no envy or irritation that some should have more than others.

Cleland obviously had Richardson in mind, making Fanny the obverse of his Pamela who virtuously resisted her master's advances and was rewarded in the end by becoming his wife. Fanny never, as far as we know, resisted anyone's advances, but her wanton nature was rewarded, first by inheriting the fortune of an elderly, genial lover who conveniently dies, and then by marrying her first seducer and living with him happily ever after. The book is an account of her own, and some of her friends' and associates', sexual encounters. They are described with zest, but become finally somewhat monotonous, especially Fanny's eulogies of the various male organs in her life:

> That fierce erect machine of his, which threatened no less than splitting the tender victim, who lay smiling at the uplifted stroke, nor seemed to decline it.

This obsession may be due to the book's masculine authorship. Female erotica (if such there be) would be unlikely to dilate so frequently, and at such length, on the size, shape, texture and colour of the male organ. One would deduce that Cleland was rather under- than over-proof in this respect, and that he rarely achieved the perfectly simultaneous satisfaction which, in Fanny's case, he makes invariable.

Her first initiation in a brothel at the age of fifteen is as a spectator. She watches the madam and a grenadier in a gross encounter, and then is taken by her friend Phoebe to watch a more alluring one between Polly and a handsome Genoese merchant, which so excited her that she was induced to engage in some Lesbian embraces and fidgetings with Phoebe. Thenceforth she embarks on a life of sensuality as a whore, all of which is meticulously and cheerfully described. Cleland, it is clear, feels that to keep the erotic titillation going he must find some means of varying Fanny's experiences with one fierce erect machine after another. Thus, he brings her into contact with a flagellant, whose painful administrations she endures, and finally enjoys. Some of her gentlemen—for instance, Mr. Norbet—have curious tastes, which please them but leave her unsatisfied. After doing her best to gratify one such, the good work is finished off in uncomfortable circumstances by a robust sailor casually met:

> He leads me to the table and with a master-hand lays my head down on the edge of it, and, with the other canting up my petticoats and shift, bares my naked posteriors to his blind and furious guide; it forces its way between them, and I feeling pretty sensibly that it was not going by the right door, and knocking desperately at the wrong one, I told him of it: 'Pooh!' says he, 'my dear, any port in a storm.'

Fanny and one of the other girls engage in a rather heartless prank whereby a half-witted boy is excited, and proves

270

to be equipped with what Fanny calls 'a standard of distinction':

Prepared as we were to see something extraordinary, it still, out of measure, surpassed our expectation, and astonished even me, who had not been used to trade in trifles . . . It was fully manifest that he inherited, and largely too, the prerogative of majesty which distinguishes that otherwise most unfortunate condition, and gives rise to the vulgar saying 'A fool's bauble is a lady's play-fellow.' Not wholly without reason: for, generally speaking, it is in love as in war, where the longest weapon carries it. Nature, in short, had done so much for him in these parts, that she perhaps held herself acquitted in doing so little for his head.

Such is Cleland's view of a whore's general philosophy of life. It makes an agreeable contrast with, and is probably more accurate than, the Victorian obsession that whores were all wronged women, having usually been seduced by selfish men of a higher station in life who then abandoned them. They end up, for the most part, in the river. If novelists like Dickens are to be believed, whores must have been two deep on the Embankment on any foggy night waiting to jump in. Cleland gets a good deal nearer the truth, I should say, with his picture of a cheerful, sensual, indolent woman, who enjoys earning a comfortable living by doing to excess what she would do enthusiastically anyway, and who has the quality, unusual in other female avocations, of wanting to please, of being ready to fall good-humouredly in with any little peculiarities her male partners may fancy, providing, of course, due payment is made. Mr. Fernand Henriques's *Prostitution and Society* on the whole supports Cleland's conclusions. A young girl unhad for four days could command twenty guineas from an alderman, a high figure in contemporary money, but a lord who wanted 'to play a game of piquet for *titillatione mamarum* and so on, with no other object,' only had to pay five guineas.

If the Oxford Dictionary definition of pornography as 'the expression or suggestion of obscene or unchaste subjects in literature or arts' be accepted, then *Fanny Hill* without any question is pornographic. It may be doubted whether even the Bishop of Woolwich would be prepared to recommend it as conducive to happy Christian matrimony or virtuous living. In that sense, its publication must be considered a welcome event as putting an end to all the tedious moralising and hypocrisy which the contemporary passion for pornography has aroused. If *Fanny Hill* is permissible, then anything is without rounding up a lot of clerics, critics and Quakers to say with their hand on their hearts that it makes for the Good Life, as happened in the case of *Lady Chatterley's Lover*.

It may be questioned how far it is prudent to subject human beings, as is done to-day, to ceaseless stimulation. The effect is certainly not to deliver them from obsessive appetites, but rather to keep them in a permanently inflamed condition. A greedy child is not made less so by constantly turning over the coloured illustrations of a cookery book. Nor will *Fanny Hill* help schoolmasters to cure their charges of the habit of masturbating, or schoolmistresses to safeguard virginity in the upper sixth. The effect on readers will necessarily be to encourage every lascivious thought and impulse.

This is not because of the subject-matter but of the treatment; Cleland obviously set out to make an erotic appeal, and brilliantly succeeded, doubtless to his own professional satisfaction, certainly to the great financial advantage of his publisher. Rabelais, who covered some of the same ground, is not in the least erotic. One has only to compare a passage from Rabelais with any of the above quotations to detect the difference:

> For this, and other causes, the Lord Humphrey de Merville, following his king to a certain warlike expedition, whilst he was in trying upon his own person a new suit of armour, for of his old rusty harness he could make no more use, by reason that some few years since the skin of his belly was a great way removed from his kidneys; his lady thereupon, in the profound musing of a contemplative spirit, very maturely considering that he had but small care of the staff of love, and packet of marriage, seeing he did no otherwise arm that part of the body, than with links of mail, advised him to shield, fence, and gabionate it with a big tilting helmet, which she had lying in her closet, to her otherways utterly unprofitable.

Cleland's own hopes and desires are inextricably mixed up with Fanny's, whereas Rabelais had ridden triumphantly away from his on a great wave of laughter. When appetite comes in, whether of attraction like Cleland, or of revulsion like Swift, the result must be in some degree pornographic.

Thus, though Cleland writes rather like Jane Austen, *Fanny Hill* is markedly inferior to *Emma*; though his views of life may be compared with Fielding's, it is also markedly inferior to *Tom Jones*, and though there is a certain comedy in Fanny's attitude to her occupation and clientele, she cannot be compared with Mistress Quickly. In these circumstances, her long-standing and secure place under the counter was possibly to her, and our, advantage. She has now been abstracted thence, to take her place on library shelves beside *Forever Amber, Peyton Place* and other such female compositions, by no means necessarily, I should have thought, congenial to her tastes, which, in all respects save one, were markedly moderate, polite and respectable.

Confessions of an egghead

The first contemporary hero I consciously had was Woodrow Wilson. I saw this solemn-faced American on the old flickering silent film. He was wearing a top hat, which he raised from time to time. It seemed to me that he had come as a saviour among us; that his Fourteen Points would deliver mankind from the evils of war for evermore, and that under the auspices of the League of Nations the reign of freedom and brotherhood must prevail. When this did not happen, I was confident that his purposes had been frustrated by wicked, selfish men. It did not occur to me that the purposes themselves might be mistaken.

Subsequent judgments and admirations have little better withstood the test of time. As a leader-writer on the *Manchester Guardian* I used to argue with great passion that the virtuous Germans were only claiming their just rights in Europe, malignantly opposed therein by the French, whose ruthless and unscrupulous exercise of power politics threatened to involve us all in another war. Alas, only a few years later the roles had changed. The virtuous Germans were voting in large numbers for Hitler, while the malignant French represented the champions of justice and freedom. Their *Grand Armée* whose maintenance had been so roundly denounced became (again mistakenly, as it turned out) a blessed bulwark of righteousness.

Again, in India it seemed to me clear that once the British Raj was ended, communal and other troubles would all automatically vanish. The alien imperialists must go, and then Gandhi would take over and his humane notions prevail. Certainly I did not foresee that the British Raj would end in a bloody and impracticable partition, whose ill consequences for both Moslem and Hindu are with us still. Yet again, I first thought that the Soviet régime had fulfilled all the promises of human felicity ever made, and then, having spent a year in the U.S.S.R., that it must collapse under the weight of its cruelty and oppression.

The fact is that eggheads (taking an egghead to be one who approaches life in terms of ideas rather than of what seem to be immediate realities) are nearly always wrong. It might be argued that they were right about the Spanish Civil War. Even in this case, however, in retrospect, the awkward thought arises that the most probable alternative to a Franco government would have been one more or less subservient to Moscow. Such a government, in 1940, during the operation of the Nazi-Soviet pact, would probably have been induced by Stalin, as part of other bargains on his own frontiers, to let the Wehrmacht march through Spain, and thence to North Africa, whereas Franco, with surprising toughness, resisted all Hitler's persuasions to agree to this.

Past eggheads seem to have been as unfortunate in their prognostications and misguided in their enthusiasms as contemporary ones. They had as foolish expectations, and said as foolish things, about the French Revolution as we did about the Russian Revolution. An egghead like Hazlitt went on regarding Napoleon as the poor man's friend with the same idiot persistence as his like a century later persisted in seeing in Stalin the practical implementer of the Sermon on the Mount. Again, take the case of Dr. Johnson. He was convinced that the American colonists' demands were preposterous and indefensible, and that anyway little more was likely to be heard of them. The political ideas of Voltaire and Rousseau seemed to him so obviously depraved and ludicrous that no one would ever heed them. As for Gibbon and Hume—they were outside the pale. Johnson, of course was a Tory, though many of the views he expressed were on the side of the angels. He was a strong believer in poor people having more money; he was always ready to do anything he could to save convicted criminals from the gallows, and his *Life of Savage* is the most sensitive and uncensorious biography in the English language. As for his personal charity —it was fabulous. His house was full of down-and-outs of various kinds, and of his pension of £300 a year he gave away all but £75.

Johnson, as I have said, was a Tory. What, then, about Marx and Engels who confidently predicted that the proletariat would triumph in their time? Or, for that matter, what about the founder of the Christian religion, who encouraged his followers to believe that the end of the old, cruel way of life was at hand and the reign of righteousness imminent?

The truth is, surely, that liberalism, in one variation or another the egghead's credo, may be strategically sound, but is tactically fallacious, and as such highly misleading as well as highly destructive. Indeed, in my opinion, it is *the* destructive force of the age. Propositions of our time like Communism, which unashamedly recommend violence and destruction, have also presupposed a consequent stability. They are essentially conservative, stabilising forces. There is to be a big bang, and then quiet. Liberalism, on the other hand, presupposes what is unattainable—that we, little men and women, should live in amity together on our minute corner of the universe for the few score years vouchsafed us, of our own volition seeking one another's good and sharing equitably the material things which satisfy our needs and desires. This is a fantasy. This, in human terms, cannot be. Therefore, the effect of believing in it is constantly to tear the world to pieces.

In this sense, the persecutors of eggheads had some justification. When egghead flowers blossom, as the Chinese say, they are liable to turn into weeds, and then they have to be uprooted. Brains have to be washed because, from the point of view of those who want to maintain order—any sort of order—unwashed, they are a menace. We have all written righteously indignant paragraphs to solace ourselves about Mr. So-and-So, Herr So-and-So, Señor So-and-So, Comrade So-and-So, a mild man who spent all his time browsing among his books, and never had anything to do with plots and stratagems, but who none the less had been wickedly imprisoned or shot, and what a monstrous thing it was. Of course it was monstrous. But it was also sensible. If you want to have a stable society getting richer and richer (which is what the majority of mankind now want, and perhaps always have wanted) you just cannot afford to let mild men browse quietly among books. I am not suggesting they should necessarily be killed or imprisoned. Stalin and Senator McCarthy were simple hearts whose methods lacked subtlety. A less ostentatious, and perhaps in the long run more efficacious procedure is to buy them off with regius professorships and other like offices, or to get them attached to some church or other, the more authoritarian the better. But just browsing they are a menace.

After all, it was not Hitler or Stalin or Mr. Dulles or even Field-Marshal Montgomery who invented atomic fission and made possible all its deadly affiliates, but a rum-looking egghead, Einstein, scribbling on a piece of paper. It was not Napoleon who made the French Revolution; but Rousseau, a crazy Swiss, who took to knitting and to dressing up in Armenian costume, had a lot to do with it. Stalin, when he killed off all his eggheads like Bukharin, was only establishing a sound and stable government. In this country the victims would have been given the O.M. and sent to the House of Lords, but the end result would have been the same. They would have been silenced. One or two of them, for form's sake, might even have been left at large, with the possibility of appearing on television or otherwise propounding ideas through the B.B.C. filter. Why purge when the same objective can be painlessly achieved? Broadcasting House washes whiter.

The basic egghead fallacy, the fallacy of liberalism which makes it in practice so destructive a force, is, it seems to me, that it implies the possibility of achieving imaginative ends by the exercise of the will. Actually, these two—the will and the imagination, or, to put it another way, power and love

—are in conflict. They pull in opposite directions, and cannot, without the most disastrous consequences, be harnessed together. If the operations of the will are judged in terms of the imagination, the judgment must necessarily be false. Nonetheless, it is the fate of the egghead to attempt this impossible feat. He buys every gold brick because, imaginatively, its glitter is convincing. When, however, he goes to sell it he finds it is worthless. And quite often he has it thrown at his head for his pains.

Brendan Behan at Lime Grove

Characteristically of this crazy time, it was appearing drunk on television, not his plays and writings, which first aroused public interest in Brendan Behan. As I was the interviewer concerned, in this hilarious episode, I should like, now that the poor fellow is dead, and while my memory of it is still clear, to record exactly what happened. It was the excellent idea of Catherine Dove, then working on the B.B.C. programme, *Panorama,* to get Behan to Lime Grove studios where *Panorama* is produced. His play, *The Quare Fellow,* was running under Miss Littlewood's spirited direction, out at Stratford. Though it had been well reviewed, no West End management had evinced any interest in it. On the morning after Behan's *Panorama* appearance, Miss Littlewood told me in her amusing, dry way, she had five eager inquiries.

I arranged to meet Behan at the Garrick Club in the early evening. He arrived there, in a fairly high condition, with his delightful wife, and carrying some kind of a wreath he had acquired in the course of the day's festivities. One or two members peeped in curiously as we took a few noisy drinks together before leaving for Lime Grove. There, in the entertainment room, refreshment continued to be available, and Behan was soon singing and shouting obscenities in his customary style.

The other *Panorama* items were perfect. Woodrow Wyatt was to question two brass-hats from the War Office on civil defence. They were equipped with the inevitable map and long pointer. Then there was an item about finishing schools, in which a finishing-school headmistress and some of her charges were to appear. At one point they all filed into the entertainment room, heard Behan holding forth, and then abruptly about-turned and filed out again. After they had gone, Behan turned to me and asked with some anguish: 'Didn't I see a lot of pretty girls in here just now?' I explained that he had been dreaming: we were in a place of dreams, I said.

As Behan grew drunker and more boisterous, doubts began to be felt in the higher B.B.C. echelons as to whether he should be allowed to appear at all. I argued strongly that he should. After all, I contended, somewhat speciously, walking up and down a corridor nervously with Leonard Miall, the B.B.C. official in whose jurisdiction *Panorama* then fell, this is the man who wrote *The Quare Fellow*. Let us, then, present him as he really is. Miall in the end agreed, only adding beseechingly: 'If he uses the word c——, don't laugh.' I readily accepted this condition. As it happens, I do not find the word particularly amusing.

On the set it was apparent that Miall need have had no apprehension. Behan was incapable of speaking coherently at all, which perhaps, in the circumstances, was just as well. He took off his boots and muttered something about 'wanting a leak.' To have tried to arrange for him to have one would have been too complicated. I decided to take the risk. When the cameras came on us, I put my first question, and, allowing Behan to mumble a little, answered it myself. All television interviews are really like this. Behan's was simply an extreme case. Towards the end of our time, remembering that the intoxicated can sometimes sing when they can't speak, I asked him if he would care to give us a song. In a thin, reedy voice he managed to give a rendering of a song in his play.

Afterwards, we returned to the entertainment room, I left him there roaring out the 'Internationale' at the top of his voice, with the two War Office brass-hats giving every indication of being about to join in. It was the pleasantest and most rewarding evening I ever spent in Lime Grove.

In his subsequent remarks to the Press about the interview, Behan was extremely considerate and friendly in his reference to me. I liked him, except, of course, that, like all drunks, he was a fearful bore. Drunkenness is a device to avoid having to think of anything to say. As Johnson observed once to Boswell, it leads to a confusion of words with ideas, which is conversationally disastrous.

A hero of our time

One of Claud Cockburn's uncles, he is fond of recounting, used, when watering his garden, to climb on to a ladder in order that the water, when it fell, should seem like rain. The episode is highly characteristic of the nephew. It conveys a certain poetic eccentricity, which is none the less capable of a rational explanation, and at the same time, a pleasing sensibility, an awareness that plants, like all other living things, deserve consideration. These qualities provide the key to Cockburn's adventurous life, and to the rare survival, through all its hazards and changes, of an inward integrity and serenity. They qualify him to be regarded, in the Lermontov sense, as an authentic hero of our time.

His own account of himself and his experiences has now been completed with the publication of a third autobiographical volume, *View from the West*. It is a fascinating work. One can now survey him as a whole. From an Oxford fellowship to working for *The Times* in Washington and Berlin; from Printing House Square to King Street and the *Daily Worker*, with the alluring and exciting interlude of the *Week*; from Communist Party membership to withdrawal to Ireland and the long, hard struggle to support his family by writing, with a bout of grave illness to add to his difficulties—such has been his life's course to date.

For someone like Cockburn, who became a Communist, operating for a number of years inside the *apparat*, and then ceased to be one more or less suddenly, the natural assumption is that there must have been a dramatic moment of disillusionment. Some sort of breast-beating act has been confidently expected from him. None has come or ever will come. Anything of the kind would be wholly alien to his disposition.

Cockburn, that is to say, does not fit into the category, common enough in his generation, of the disillusioned Communist. No god failed him because Communism never assumed, in his eyes, a god-like shape. He supported it as a cause wholeheartedly and with characteristic verve; and when it ceased to appeal to him as a cause, he ceased to support it. That was all. It might, in different circumstances, have been a different cause. I can easily imagine him, for instance, throwing himself with enthusiasm into the Crusades, had he lived at that time. Or marching through Georgia. Whatever the cause, however, he would never have been among those who subsequently complained that its true purposes had been obscured and its following betrayed.

To him, a cause is like a love affair whose ecstasy remains valid even when it is over. He loves causes for their own sake alone. I remember once dining with him in Cork and discussing, not at all idolatrously, the then de Valera government. Later in the evening there was to be an election rally, and, both of us having a taste for such occasions, we strolled out to have a look at it. Cockburn soon elbowed his way to the front of the crowd, and by the time de Valera appeared he was leading the cheering. Though I suppose there must be few subjects on which he and de Valera would find themselves in agreement, I could see the bond between them—both so tall, and with the sweetly severe expression of loving men who have found it necessary to hate. Maurice Richardson, with his aptitude for calling everything and everyone by the correct name, always refers to Cockburn as 'the Chevalier.' It suits him better than Comrade.

This is not at all to suggest that Cockburn will throw himself into any old cause. Quite the contrary. A cause, to appeal to him, must seem to be on the side of the weak and against the strong, and on the side of life and against death. Communism appeared to him to be such a cause, and as such he espoused it. It was, of course, an oversimplification and ultimately a delusion. Revolutions cannot afford to succeed or ever to stop. If they do, there is always a Cromwell or a Bonaparte or a Stalin waiting to take them over. Unfortunately they have a way of really revolving—that is, of ending where they began.

The inveterate contemporary habit of thinking in terms of categories makes it difficult, in the existing mental climate, to understand someone like Cockburn or to make sense of his account of himself. A twentieth-century man is expected to fit into a particular category and to vote the ticket that goes therewith. He is on the left, which means that he supports the Kremlin against the Pentagon; that he upholds birth control, abstract art, *Lady Chatterley's Lover* and the Wolfenden Report, and abhors Kipling, de Gaulle, and the American Way of Life. Or he is on the right, in which case vice versa.

Any variation in these rigidly adumbrated loyalties and abhorrences causes confusion and rage. One realises how they dominate people's minds if one happens to take a position which cuts across them. From one side come accusations of being a Communist, a Jew and a homosexual; from the other of being a Fascist, and an advocate of apartheid, flogging and capital punishment, quite irrespective of whether any of these matters are at issue.

Cockburn is a case in point. He has been a devoted Communist, but he happens also to adore America. He has, likewise, the happiest memories of living in Germany. Though a revolutionary by instinct, the temper of his mind is in many ways intensely conservative. He venerates de Gaulle and abominates Harold Wilson; he is more often seen reading P. G. Wodehouse than Karl Marx. If he ever voted Labour, it must have been with a heavy heart. His social origins are upper middle class, and he takes great pride in his ancestry, particularly in his great-grandfather, Lord Cockburn, a legal luminary in Edinburgh, whose *Memorials of His Time* remains one of his great-grandson's favourite books. Carlyle, I see from the *Dictionary of National Biography,* described this Lord Cockburn as 'a bright, cheery voiced, hazel-eyed man ; a Scotch dialect with plenty of good logic in it, and of practical sagacity; veracious, too. A gentleman, I should say, and perfectly in the Scotch type, perhaps the very last of that peculiar species.' As it turned out, not the last.

It is a great source of satisfaction to Cockburn that, at almost the same time, in Washington he appeared on a list

drawn up by the late Senator McCarthy of the 269 most
dangerous Reds in the world; and in Prague one of the unhappy victims of a Communist Party purge 'confessed' that
he had transactions with a certain Colonel Cockburn of
the British Intelligence Service. On judgment day, I suspect,
credentials of this sort will be required of all of us. If so,
Cockburn will be well placed.

It is, of course, as a journalist that Cockburn is best known.
His skill in this ribald trade is outstanding, and anyone in-
tending to follow it should study all his observations upon it.
It is true that his guidance would not fit a prospective journalist to work on the *Daily Express,* or indeed on any extant
newspaper except perhaps the *Canard Enchainé.* It would
simply enable him to become a good journalist. In *View from
the West* Cockburn divertingly describes his transactions with
the now defunct Hulton Press, that *pons asinorum* of contemporary journalism. The two publications he worked for
were Dead Souls and never appeared, but Cockburn, I am
happy to think, benefited financially. Surveying the capital
gains which Sir Edward Hulton's idiosyncratic methods have
subsequently earned him in the take-over stakes, Cockburn,
like Clive, may marvel at his moderation.

On *Punch* he was my very present help in time of trouble.
He is a humorous writer of rare distinction, and his appearance in that place of shadows gave pleasure to one and all,
especially to me. His account of our collaboration is so
generously and affectionately expressed that it is difficult for
me to comment on it. Some seek to laugh off the asperities of
life, finding in the absurdity of its minor misfortunes a means
of evading its larger ones. Others, like Cockburn, see in life's
inherent absurdity an image of its mystery and grandeur.
Clowns are the poets of humour, wits its engineers. Cockburn is a clown, with a clown's serious, watchful eyes set
in a wide expanse of face.

Like all imaginative and sensitive people, Cockburn tends
to lurk in a maquis of his own devising. In the last of his
three autobiographical volumes, more than in the other two,
he emerges into the open. There is more of himself in it.
His experiences and reflections while a tubercular patient in an
Irish sanatorium are, not more seriously, but more profoundly

conveyed than his account of his political and journalistic escapades in *In Time of Trouble* and *Crossing the Line*. He was very ill indeed, and at one point, not unreasonably, became convinced that he would shortly die. I went to see him at the sanatorium. It was a weird place, constructed almost entirely of glass. One could look along and see all the patients in their cubicles, like endlessly repeated images in a mirror. The sanatorium was excellently equipped as a result of the Irish Sweep. 'Buy a ticket and get comforts for Claud' would be, Cockburn suggested, a good new selling point.

He was assiduously reading Harnack's nine-volume *History of Dogma,* a work which recommended itself to him because of its enormous length. And anyway, he writes, 'any great and good book, regardless of its subject matter, must have something of the effect of the walls of a rackets court—it sets the mind bouncing.' Cockburn's mind was bouncing as ever. Beside his bed was a dictaphone, by means of which he still managed to engage in gainful employment. He was even able to offer a drop of refreshment from a bottle discreetly arranged with others containing more orthodox medicine. Misfortunes, to him, are always blessings in disguise. This one's disguise was rather deep, but he managed to penetrate it. The other patients were assiduous visitors to his glass cubicle, and eagerly partook of his equanimity and conversational flow. His popularity had a trifling and temporary setback when, by a process of reasoning, he won the sweepstake on who would be the new Pope. It was felt that a Protestant with free-thinking proclivities should not have succeeded in this particular field.

Leftists in our sort of society (using the term to signify all who feel instinctively on the side of change, as distinct from upholders of the *status quo*) fall into two categories—the failed revolutionary and the failed saint. They are the ghosts of those shot on the barricades or of those burnt at the stake. Curiously enough, Cockburn, though of all his kind the nearest to being a practising revolutionary, belongs in my opinion to the latter category. He loves action for its excitement rather than its purpose. His approach is mystical rather than ideological. For power he has no appetite or aptitude, and for love an insatiable need, which his stout-hearted and enchanting wife, Patricia, and his three delightful sons have abundantly provided. He looks for the meaning rather than the outcome, and never wastes his hopes on earthly paradises; those fatuous mirages of the lost. Life itself is a blessing, not even in disguise.

Life and the legend

It often seems that the contemporary world is divided into two parts. Half the stage is dark and silent, and that is life; the other half is arc-lit, sparkling, loquacious, and that is the legend. If an individual strays from life into the legend, he is transfigured. Either he becomes a hero, radiant and wonderful, or a villain, louring and malignant. In the legend there are no men, only heroes and villains; in life there are no heroes or villains, only men.

What goes on in life has only a tenuous connection with the legend. Thus, in life there are vast catastrophes and vast ecstasies. Men kill and love. The killing, as presented in the legend, becomes heroism or murder according to the circumstances. If heroism, then music of requisite solemnity plays; human interest provides a Cellophane covering for human extinction. If murder, then cameras swoop like insatiable women, and a television panel subsides slowly and loquaciously into the slough of objectivity until lost to view, while popular commentators imagine vain things.

In life, there is just the bloodshed; men blindly groping, confusion, dread; fears and hopes which are both false, because, in life, there is neither fear nor hope. These belong to the legend, and are transmitted into life on very High Frequency Modulation by courtesy of the British Broadcasting Corporation or the Independent Television Authority or Early Bird; networked, in fact, by all concerned—that is, by all who exercise any sort of authority and traffic in any way with power; a goodly and most various company, taking in the Pope, General de Gaulle, the esteemed editors of *The Times* (London and New York), *Playboy, Time* and the *Reader's Digest, Le Monde*, the *Universe, Confidential, Mad*, etc., etc., as well as Lyndon Johnson, Billy Graham, Mao Tse-tung and the Archbishop of Canterbury.

When we come to loving, the legend presents cheesecake or religious worship. (There are, as a matter of fact, other variations, but these, without stretching matters too far, can be included under the two basic ones.) Cheesecake means vital statistics, Italian film stars more or less undressed, female flesh variously presented, cancanery in all its aspects, crooning, drooling, vice indignantly exposed or salaciously peep-holed, television or radio variety smut, virtue valorously defended or hilariously lost; mink marriages, cinderella models, smart friends with diamond clips, expense account feasts and Riviera love-nests, Kinsey and Mead and *From Here to Eternity*—which stretches, in the legend, from here to just round the corner again for a quick drink.

As for religious worship—it's that curious indescribable, chanting-moaning-gurgling voice: 'Dearly beloved brethren, I pray and beseech you, as many as are here present . . .'; it's that earnest, open, down-with-racial-segregation, face; that ask-me-a-plain-question-and-I'll-give-you-a-straight answer face, staring out of the dear little screen; it's 'any questions you like, and don't pull your punches and I won't pull mine' —'Father, is there an after-life?' 'Well, Dick, what about immortality?' 'Are we, then, sir, to assume that Hell is a kind of suburb inconveniently distant from the big cinemas and restaurants and department stores and all the fun?' It's that dark, cunning expression, emerging from lace and vestments, incense-swinging, criss-crossing, and chanting monotonously, rather sweetly, incomprehensibly.

In life, love signifies passion, which is suffering. It signifies studying a face like a lost explorer studying a map, from frequent and intense past study so familiar to him, and yet he still hopes that one more look will help him to find his way. It signifies that ecstatic awareness, arising so briefly and unaccountably, in a crowd or a room or a train or in the open countryside or by the sea or in a street that every part of the universe is indissolubly linked with every other part, and therefore any emotion other than love is vile and inconceivable, any division between man and man of any sort or description as ludicrous as a division between the nodding of one's own head and the tapping of one's own foot, and even

285

treading on a snail is an inconceivable crime and cutting the grass a holocaust.

Of course, there has always been this division between life and legend. It is merely that in our time greater facilities for dramatising it (literacy, radio, television, etc.) have become available. These facilities have not created the division. They have been invented to make it more manifest. Men like Blake who lived wholly in life were mad, as were men like Hitler who lived wholly in the legend. Blake's madness was sublime, and enabled him to see what others were blind to —that the sunflower is weary of time and counts the steps of the sun. The Founder of the Christian religion likewise echewed the legend, and for this reason was killed. His teaching subsequently was incorporated in the legend—which is the point of the famous Grand Inquisitor passage in *The Brothers Karamazov*. Christ's return to earth would be an unwarranted intrusion of life into the legend, and therefore, from the Grand Inquisitor's point of view, intolerable. Hitler's madness, unlike Blake's, was abhorrent and destructive, an accumulation in his own poor distracted mind of all the base appetites for power of all his fellows. It would have been better for the rest of us if, instead of German Führer, he had been editor of *The Times* or Director-General of the B.B.C. or Moderator of the Church of Scotland, or compère of a late-night television show, but as far as he personally was concerned it would not have made any appreciable difference. He would still have been living in the legend.

It is particularly fascinating and illuminating to study the passage of an individual from life to legend. The radiance descends, and lo! such a man or such a woman, hitherto only known to a little circle of intimates, becomes familiar to millions. Television and radio, newspapers and magazines, camera and printing press and cartoonist's pencil, comedian's gag, pub conversation, casual railway exchange, all mysteriously join forces to pin-point a particular citizen. In a day or two he is so well known that we forget there was ever a time when he was a stranger. His envelope in the press-cutting library swells from a meagre two or three cuttings to burst at the seams. Henceforth, he is character-typed, hi : public *persona* is fixed. He is in an iron lung of publicity, and there must live for ever, unless he can manage (which happens rarely) to escape back to life and anonymity.

How enthralling to watch the spotlight moving, hesitating, then coming to rest. One is chosen, and all the others avidly gaze, half envious, and half thankful that they were passed over. The moving spotlight settles, and having settled, the transfiguration takes place. There is such a one, most kindly of men, condemned to be irascible, actually becoming irascible, because this is his allotted and inescapable role. There is such another, prim and estimable lady, translated into a panel game pin-up. Has she swallowed a microphone? Does she exist at all off the telly? There is yet another displaying, like a sandwichman, her bosomy treasure and another lifting his antennae-moustaches up into the stratosphere, and the Queen and the Duke of Edinburgh, respectfully but firmly led forward to the footlights, to take their bow—many, many spotlit faces, to be applauded, adulated, execrated, envied or desired; a mighty cast for a mighty legend.

The cameras prowl and pounce; the microphone is gingerly dipped into the outer darkness, like a toe into a cold bath —commentator asking: 'Are you happy?' 'Are you poor?' 'Are you angry?' 'Why?' On the legend side, all is so simple, all so bright, all so wise (Bertrand Russell, Julian Huxley, Dr. Bronowski and other Brains to give the answers); all so rich, with washing machines and television sets and sweet, untaxed money to be had for the answering. On the life side, all is so incomprehensible, all so dark, all so foolish, all so poor. And yet, when the lights are at last turned out, and the cameras are still, and the microphones are dead, and the displaced persons who populate the legend have all collected their fees and gone home to look at their press cuttings, over on the other side, the dark side, there is still a stir, as separate souls go their separate ways, or cling together in indissoluble love.